The Romance of the Lace Pillow

A BUCKS LACE-MAKER.

Photo by Dr. Habberton Lulham.

The Romance of
the Lace Pillow

THOMAS WRIGHT

A new edition with notes

RUTH BEAN

CARLTON · BEDFORD

1982

Published by Ruth Bean, Victoria Farmhouse, Carlton,
Bedford MK43 7LP, England.

ISBN 0 903585 12 X

Plate negatives, Alpha Plates, Northampton.
Printed in Great Britain at the University Press, Cambridge.

NOTE ON THE TEXT

The text reproduced here is a photographic reprint of the first edition (Olney, Bucks: H.H. Armstrong, 1919). A second edition was issued in two volumes by the same publisher in 1924 (volume 1) and 1930 (volume 2). For technical reasons the half-tone illustrations have been reproduced from the second edition. The differences between the two editions is slight, since the first was evidently kept in standing type and the second printed from the same setting: presumably some accident to the standing type led to the word for word resetting, in a different face, of pages 113-116 in the second edition.

The illustrations were augmented in the second edition by six new line drawings by Wilfred Pippet, and one by Miss L.D. Darney, which is reproduced here in reduced facsimile. The second edition has a short preface of no importance, and does not bear the earlier dedication to Queen Alexandra.

One villain, goaded by a stroke from the cane, . . . threw the whole of his apparatus into the duck pond.   See p. 105.

Drawn by Miss L. D. Darney.

In this new printing, corrections or additions to the first edition have been made on plates 6 and 36.

A.J.C. Bainton
University Library, Cambridge

Plate 6. Shoe attributed to the reign of Charles II.

The shoe is of ivory, pink and yellow silk brocade with silver, with straps to fasten with a buckle. The Mechlin lace, pearl bead and green satin trim is crudely stitched on over the original edge binding, and appears to have been added in the 19th century, possibly the 1830s, and probably for fancy dress wear. The shoe has the customer's name, Miss Langley inscribed on the quarter lining. The style of the shoe with its slender heel is about 1780.

In the late 19th century it formed part of the T. Watson Greig Collection of footwear, and is included in his book "Ladies' Old Fashioned Shoes" published in Edinburgh in 1885, plate II, where it is erroneously ascribed to the reign of Charles II (probably on account of the lace trim). In 1921 Greig's Collection was bought for the Royal Ontario Museum, Toronto, Canada by Blatchford's Shoe Company, and is still housed there (catalogue no. 921.2.21).

J.M. Swann
Keeper, Shoe Collection
Central Museum, Northampton

Plate 36. Lace School at Cranfield.

Mrs D. Moller, a lace teacher of Cranfield, Bedford, has identified the persons in the photograph with the help of contemporaries who knew them. The information was corroborated in each case by one or more villagers.

Back row: Mrs Downes, Mrs Cox. Next row: Hilda Pulley, Hilda Shattleworth, Freda White, Rosie (Rosemary) Pointin, Hilda Linnell, Annie Bullen. Front row: Daffy (Dafne) White, Kathleen Joyce (now Mrs Haynes and living in North Crawley, Bucks), Polly (Mary) Green.

The names are practically identical with those on a list found in a copy of the 1919 edition acquired by Miss Frances O'Callaghan of Kettering, Northants.

CONTENTS

CHAPTER I

LACE-MAKING AS AN ART

CHAPTER II

THE NEEDLE-POINT AND BOBBIN LACES OF THE CONTINENT

CHAPTER III

OUR GARDEN OF DELIGHT

CHAPTER IV

THE FIRST EXODUS

CHAPTER V

THE SECOND EXODUS

CHAPTER VI

FROM THE ACCESSION OF JAMES I. TO THE DEATH OF CROMWELL

CHAPTER VII

THE REIGN OF CHARLES II

CHAPTER VIII

THE THIRD EXODUS. (REIGN OF JAMES II., 1685—1689)

CHAPTER IX

BUCKS POINT

CHAPTER X

REIGNS OF WILLIAM III. AND ANNE, 1688—1714

CHAPTER XI

SMUGGLING

CONTENTS.

CHAPTER XVI

THE MALTESE AND TORCHON PERIODS

CHAPTER XVII

LACE-MAKING TO-DAY

APPENDICES

LIST OF PLATES

PREFACE

THERE have been many works on Lace and Lace-making, but this is the first attempt to deal exhaustively with Lace-making in Bucks, Beds, Northants, and the adjoining counties. In Mrs. Palliser's volume, *A History of Lace*, only a few pages are devoted to this industry; and the little book by Miss Channer and Miss Roberts is wanting by reason of its brevity. Beyond the works of these ladies, scarcely anything on the subject has been issued, with the exception of thin brochures and scattered articles in magazines.

It was felt that the time had come for a detailed History of the Industry. It was felt, too, that the work must be done at once or never. A few more years and all the old workers, who have supplied the greater part of the information conveyed in these pages, will have passed away. It is owing to their appreciation of humour and their ready collaboration that I am able to present the reader with those lively chapters on the Bobbins and the Lace Tells. Certainly no other book gives a tithe of the information which I have been able to offer on these subjects.

Many collectors of bobbins have been good enough to send me inscriptions. May I to all future collectors give one word of advice? Always be careful to make a note of the village whence any bobbin is procured. The interest of inscription bobbins would be trebled if this were done; and in some cases the "Puzzle Inscriptions" would reveal their secrets.

On the subject of the Lace itself I have been helped by a number of ladies and gentlemen, who have devoted many years to its study. I would especially thank Mr. H. H. Armstrong, Mrs. G. M. Roberts, Mrs. J. B. Harrison, Miss M. Maidment, Mrs. W. W. Carlile, Mr. A. A. Carnes, Lady Inglefield, Miss M. Burrowes, Major and Mrs. C. A. Markham, Mr. Geo. Smith, Mr. E. J. Elliott, Miss G. M. Peet, Miss C. C. Channer, Miss MacAuslin, Mr. P. G. Trendell, the Hon. Rose Hubbard, Dr. Habberton Lulham, and the Rev. A. J. Roberts, all of whom have rendered invaluable services.

I also wish to thank all the following persons for various kindnesses :—

For the Plates which embellish this book:

Dr. Habberton Lulham, *Frontispiece* and 47.
Authorities, Victoria and Albert Museum, 2 a, 8, 12 a, 18, 19, 20, 34.

Miss M. Maidment, 2 b, 3, 4, 22, 45, 46.

Midland Lace Association, 5 a, 13 a, 33, 37 (lower four), 41, 42 a.

Miss M. Burrowes, 5 b, 7 a, 14, 15, 16 a.

Mr. John M. Knapp, 6 a.

Committee of the Northampton Public Library, 6 b.

Mrs. J. B. Harrison, 7 a, 37 (Old Torchon).

Bucks Archæological Society, 9 b.

Miss C. M. Pope, 10 b, 13 b.

Mrs. W. W. Carlile, 10 a.

Mrs. Howe, 12 b.

Mr. George Smith, 16 b, 17 a, 26, 27, 30, 32.

Mr. J. Raftery, 17 b, 31, 48 b.

Mrs. T. Taylor, 21, 25 a.

Authorities, Aylesbury Museum, 23 a.

Trustees, Cowper Museum, Olney, 23 b.

Mrs. J. S. Whitehead, 24.

Miss C. C. Channer, 25 b, 38 b, 44, 49 b, c.

Miss W. Field, 28 a.

Mrs. W. Crowsley, 28 b.

Mr. H. H. Armstrong, 29.

Mr. A. De Ath, 36.

Mrs. C. A. Markham, 42 b.

Mrs. G. M. Roberts, 38 a.

Hon. Rose Hubbard, 39, 40, 49 a.

Bucks Lace Association, 43.

For various services :

Mrs. Archibald Allen, Olney ; Miss Edith Allin, Oxford ; Mrs. E. A. Andrews, Bedford ; Mrs. Armstrong, Stoke Goldington ; Mr. Percy Ashby, Towcester ; Mrs. Beatrice Aste, Cold Norton, Essex ; Mrs. Catherine Ayton, Preston.

Miss F. Bagust, Stamford Hill, N. ; Mrs. W. Bamford, Kingsland, Herts ; Mrs. J. Bastable, Furze Platt, Maidenhead ; Mr. O. J. Bates, Northampton ; Miss E. J. Barker,

Scarborough; Mr. J. E. Beasley, Weston Favell; Miss Mary
Beal, Hornsey Rise; Miss Kathleen Bell, Highgate; Miss
U. Bevan, Spratton; Miss Alice Birdsall, Northampton; Mr.
R. Blair, Harton, near South Shields; Miss S. Bostock,
Northampton; Mr. R. Boulton, Swindon; Miss Mabel Brom-
ley, Boscombe; Miss Rosa F. Broughton, Skegness; Mr.
Reginald Brown, Northampton Public Library; Mr. A.
Brown, Stamford Hill, N.; Mr. W. F. Bull, Newport Pag-
nell; Mrs. Bull, Calverton; Mr. Alfred Bullard, Newport
Pagnell; Mr. G. E. Bullen, Herts County Museum.

Miss Campion, Bletsoe Castle; Mrs. Caves, Hanslope;
Miss C. C. Channer, Northampton; Mrs. Chettle, Leaming-
ton; Miss Iris Clare, Newport Pagnell; Mr. W. H. Clark,
High Wycombe; Mrs. E. Clarke, North Crawley; Mrs.
Coales, Newport Pagnell; Lieut. J. L. Coales, Newport Pag-
nell; Miss Florence Cockrane, St. Neots; Mrs. W. J. Collier,
Beer; Mrs. E. P. Carling, London; Mrs. A. J. Comber,
Fritwell; Mrs. R. Cooper, Elstow; Mr. W. Cosford, Dod-
worth; Mrs. Course, Ravenstone; Miss Cowley, Stevington;
Mr. and Mrs. W. Crowsley, Kempston; Mrs. Cox, Cranfield;
Mrs. W. S. Cox, London; Mr. W. P. Crouch, Kettering;
Miss A. S. Culpin, Sketty, Glamorgan.

Mr. William Day, Bath; Miss K. Dickinson, St. Albans;
Mrs. J. T. Dickinson, Orton Longueville, near Peterborough;
Miss Margaret Dickson, Reading; Mrs. Dowdy, N. Crawley;
Mrs. E. S. Druce, Woking; Miss Alice Dryden (Mrs. Marcon),
Newbury; Mrs. Mabel Dunkley, Torrington Square, W.C.

Miss Edge, N. Crawley; Mr. J. S. Elliott, Dowles Manor,
Bewdley; Miss Agnes Ellis, Leicester; Mrs. Elmer, Olney;
Mrs. Elstone, Stony Stratford.

Mr. John Fearon, Ockenden, Woking; Mr. W. Foat,
Westcliff-on-Sea; Miss P. R. Finny, Surbiton; Miss G.
Foster, Aspley Guise; Mrs. Fowler, Honiton; Miss L. E.
Freeborn, Turweston.

Mrs. Garner, Kempston; Mrs. Janet Garrood, Alconbury Hill; Mr. J. S. Gee, Rusholme; Mr. George, The Library, Northampton; Mr. W. Glassby, Renhold; Mrs. Gomme, Olney; Mrs. A. Gooding, Forlton, Crediton; Mrs. A. L. A. Greaves, Haversham, Bucks; Miss A. Gregory, Plumstead; Messrs. H. M. & John Grey, Hackney; Dr. Innes Griffin; Mrs. Grindon, Olney.

Miss F. Haines, Bedford; Mr. S. H. Hamer, Halifax; Miss Lydia Hammell, Taunton; Miss Phoebe Hardwick, Skegness; Miss Laura Harris, Oxford; Mrs. Hawkins, Stony Stratford; Mrs. M. Haywards, 11 Old Bond Street, W; Mr. Samuel Hearne, Halse Hill, Brackley; Miss E. Hedges, Tring; Mr. R. Hinde, Cockermouth; Mr. Geo. Hollingshead, Olney; Mr. Edwin Hollis, The Museum, Aylesbury; Mr. Hopkins, Turvey; Mr. J. F. Horton, Bedford; Mr. T. F. Horton, Bedford; Mrs. Howe, Chesham; Mrs. Howson, Olney; Mr. H. Howkins, Bedford; Miss Maggie Huckle, Kempston; Lady Rose Hudderfull, Ramsgate.

Mrs. Iliffe, 9 Kent Terrace, Regent's Park.

Mr. W. W. James, Wellingborough; Miss M. Jourdain, Beaminster.

Miss Mabel Keighley, Plymouth; Miss Kewley, Haddenham; Miss H. King, Westbourne Park, W.; Miss King, Towcester; Miss M. Kirkman, Cambridge; Miss Kitchener, Olney; Mr. John N. Knapp, Linford Hall.

Mr. Charles Lee, London; Miss E. C. L'Estrange, London; Messrs. Liberty, London; Mr. James Linton, Joppa, near Edinburgh; Miss J. Selby Lowndes, Brighton; Mrs. Lovegrove, Aylesbury; Mrs. Lacey, Highgate.

Miss MacAuslin, Northampton; Mr. C. Madeley, The Museum, Warrington; Mrs. E. Martin, Roade; Mrs. Mason, Taunton; Mrs. Edith Mauro, Bracon Ash; Mrs. Mead, Ravenstone; Miss Emily Meen, Comer, Liverpool; Miss B.

Moffatt, West Halkin, S.W.; Capt. H. A. Morgan, Highbury; Mr. Thos. Muddiman, Hackney; Mr. W. V. Morten, Nottingham.

Miss Zilpah Nicholls, Ravenstone.

Mrs. Orlebar, Hinwick, Wellingborough.

Mr. Geo. Perry, Wallingford; Mrs. Peters, Olney; Colonel Duncan Pitcher, Huguenot Society, 16 Victoria Street, Westminster; Miss C. M. Pope, Torquay.

Mr. J. Raftery, London; Mrs. C. Randall, Northampton; Mr. O. Ratcliff, Southend; Mr. F. Richardson, Weedon; Mrs. T. Robbins, Lytchett Minster, Poole; Miss Ruff, Hanslope; R. B., Oakley.

The Hon. Emily St. John, Bletsoe; Miss Sams, Paulerspury; Miss Ada Sanders, Lipson, Plymouth; Miss Saunders, Worcester; Miss Alice Savory, Diss; Miss A. Scott, Carrington, Notts; Mr. Thomas Seymour, Oxford; Mrs. S. M. Shearman, Belfast; Mr. H. Shelton, Weston Underwood; Miss E. M. Smith, Ramsgate; Mrs. Emily Smith, Luton; Mr. G. T. Smith, Towcester; Rev. O. C. V. Snowdon, Broadstairs; Mrs. W. A. Spencer, Great Alne, Alcester; Miss M. Statham, Derby; Dr. Street, Cranfield; Mrs. S. A. Sutthery, Chesham; Mrs. E. Steward, Shoreham.

Mrs. F. Taylor, Newport Pagnell; Mrs. T. Taylor, Bridgewater; The Misses Tebbs, London; Mrs. Broughton Thompson, Northants; Mr. W. Timberlake, Bicester; Miss Adeline Tompkins, Alton; Miss C. Townshend, Islington; Miss Audrey Trevelyan, London; Miss E. Turnham, Waddesdon; Miss C. M. Tyson, Oxford.

Mrs. A. Varney, Haddenham; Mr. Fredk. K. Vaughan, Bracknell, Berks; Lady Verney, Claydon; Sir Arthur Vicars, Kilmorna, Kerry.

Mrs. Lucilla Wadsworth, Newton Blossomville; Mr. Wagstaffe, Newport Pagnell; Mr. F. R. Walding, Northampton; Mrs. E. S. Warner, Stoke Goldington; Mrs. E. Warner, Upper Tollington Park, N.; Mrs. Whitehead, Shelton, Beds; Mrs. M. L. Whiteman, Sawtry; Mr. W. Whitton, Torquay; Mrs. Wickham, Newport Pagnell; Mrs. C. J. Woolcock, Hayle, Cornwall; Miss B. Wright, Hornchurch; Mrs. Henry Wright, N. Crawley; Mrs. and Miss Whitmee, Olney.

Miss York, Emberton.

In conclusion, I wish to say that I shall be pleased to receive from any of my readers information respecting the history of lace-making and the progress of lace-making in any district. This information will be incorporated in the second edition of the book, which will appear at an early date; for, owing to the large number of orders already received, it is expected that the first edition will be exhausted within a few days of publication.

THOMAS WRIGHT.

COWPER SCHOOL,
OLNEY, BUCKS.
19th September, 1919.

THE

ROMANCE OF THE LACE PILLOW

CHAPTER I

LACE-MAKING AS AN ART

" The history of Lace-making," it has been appositely said,[1] " is the history of an art. A piece of lace is an artistic com- **1. Introduction.** position expressed in twisted thread, just as a piece of wood-carving is the expression of the artist's idea in chiselled wood. Lace is not, like embroidery, an ornamented fabric ; it is itself ornament. It is not the application of art to a craft ; the whole pattern is the fabric, and the fabric is the pattern. It is this peculiarity that distinguishes lace from needlework and woven work." Now it is only by the persistent determination to regard Lace-making as a beautiful and elevating art that progress in the industry can be effected ; and this fact has happily been fully recognised by those ardent enthusiasts in the Midlands and elsewhere who of late years have devoted themselves so pertinaciously to the advancement of Lace-making, and to the furtherance of the best interests of the workers.

[1] By Miss C. C. Channer in *Lace-making in the Midlands*.

Their object, which has been proclaimed in season and out of season, is to give the lace-makers every facility for producing a work of art, and to lead them to take in it that laudable pride which fired their predecessors in the Golden Age of Lace-making.

A border of Buckinghamshire Point of beautiful design and gossamer texture is the product, not of an elderly woman—seated at the door of a thatched cottage—and a pillow gleaming with bobbins and pins, but of centuries of vision, intuition, and skill. The artists who conceived the designs were men who saw with the eyes of the soul beauties that were invisible to the corporeal eyes of their contemporaries—and who, seeing these beauties, had the sagacity to perpetuate them. And yet this is not the full explanation, for an exquisite piece of lace is an Iliad. It cannot be said to have sprung from a single genius; it is the expression of the most rapturous moments of whole dynasties of men of genius. Nor is this all, for to the output of brain—poetic, impressionable or supple—of queen, ecclesiastic, statesman and burgher, whether in Italy, Flanders, France or our own England, there required to be added the ingenuity and dexterity of multitudes of workers in five centuries. All these and other powers and activities were antecedent or ancillary to the presentation of the chaste and unique beauty of real Buckingham-

shire Point.   Certainly, if the designer of the
pattern is an artist so also is the gifted lace-
maker, who never fails to impress her personality
upon her labours.   " Every worker," says Mrs.
W. W. Carlile[1], " has an individual way of handling the bobbins that enables her work to be
recognised, not only by herself, but also by connoisseurs, from among that of a dozen others
made on identical parchments, and fixes its
relative value."   And if the designer is an artist,
and the worker is an artist, an artist also, in a
sense, is the wearer of beautiful lace.   This fact
was recognised as early as Queen Elizabeth's
day, for Thomas Wright, the psychologist, writing
in 1601, says and truly, " Extraordinary apparell
of the bodie declareth well the apparell of the
mind."[2]

In short, Lace-making is an art, and the minds
of those who are brought into touch with it
partake, to an extent, of the joy of the artist:
their minds, like his, are lifted by ennobling
thoughts and lapped in delightful emotions. They
take their pleasure in old-time paradises. For
the moment, the poetical past is to them reality,
the utilitarian present only an unsubstantial
dream.   The study of lace is one of the means
of overcoming the soul's greatest malady—cold-
ness ; for when we speak of lace we pre-suppose

[1] *The Empire Review*, Jan., 1903.
[2] *The Passions of the Mind*, Ed. 1630, p. 26.

beauty; and beauty, like contemplation, work and contact with culture, has the effect of evoking the flaming lights of the mind.

The object now before us is to outline the history of the industry from its commencement; to tell of its introduction into England; and to present in detail its subsequent history in this country. Although our concern is mainly with the romance of Lace-making in so far as it relates to the quaint, sequestered, old-world villages of Bucks, Beds, Northants, and the surrounding counties, some attention will also be devoted to the Lace Industries of Devon and Ireland.

"Enchantments to Egypt!" says an old proverb—implying that Egypt was the natural home of magic. Certainly, if anything has the appearance of having been executed by supernatural powers, it is that filmy web-like impossibility, of whatever variety, which we call lace; and it was in Egypt, the land of the necromancer, the diviner, and the magician, that the earliest fabric that really deserves the name of lace was probably made. Most of the "lace" incident to the early Bible ages was really a sort of embroidery, and not lace in the common acceptance of the word. At the time the Authorised Version appeared (1611) almost anything used in the way of cord, braid, or fillet was called a lace. Thus William Browne

2. The Blue Lace of the Bible.

in his *Britannia Pastorals* (1613), after speaking
of a lady's "flaxen hair," goes on to say :

> " Whereat she sweetly angry, with her laces
> Binds up the wanton locks in curious traces."

In Exodus xxviii. 28 and xxxix. 31 a blue cord
seems intended, and in Exodus xxviii. 37 a blue
fillet—*vitta hyacinthina*, as it is rendered in all
three places in the Vulgate of 1583. Such was
part of the adornment of the high priest Aaron
when he stood gorgeous before the Lord.

Very charming is the derivation of the word
"lace," coming as it does through the Old French
las from the Latin *laqueus*, a snare, allied to *lacere*,
to entice—a fact which would alone prove that
what we call lace is a comparatively modern production. Hence " lace " really means something
that allures or entices, a derivation that is singu-
larly appropriate seeing that so many persons
are ensnared by its irresistible graces. It is
pleasant to notice that the word "delectable" is
of the same family—being from *delicere*, to allure.
Ladies are difficult to resist, even without lace ;
but with it who shall withstand them ! They
cannot be withstood. The only safety is in flight.

To return to our starting-point—it is in the
Egyptian "lace," then, that we shall 3. **Mummy**
find the origin of bobbin work.   **Lace.**

The *First Step.* A specimen taken from a
mummy case is preserved in the Victoria and
Albert Museum, South Kensington, and labelled,

"Found at Ehnasya (Herakleopolis Magna) during the excavations of 1903-4" (See Plate 2).[1]

Miss M. Maidment, an authority on lace both ancient and modern, observes that this primitive work was made on a frame consisting of two vertical rods which were kept rigid by two horizontal bars. Two foundation cords were fastened across from one vertical bar to the other, one being near the top and the other near the bottom. The thread to be plaited was wound upon these cords. After one end had been tied to the top foundation cord the thread was wound over and under both cords, and in a manner that would allow the fingers of the worker's left hand to be slipped in between the thread coming from the front of the top cord and the thread coming from the back. By this means, and by using the fingers only, the threads were twisted or plaited, the front threads dropping back and the back threads being pulled forward. This plaiting was performed in the middle of the work—the top and bottom necessarily being done simultaneously. Upon the completion of each row a stick was inserted, and the work pushed up and down into position. The plaiting being finished, the work could either be secured firmly in the middle or cut across and the ends tied, when there would, of course, be two articles.

---

[1] Museum Number, 1197—1904. Another specimen in the Museum (50—1891)—part of a bag—shows the use to which this kind of work was sometimes put.

The *Second Step* towards modern methods (suggested doubtless by the severing of the threads in the middle) was to use several shorter lengths of thread instead of the continuous one ; and to fasten to the ends of these cut lengths small handles (now called bobbins) with which to plait the threads.

The *Third Step* was to discard the frame and place the work on a cushion or pillow.

The *Fourth and Final Step* was to keep the threads in position by means of pins.

In order to make perfectly clear to our readers this early method adopted by the Egyptians, Miss Maidment has kindly imitated it with modern threads, and we have given photographs both of the Egyptian work and Miss Maidment's exposition of it.[1] The Countess Brazzia tells us that bobbins as well as specimens of lace have been found in mummy cases, but bobbins did not come into general use until the sixteenth century.

The art of making lace in the Egyptian way was probably lost for hundreds of years. In any case it made no progress till the 14th century, for an illustration after an engraving by Martin de Vos (1585) which appears in Mrs. Bury Palliser's *History of Lace*[2] shows a Flemish woman fingering a tall upright frame which could scarcely have been an advance on the frame used

4. Martin de Vos's Picture.

[1] See Plate 2.   [2] Ed. of 1910, p. 110.

by her Egyptian sister. Lace then was still made
" in the air " in the 16th century ; and wearisome
work it must have been, for it was most difficult
to twist the threads correctly. This weird, this
uncanny occupation, though out of place in
mediæval Flanders[1], seems quite suitable to the
sepulchral, chocolate-coloured ladies who walk
one way and look another in the Egyptian Book
of the Dead.

In Martin de Vos's picture, by the side of the
woman at the frame, is a girl making lace on a
flat pillow with pear-shaped bobbins. Evidently
the old method was dying out and the new just
coming in.

As to the meaning of the term " bone lace,"
we had better quote Thomas Fuller who, writing
about 1660,[2] says : " Some will have it called lace,
a *Lacinia*,[3] used as a fringe on the borders of
cloaths ; bone-lace it is named, because first
made with bone (since wooden) bobbins."

In the wardrobe accounts of Queen Elizabeth's
day the terms " bone lace" (which was made with
a fine thread) and " bobbin lace " (which was
made with a coarser thread) often occur—"bone,"
however, more frequently than " bobbin."

There are many references to bone lace in

[1] At that time Flanders included not only East and West Flanders,
which are now part of Belgium, but also French Flanders and Artois,
which did not become French till the reign of Louis XIV.

[2] In the *Worthies*, which was published in 1662, the year after his
death.

[3] Latin for a lappet or fringe of a garment.

the works of the 17th Century Dramatists. Thus the pert sempstress in Robert Green's *Tu Quoque* (1614) cries as she enters with her basket of wares : " Buy some quoifs, handkerchiefs, or very good bone lace, mistress ; " and Loveless in Beaumont and Fletcher's play, *The Scornful Lady* (1616), says : " She cuts cambric to a thread, weaves bone lace, and quilts admirably."

In time, however, the distinction between the terms was lost; and Defoe, as early as 1720, calls everything made with bobbins " bone lace."

CHAPTER II

THE NEEDLE-POINT AND BOBBIN LACES
OF THE CONTINENT

The fact that in the picture by Martin Van Vos two women are seen, one working at a frame, and the other on a pillow, does not, of course prove that Lace-making, as we understand it, originated in Flanders. The State of Venice also claimed to have been the cradle of the Industry.

5. Rival Claims.

The Venetians, in support of their theory, have produced documents dated 1476 in which occur passages referring to fabrics made with bobbins; but the Flemings can point to nothing earlier than an altar piece of 1495, at St. Peter's, Louvain, the work of Quentin Matsys, in which a girl was represented making lace, with bobbins similar to those now in use.

The statement, so widely accepted, that the originator of bobbin lace was the gifted and persistent Barbara Uttmann, wife of a mining overseer in Saxony, is a pure invention, for this lady was not born till 1514, that is, nearly twenty years after the date of the lace-pillow picture by Quentin Matsys. What this flaming soul really did was to carry Lace-making as if she were carrying gold into her own country. How good it is to be an enthusiast! It is only the enthusiast who can enter into the joy of his Lord. Despite, however, the fact that she did not invent lace, there can be seen on her tombstone, in the Churchyard of Annaberg the words, written by some ignoramus, "Here lies Barbara Uttmann, died 14th January 1575, whose invention of lace in the year 1561 made her the benefactress of the Hartz Mountains."

The probability then is that Lace made its way from Egypt to Venice, and from Venice to Flanders.

In the previous pages we gave our attention to the inception of Bobbin Lace. Concerning the genesis of Needle-made Lace history is silent. The earliest

6. The Laces of Italy.

needle lace of which we have any definite knowledge is **Reticella,** sometimes called Greek Lace, which was made from 1480 to 1620 at Venice and many other towns. Its designs were geometrical and very beautiful. And, as we shall see, they commended themselves to persons of fashion not only on the Continent but also in England. At the end of the 16th century pattern books for laces were issued both at Venice[1] and also in Flanders, and they were identical in general character.

[1] *Le Pompe*, the first, was published at Venice in 2 vols. in 1557 and 1560. *Corona* was issued in 1591 by Cesare Vecellio.

The earliest Italian Bobbin Laces were also geometrical in design. Imitations of them are now produced by the workers of the Winslow[1] Lace Industry, who have also made a speciality of other early Italian laces. (See Plate 39.) The principal later laces of Italy were **Venetian Raised Point, Venetian Flat Point** and **Venetian Grounded Point,** all of which were made with the needle ; and **Genoa,** which was a mixed lace, the design being bobbin-work, and the ground and fillings needle-work. To these must be added that offspring of Genoa Lace, **Maltese,** which was made entirely on the pillow with bobbins. Lace was made chiefly, then, in Venice, Genoa and Malta.

i. VENICE.

(1.) **Venetian Raised Point (Gros Point de Venise)** dates from 1520. Its characteristics are boldness, a prominent *cordonnet*,[2] and an abundance of *picots*.[3] Later, tiny roses were worked into the various parts, and the lace became known as **Rose Point.** Sometimes above these roses are two other roses, giving the lace the appearance of snow, whence its name, **Point de Neige.**

(2.) **Venetian Flat Point (Point Plat de Venise).** In this lace there is no raised work. A later style of it, **Coralline Point,** or **Mer-**

[1] Bucks.
[2] Thick thread, with which the pattern is outlined. In some laces horsehair is used instead of thread. A gimp is a cordonnet, but all cordonnets are not gimp.
[3] Tiny loops.

maid's Lace, is said to have been first made by a Venetian girl who had received a present of coral from her sailor lover. She imitated it in her work, and thus contrived for herself the double joy of earning a livelihood by her industry and of being continually reminded of her absent friend.

(3.) **Venetian Grounded Point (Point de Venise à réseau)**—Venice Lace with a net ground—was evolved about 1650 in imitation and rivalry of the lace of Alençon, from which it differs chiefly in not possessing a *cordonnet*. A zigzag filling is its characteristic ornament, and lilies and other flowers form the pattern. The industry was destroyed about 1789 by the French Revolution.

ii. GENOA.

Genoa Lace was coarse and solid, hence it was used for boot tops, shoe roses, scarves, and other objects subject to rough usage. Vandyked and deeply rounded scalloped edges were a characteristic, and the "wheat grain" was a common ornament.

iii. MALTA.

Maltese Lace owes its origin to Lady Hamilton Chichester, who introduced Lace-making into Malta in 1833. Having evolved it from Genoese designs, appropriating among other features the "wheat grain" ornament, she introduced into the pattern, out of compliment to the Island, the familiar Maltese Cross. This lace, as we shall see, began to be made about 1850 in England, where it underwent various alterations to suit the tastes of its Northern patrons. (See Chapter 16.)

The oldest Flemish laces seem to have had as foundation a braid or tape, whence **7. The** the name **Pillow Guipure,** but a **Laces of Flanders.** "Trolly," or heavy *cordonnet*, sometimes took the place of the tape. All laces made in Flanders previous to 1665 were known in France as **Malines (Mechlin),** but the lace which we now call Mechlin is not heard of till about 1630.

The principal later laces of Flanders are Brussels (of which there were two leading kinds : **Point à Aiguille** or Needle-made Lace, and **Point Plat** or Bobbin-made, though the needlework and the bobbin-work were often mingled), Mechlin and Antwerp, which were pillow laces.

i. BRUSSELS.

(Dating perhaps from 1520.)

In old **Brussels** the flowers were worked with the net, the meshes of which consisted of four twisted and two plaited sides. (See Plate 4.) In later years the flowers (made either with the needle or on a pillow with bobbins), which were produced first, were connected either with net (which was also made either with a needle or on a pillow with bobbins) or with *brides* (pearl-ties[1]). In the bobbin laces the flowers and leaves are outlined with a raised plaited *cordonnet*. In the needle point laces the *cordonnet* is not covered with button - holing. Later, the flowers were sewn into the ground. The lace in which the pattern was connected with net developed in the 17th Century into **Point d'Angleterre** (see Plate 8), and that in which it was connected by *brides* into **Point d'Angleterre à brides.**

ii. MECHLIN. (See Plate 12.)
(First mentioned about 1630.)

Mechlin which is fine and light as a spider's web is often called the Queen of Laces. Its mesh, like that of Brussels, consists of four twisted and two plaited sides (see Plate 4), but the plaited sides are shorter than those of Brussels. A distinguishing feature of Mechlin is the flat *cordonnet* which forms the flower, giving it the appearance of embroidery. Early Mechlin has an irregular ground, and numbers of tiny holes. The net which we have come to regard as characteristic of Mechlin is to be looked for only in the later laces. The design is generally of a floral character, and scroll work enclosing quatrefoil[2] and other ornamental fillings, is a common feature. For Mechlin lace made in Bucks see Chapter 9, Section 26.

[1] Legs or straps (Bucks).
[2] Four-leaf.

iii. ANTWERP OR POT LACE.

The characteristic of this lace is the coarse Kat Stitch[1] ground. From the fact that a flower-pot or vase always appears in the pattern it is also called **Pot Lace.**

The principal Needle-point Laces of France are **Point de France,** (afterwards called **Point d' Alencon**), and **Point d' Argentan.**

8. The Laces of France,

(1) POINT DE FRANCE AND POINT D' ALENCON.

The **Point de France** industry was established by Colbert,[2] the minister of Louis XIV., who induced workers from Venice to settle at L'Ovray near Alençon. At first it was indistinguishable from Venice Lace, but after 1678 it became more delicate in appearance and the patterns became clearer and more defined. With the change in style came a change in name, and it was thenceforward known as **Point d' Alencon.**

The net of Point d' Alençon is made throughout with a double twisted thread, the looped stitches being twisted on to horizontal threads. The net-work has thus the appearance of lines or rows, and the mesh is square rather than hexagonal. Its *cordonnet* is firmer and clearer than

---

[1] See Chapter 3, Section 11.
[2] He died in 1683. See Plate 9 for his portrait.

Plate 2

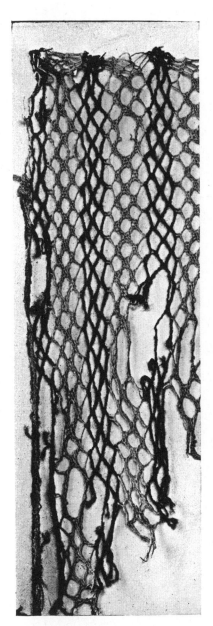

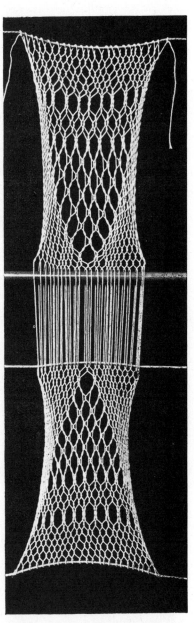

MUMMY LACE. See p. 5.

Victoria and Albert Museum. (*By permission of the Authorities.*)

Miss M. Maidment's Imitation of Egyptian Mummy Lace.

The foundation cords (one at the top and one at the bottom) are left in, but the wooden frame is not shown. A cord near the middle and the round ruler, used for pushing the work up or down into the required position, are also left in, so that the reader may more easily understand the method of working. The only use of the cord left in the middle is to prevent the work from undoing should it be put aside for a short time.

Plate 3

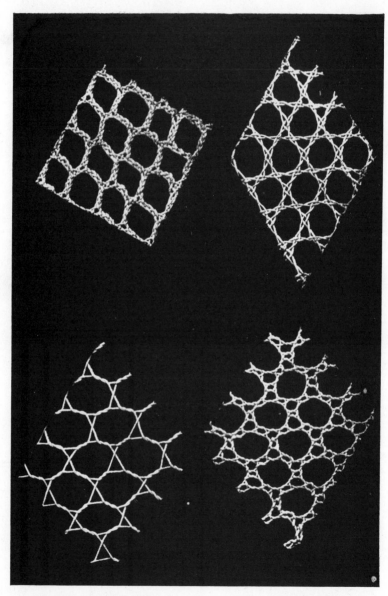

VALENCIENNES NET.   KAT STITCH NET.
LILLE or POINT GROUND NET.   HONEYCOMB NET.

that of any other lace, owing to the fact that it is worked over with horse-hair. Owing to this peculiarity Point d' Alençon can easily be recognized. This lace is also remarkable for the beauty of its fillings.

The principal characteristic of **Argentilla,** a variety of Point d' Alençon, is the ground called the Partridge's Eye (a solid hexagon within a skeleton hexagon).

(2) POINT D' ARGENTAN OR GIANT MESHED LACE.

This lace was made at Argentan near Alençon. Its peculiarity is its giant mesh the sides of which are worked over with button-hole stitch. The mesh is larger than that of any other needle-made lace, and portions of it are fringed with *picots*. Its *cordonnet* is similar to that of Alençon, but the horse-hair is finer.

The principal Pillow Laces of France are Valenciennes, Lille, Chantilly and Blonde.

(1) VALENCIENNES.

This lace is made at Valenciennes, a town which has been French only since 1678. Its mesh is diamond shaped and looks it.[1] (See Plate 3.) There is no *cordonnet*, consequently the fabric is perfectly flat. Other characteristics are its richness of design, the evenness of its tissue, and its

---

[1] This is the mesh so frequently imitated by machinery.

general solidity, resultant from the fact that its mesh is plaited throughout. There are two varieties : **Vraie Valenciennes,** which has only the diamond shaped mesh, and **Fausse Valenciennes,** in which other meshes are introduced.[1]

(2) LILLE.
(Mentioned as early as 1582.)

This lace was made at Lille, which has been French since 1668. The mesh which is diamond shaped but looks hexagonal (owing to the usual treatment of the threads, which are left loose and long at crossing), is called *Fond Simple* or *Fond Clair*. Instead of the sides of the mesh being plaited as in Valenciennes, or partly plaited and partly twisted as in Brussels and Mechlin, they are formed by twisting two threads round each other. It is the finest, lightest and most transparent of grounds. Nobody can mistake it. (See Plate 3.) The pattern is outlined with a *cordonnet*,[2] of flat untwisted coarse thread. The principal beauty of the lace is the fine and clear net which is frequently sprinkled over with *points d' esprit* (small square dots). Old Lille lace has a straight edge and a stiff pattern.

Arras Lace is similar to Lille, but is stronger and firmer to the touch. The laces of Lille and

---

[1] Among the other grounds that occur in Valenciennes lace are the circular mesh and the wire ground. Each centre of the industry had its own bias.

[2] In the case of Lille lace the terms *cordonnet* and gimp are synonymous. Lille lace has more gimp than Mechlin.

Arras particularly interest us because from them in conjunction with Mechlin was evolved our own beautiful Bucks Point. A splendid example of Lille lace is shown in Plate 34.

(3) CHANTILLY.
(White Thread and Black Silk.)

This lace was made at Chantilly (in Oise) and in Normandy. The mesh is Fond Chant[1] (short for Chantilly). The Alençon ground was also used. The pattern is outlined with a *cordonnet* of flat untwisted silk strand. This lace is remarkable for the fineness of its ground and the close workmanship of its flowers. Flax thread lace was made at Chantilly in 1740, and Black Silk lace a little later.

(4) BLONDE.
(Pale Lace.)

Blonde Lace was first made at Caen and other towns in Calvados in 1745. The mesh is that of Lille. In the 18th century it had a *cordonnet* of chenille or of gold thread. The broad flat strand of the *toilé* (close-work) gives it a glistening effect. At first blondes were of the natural creamy colour of silk, but later white and black were made. Sometimes the *toilé* was of coloured silks. Workers in white silk used, in order to avoid the contamination of smoke, to work in winter in lofts over cow-houses—the heat

[1] The Point de Paris reseau is the same.

from the animals supplying the only warmth.[1]
Blonde was introduced into Buckinghamshire
about 1860. See Chapter 16, Section 70.

GERMANY.

To the story of Barbara Uttmann, who seems
to have introduced Lace-making into
9. The Laces of Germany and other Countries. Germany and who died in 1575, we
have already alluded. In 1647 we
hear of the Twelve Old Silver Bearded
Lace-makers of Dorlmund (in Westphalia) who
taught any applicants. Tennyson's old man with
his beard a yard before him and his hair a yard
behind, would have found himself quite at home
with these delightful Westphalians whose beards
were so long that while they worked they were
forced to keep them in bags out of the way of
the bobbins and pins. These old men, by invita-
tation of a merchant named Steenbeck, subsequently settled at Tönder in Jutland, where they
taught their art, which was subsequently practised
all over Denmark.

As the result of Revocation of the Edict of
Nantes (1685), Lace-making made enormous head-
way in Germany, to which country the French
Protestants chiefly emigrated. The laces made
were naturally those of 17th Century France.

SPAIN.

Spain seems to have derived the art of Lace-

[1] Compare our notes on the Fire pot in Chapter 12, Section 38.

making from Italy and Flanders (which was
formerly part of the Spanish dominions). Gold
and silver **Point d'Espagne** of geometric design
was made both in Spain and France; but of the
early Spanish laces we are most interested in the
white lace with gimp in the middle which was
introduced into England by Katharine of Arragon,
by whose name it has since been called. (See
Plate 5.)

CRETE.

Old Crete could construct labyrinths for its
minataurs, and its acrobats were the first in
Europe, but of the involutions of lace it knew
nothing. The laces called **Old Crete** (see Plate
40) are really of comparatively modern origin,
having been derived from those of Venice. They
are chiefly of silk, and some, like the early
Venetian laces, are geometrical in design. A
cordonnet of brightly coloured silken threads sometimes enhances their beauty. There is a collection
of them in the Victoria and Albert Museum,
S. Kensington.

RUSSIA.

Lace has been made in Russia only during
the last hundred years. The Russian laces—
some of which have a vermiculated pattern—are
remarkable for the quaintness of their design
and the brightness of their colours; in short,

they are semi-Oriental. A kind of Torchon with colours introduced is made at Vologda.

AMERICA.

As the result of the energy displayed by Director Flagg and others, lace is now made in Minnesota and other American States, most of the workers being women from various parts of Europe.

CHAPTER III

OUR GARDEN OF DELIGHT
1246

Lace-making was not introduced into England until many years after it had become established on the Continent. It is **10. Embroidery.** true that the English had for centuries made what they called "lace," but this was really embroidery—whether drawn linen or cut work; very attractive, certainly, but not lace as we now understand the term.

Gold "lace" of great beauty adorned the cope and maniple of St. Cuthbert, who died in 685 A.D. To the art of embroidery the Saxon ladies of the courts of Edgar, Edward "the Martyr," and Ethelred paid persistent attention, and Archbishop Dunstan (who died in 988) and other men of taste made artistic and charming designs for them. The richly embroidered orphreys of the English clergy in 1246 led Pope Innocent IV. to allude to England as "our garden of delight." The priests in Chaucer's latter period (1375—1400) peacocked it in marvellous gowns of scarlet and green cut work. The ladies of the day were fond of plaiting threads into a little looped edging which they

called purling or pearling. Purling is mentioned
in *Canterbury Tales* (1390), and it is pleasing to
note that from this time downwards the English
have shown a persistent affection for these ingra-
tiating purls, loops, or *picots*. Furthermore, when
in this country what is now understood as lace
came to be made—whether Bucks Point or the
far later Maltese—they put in a plea for their
favourite ornament, and the worker, delighted to
humour so charming a taste, has ever since
allowed to rise over the headside those pretty
bubbles which to the poetical eye are not bubbles
at all but actual pearls.

Anne of Bohemia (wife of Richard II.), the
ladies of her court (1374—1394), and the nuns
in the convents delighted to make wonderful
embroidered altar cloths and winding sheets in
which figured bizarre and fearsome monsters
that ramp only in dreams, weird looking Post-
Impressionist trees, and gorgeous armorial devices
embracing swallows without legs, lions and horses
with wings, and other improvements on nature.
The designers were poets, though they never
wrote a line, and all poets have been wayward
from Pindar, who ascribed to the Muses violet
hair, to Payne who made it rain silver lilies.[1]
This work helped the nuns to beguile the
monotony of their cloistered lives. The daring
colour schemes and other rich effects contrasted

[1] " A Soul's Antiphon."

curiously with the pallor of the worker, and imparted glory to many an etiolated frame and many a morbid life.

But of all the ladies who in early times in this country made "lace," the most famous was Katharine of Arragon, **11. Katharine of Arragon, 1531.** wife of Henry VIII. She delighted "in working with the needle curiously," and when great folks called on her they found her, as often as not, "busy at work with her maids," and "with a skein of red silk about her neck." Her favourite occupation seems to have been cut work, the patterns used being probably those brought by her from Spain.

In 1531, when this aesthetic queen was living in retirement at Ampthill, while her appeal to Rome respecting her divorce was impending, she taught the people in some of the Bedfordshire villages her favourite art. Indeed, it is handed down that in a hard time, when the villagers were put to it to get bread, she burnt her "lace," with the object of affording herself an excuse for placing new orders among them, though one would have looked in so inventive a mind for a more sensible expedient.

In respect to Katharine of Arragon we are confronted with two theories :

(1) That the "lace" made under her direction was Spanish embroidery or cut work, and not lace as we now understand the term.

(2) That, though an adept at embroidery, she also made bobbin lace,[1] into the mysteries of which she may have been initiated by workers from Venice or Flanders who had drifted into Spain or England. In support of this theory it may be observed that there is still made in Northants a lace with an antique Italian look which is called Queen Katharine Pattern[2] (see Plate 5)—the chief characteristic of which is that the gimp runs through the middle of the design, instead of forming, as in most other laces, its outline and veining. Then, too, the people of Madeira, where Queen Katharine lace is also made, allege that the patterns came from Spain. And lastly, there is a stitch — the Kat Stitch (also called French ground, wire ground, six-pointed star ground, and—in Bucks—hair-pin stitch, and many other names, see Plate 3), which takes eight bobbins to a pin instead of four like other stitches; and for its invention Katharine has been given the credit.

Nevertheless, it was in embroidery that Katharine most excelled—her needle being chiefly employed in decorating copes, many of which, according to Peter Heylyn, were made of "cloth of tyssue, of cloth of gold and silver, or embroidered velvet;" but the poor lady's ingenuity was put to purposes very different from what she

---

[1] The altar cloth at Paulerspury Church, Northants, is said to have been designed from Katharine of Arragon parchments.
[2] It is still made at Paulerspury, Northants.

had intended, for in a very few years came the Reformation, when all these gorgeous vestments were appropriated by the nobles and devoted to domestic uses. According to this same Peter Heylyn, " Many private men's parlours were hung with altar cloths, their tables and beds covered with copes, instead of carpets and coverlids. It was a sorry house which had not a fair large cushion made of a cope." [1]

But whatever became of her work, whether in the way of embroidery or lace, lovers of the arts have come to regard this unhappy lady as one of the long line of artists whose enthusiasm and abandon have enlarged the human outlook and have given beauty for ashes.

[1] *History of the Reformation of the Church of England :* Address to the Reader and p. 134.

CHAPTER IV

THE FIRST EXODUS.

1563—1568. (See Plate 11.)

For many years the people of the Low Countries, most of whom were Protestants,
had under the rule of Charles V. of
Spain, enjoyed, in spite of steady persecution and oppression, unpreced-
ented prosperity, and their principal cities, especially Antwerp, Ghent, and Bruges, became both
opulent and powerful. When, however, in 1556,
and amid circumstances of histrionic pomp, his
son Philip II.,[1] a dark, domineering, narrow-
minded, icy anatomy ascended the throne, a
period of gloom at once set in. He resolved
straightway to impose upon those countries the
maintenance of a Spanish Army and to re-estab-
lish in them the hated Inquisition. Hundreds
of godly persons were flung into prison. Reading
the Bible was forbidden. Men who attended
religious meetings were beheaded, women burnt
alive. The towns reeked with murder. The
penalty to a Catholic for sheltering a Protestant
was also death. As a result, and rather than

12. The Mechlin Workers flock to Cranfield.

[1] He married Mary I., Queen of England, in 1554, and he reigned from
1555 to 1598.

apostatize, thousands of the Flemings fled from the country, and very many found their way to England. The earliest—a number of whom were lace-makers—seem to have arrived at the coast towns of Kent in 1563, where they worked at their calling—making, in the term of the day, "parchment lace." Among the arrivals at Dover were "twenty-five widows," makers of "bone lace and spinners." The husbands of these poor creatures had, doubtless, but a few days previous been foully murdered. Four hundred settled at Sandwich, and Archbishop Parker who visited that town in 1563 says that "the refugees were as godly on the Sabbath days as they were industrious on week days," adding that such "profitable and gentle strangers ought to be welcome and not to be grudged at."

Galled by the opposition to his commands, Philip in order to enforce them sent hot-foot into the Low Countries in 1567 an army under the Duke of Alva, a bigot who was more fanatical and truculent even than Philip himself. A period of terror then ensued, and over a hundred thousand Protestants abandoned their native country and emigrated to England, where they were received with every kindness, and in many towns subscriptions were raised for them. The lace they brought with them was regarded by our countrymen with wonder and admiration. At first like their predecessors they settled in the coast towns of Kent, and Sussex, but many drifted to Southwark and Bermondsey. The lace-makers among them, however, who came from the Mechlin country made their way (in 1568) to Cranfield in Bedfordshire—the earliest fixing their abode at the part of the village called Bourne End where at the time was a Tudor mansion, the owner of which seems to have stood their friend. A little later others found their way into Buckinghamshire, settling especially at Newport Pagnell, Olney and Buckingham.

It is said when Linnæus saw for the first time the gold of the gorse plant, he fell on his knees and thanked God for making anything so beautiful. Some such feeling must have stirred the ladies of Bedfordshire and Buckinghamshire when with astonished eyes they saw the marvellous webs shape and repeat themselves on the Flemish pillows.

Persons who are fond of noting coincidences may like to be reminded that the patron saint of Buckingham, "the county of beautiful lace," and of Mechlin, "the city of costly lace," are one and the same, namely, the wonderful baby, Saint Rumbald, who during his excessively short life of only three days did innumerable pious acts and performed astounding miracles. His sumptuous shrine at Buckingham, which drew pilgrims from all parts, was demolished at the Reformation, but his remains somehow found their way to the cathedral at Mechlin, where they were until recently, and probably still are, most gorgeously enshrined. So Buckingham gave to Mechlin a saint for whom she had ceased to have any particular use, and Mechlin in return presented Buckingham with a lace which she was delighted to possess. Each was more than satisfied with the bargain. If only all business could be conducted in so pleasant a fashion!

The industry established itself almost everywhere in Bucks, Beds, and Northants. Men, women, and children all made point lace—the sleepy giants of Wilstead,[1] the Johns and Joans of Clapham,[2] the gokes[3] of Yardley Gobion, the black-eyed girls of Fritwell, the skegs[4] of Brackley, the moon-rakers of Grendon,[5] the thatchers' wives of Haddenham,[6] the ripe beauties of King's Sutton,[7] the wearisome musicians of Lavendon,[8] the girls whose hair was all North Crawley[9] and the girls whose hair was tidy—in

---

[1] Wilshamstead near Bedford, once noted for its fine men. The various characteristics of the people of the villages mentioned are taken from local proverbs.

[2] Favourite names at Clapham, near Bedford.

[3] I.e., simpletons. Cf., "Half sharp and hardly, like the folk of Yardley." See *Proverbs of Northamptonshire*, by Major C. A. Markham.

[4] "Brackley skegs "—rustics.

[5] The men of Grendon tried to rake the moon (thinking it was a cheese) out of the village pond.

[6] "At Haddenham they thatch the ponds to keep the ducks dry."—Old saying.

[7] "King's Sutton for beauty."—Old saying.

[8] "It's like Lavendon play—all alike."—Old saying.

[9] All awry. An allusion to the crookedness of Crawley Brook.

short, to use a Northamptonshire saying, all the world and Little Billing¹ made lace.

Subsequently the workers spread over all that belt of country that stretches from Cambridge to Dorset and Somerset, but, as time went on, Lace-land gradually shrank until it corresponded only with Bucks, Beds and Northants, and narrow fringes of Hunts, Herts and Oxon—the centre being the fortified town of Olney, most of the point lace being made within a radius of thirty miles of it. The Northampton portion of the district " is placed," to use the words of an old writer, " upon the middle and top of the nation."²

Curiously enough, we owe to these Flemings not only the Lace industry, but also our more important vegetables. Cabbages, carrots and celery came in with Flanders lace. They had previously been almost as scarce as diamonds. Owing to the lack of them cutaneous diseases were common. The leper with his head hidden save at the two eye-holes, rang as he walked through the streets his melancholy bell to warn intruders from approaching. Every church had its leper or low window through which the wretched sufferer could receive the host by the instrumentality of a cleft stick.³ Nobody could

¹ Village near Northampton.
² *Another Outcry of the Innocent and Oppressed.* A tract written in the time of Charles II.
³ For other theories respecting these windows see Major C. A. Markham's valuable brochure, *The Low Side Windows of Northamptonshire,* 1908.

Plate 4

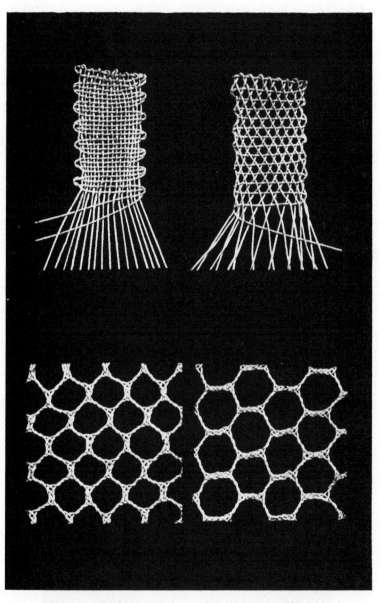

WHOLE STITCH. HALF STITCH.
MECHLIN NET. BRUSSELS NET.

Plate 5

KATHARINE OF ARRAGON LACE. See p. 26.

Made at Potters Pury.

PEACOCK'S TAIL (INSERTION). See p. 81.

Made at Turweston.

give his sweetheart, or his sovereign for the matter
of that, a more acceptable present than a cabbage
or a bunch of carrots. The Flemings at once
set about sowing, with the result of crops of
turnips, parsnips, carrots and other vegetables,
" all of which," says an old writer, " were great
wonders, we having few or none in England but
what came from Holland or Flanders."[1]

These settlers, as well as the Huguenots who,
as we shall see, flocked a little later to Bedfordshire, used to gather together for worship in one
another's houses, but gradually most of them
became absorbed in the Baptist and Independent
bodies. This fact explains the position, otherwise
incomprehensible, of a number of the early Non-
conformist chapels. The Baptist chapel at Cranfield, for instance (the cause was founded in 1660)[2]
is far out of the village proper, but at a convenient
distance from the Flemish settlement at Bourne
End where at the time there must have been a
considerable number of cottages. A windmill at
the north end of the village (the nearest point to
Bourne End), and not far from the chapel, gives a
Flemish touch to the scenery even to-day.

The magnet that drew to Cranfield the Flemish
Protestants of 1568 and their successors, the
Huguenots of 1688, was probably the influence of

---

[1] Hartlib, writing in 1650, quoted by Smiles in *The Huguenots*, p. 107.
[2] Its first pastor, William Wheeler, published in 1670 *A Spiritual Portion of Heavenly Treasure.*

the powerful Russell family, whose seat was at Woburn close by. The head of the House at this time was Francis, 2nd Earl of Bedford, whose son William distinguished himself at Zutphen, 22nd Sept., 1586 (the battle at which Sir Philip Sidney died fighting with William of Orange against Philip II. of Spain, the persecutor of the Flemish Protestants); and it is worthy of note that Lord William Russell, the patriot (who was son of the 5th Earl and 1st Duke) married Rachel, daughter of the Huguenot Marquis de Rivigny.

Another great Bedfordshire family that was all on fire to help the Flemish Protestants was the House of Gascoigne, whose seat was Cardington Manor. George Gascoigne the poet,[1] a member of this family, who wrote his *Fruites of Warre* "piecemeale at sundrye tymes" while he was fighting under the standard of William of Orange, had the advantage of being able to converse freely with the refugees in their own tongue.

Nevertheless, the name of the prime mover in this affair is unknown. As a rule God performs a work in (or through) us, and we get, or give ourselves, the credit for it. In this instance the human instrument is concealed and we can see only the First Cause.

---

[1] Born perhaps in 1525, died 1577. A good account of George Gascoigne was given in the *Beds Times*, Sept. 8th, 1916.

Whereas the Mechlin workers flocked to Bedfordshire, those from Brussels made 13. The
their way to Honiton and other places Brussels
in Devonshire, and the lace (altered to flock to
suit the requirements of their adopted Honiton.
country) became known as "Honiton," but the
term "Devonshire Lace" is preferable. From the
first the Devonshire fabric, unlike that of Brussels,
had an outlining of gimp. Its two earliest stages
were :

1. *The Artistic Pattern and Net Stage.* The
patterns or sprigs which were of artistic design
were worked on a pillow with bobbins and then
arranged artistically on another pillow. Net was
worked among them with bobbins; or the patterns were stitched on hand-made net, forming
Appliqué Work.

2. *The Artistic Pattern and Guipure Stage.* A
little later, instead of the net being made, the
patterns were artistically united by purl-pin-bars,
the work being done with bobbins. This operation
was called purling. In some districts the sprigs
were first tacked to a blue paper foundation and
then joined with a needle-made net.[1]

Flemish names, such as Murch, Groot, Speller,
Kettel, Boatch and Woram, are found in the
district, and memorials to lace-workers abound,
the most interesting being an altar tomb in the

[1] The two subsequent stages in Devonshire Lace will be noted in
Chapter 17.

old church of St. Michael, Honiton, which is inscribed : " Here lyeth ye body of James Rodge of Honiton in ye county of Devonshire (bone lace siller, hath given unto the poore of Honiton Pishe the Benyfitt of £100 for ever) who deceased ye 27th of July A.D. 1617, aetatae svae 50 Remember the poore."

Soon after the Flemish Exodus brass wire pins came into general use in this country. Pins of a sort had been made here as early as 1347, but our brass wire pins date only from about 1530. By the statute of 1543 entitled " An act for the True making of Pynnes " the price was not to exceed 6/8 per 1000. Nevertheless until 1626, when John Tilsby established a manufactory in Gloucestershire, most of the pins used by English workers were imported from France. The Pinmakers' Corporation of London was not established till 1636.

Plate 6

THE MAIDS OF MAIDS MORTON. See p. 40.

The original belongs to J. M. Knapp, Esq., of Little Linford, Bucks. This picture was lent by Miss Burrowes of Maids Morton.

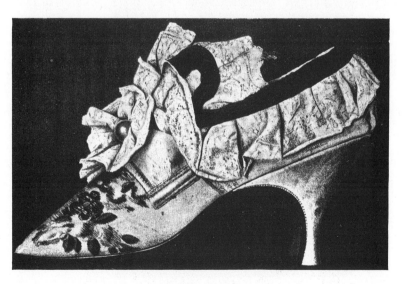

LACED SHOE

that belonged to a Miss Langley, time of Charles II. See p. 58.

It is made of pale yellow silk, tastefully embroidered and trimmed with lace. The ribbon at the top is green, the sole is brown. In the possession of Mr. T. Watson Greig, of Glencaise. From the *Book of Illustrations of Collections of Ladies' Old-Fashioned Shoes*, by T. Watson Greig. For permission to use it we have to thank the Committee of the Northampton Free Library.

See Note on the text.

Plate 7

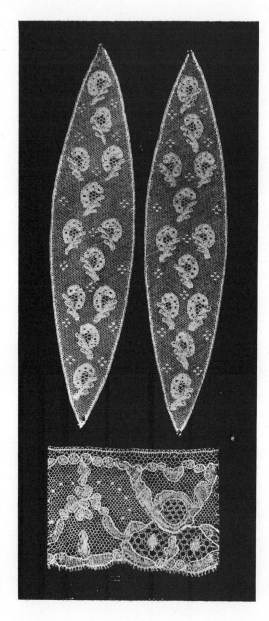

PERIWINKLE PATTERN.

Two Stocking Fronts. Lent to the Exhibition of Paris, 1914. At the time the Germans came near Paris these fronts and other specimens of lace were bricked up in the cellars of the Louvre for safety. Stocking fronts were used in Queen Elizabeth's day. See p. 40.

Queen Elizabeth Lace. See p. 70.

Lent by Mrs. J. B. Harrison, formerly of Paulerspury.

CHAPTER V

THE SECOND EXODUS

1572. (See Map, Plate 11.)

On 24th August, 1572, occurred that terrible slaughter of the Huguenots in Paris and other towns of France, which has ever since been known as the Massacre of St. Bartholomew. It was ordered by the young Charles IX. of France, who had been instigated by his mother, the cruel Catherine de Medicis.

14. The Massacre of St. Bartholomew, Aug. 24, 1572. Flemish and French Names.

The king himself, armed with an arquebus, fired at his subjects from one of the windows of the Louvre. Over 100,000 were murdered—men, women and children. A thrill of indignation and anger went through England when the awful news arrived; but when Philip II. of Spain heard it, his marble face relaxed, and he laughed for the first and only time in his life.

Many of the survivors escaped to England; and the lace-makers among them, who came chiefly from Lille and the neighbourhood, found their way into Buckinghamshire and Northamptonshire, where they joined the Mechlin workers from Flanders who had for several years been settled

there. As a natural result we find that many of
the old designs of these parts are a combination
of the two laces, Mechlin and Lille. Frequently
the Mechlin design is worked with the Lille net,
which is easier to make than the Mechlin ground.
Then, too, and as might be supposed, very many
Flemish and Huguenot names are still to be
found in the Lace-making districts of Bucks,
Beds and Northants. Thus we find Minard,
Cattell, Rubythorn and Raban at Olney; De Ath
and Rennels at Buckingham; Perrin at Moulsoe;
Lathall at North Crawley; Simons at Hanslope;
Bitchiner, Sawell, Glass, De Ath, Vaux, Waples,
Francy and Cayles at Cranfield;[1] Le Fevre at
Harrold; Dudeney (Dieu donné) at Bedford;
Nurseaw at Sherington; Mulliner and Conant at
Northampton; and Laycock (Le Coq) at Welling-
borough. There were Independent ministers
named Hillyard both at Olney and Bedford.
The Rev. John Newton used to hold prayer
meetings in the cottage of Molly Mole (Mohl).
But many hundreds of other instances could be
given. Almost every town and village within
thirty miles of Olney has persons with Flemish or
French names, and practically the whole population must be partially of Flemish or French
descent.

[1] Mrs. A. Glass, of Iddesleigh Road, Bedford, says that her grandmother, who was born in 1795, was a parchment maker, and a descendant
of the Flemings who first settled at Cranfield. Her designs were sometimes traced from the touches of frost on the window panes.

The wretched king who had ordered the massacre lived only two years, which were tortured with remorse. " Sleeping or waking," he said to his physician, " the murdered Huguenots present themselves to my eyes, with ghastly faces and weltering in blood." In his last moments he was attended by a Huguenot nurse. He died " howling " on 30th May, 1574. The punishment of the infamy of Philip II. of Spain was longer delayed. He died unrepentant, of a lingering, loathsome disease on 13th September, 1598—his hands red with murder and, amazing to say, the name of " Jesus " on his lips. The obsequies were necessarily hurried.

The Huguenot exodus continued until 1598 when it was arrested by the promulgation of the Edict of Nantes, the act of the great and sagacious Henry IV. of France. Allowed, after sixty years of persecution, to worship God in their own way, the Huguenots no longer turned their eyes to England.

When Queen Elizabeth ascended the throne, the Lace industry in this country advanced by leaps and bounds, the great feature in the way of finery at her spectacular court being the enormous ruff supported by a wire frame **15. Lace at the Court of Elizabeth. Mary, Queen of Scots. 1558—1603.** and stiffened with starch. The ruff, as contemporary records show, was often edged with lace, which, however, was not necessarily made in

England. Elizabeth herself favoured a ruff
trimmed with the most elaborate thread guipure
and linen cuffs turned over and edged with similar
lace. One of the most interesting pictures of
ladies wearing the laced ruff and cuffs is that of
the Maids of Maids Morton, near Buckingham,
who are supposed to have been joined together
like the Siamese twins. The original was painted
by Zuchero, the court painter to Queen Elizabeth,
but the portraits are for the most part imagi-
nary, the only authority for them having been a
brass which formerly existed in Maids Morton
Church. Zuchero painted the ladies not in the
dress shown on the brass, that is to say of the
time when they actually lived, but in the dress
of his own day.[1] (See Plate 6.)

Another fashion of the period was the use of
Stocking Fronts made of lace. A pair of these
with the Periwinkle pattern is shown in Plate 7.

The poets and poetical prose writers of Elizabeth's court, although admiring lace for its own
sake, took their chief pleasure in it from the fact
that, in the elegant phrasing of Sir Philip Sidney,
it was after all "but a fair ambassador of a most
fair mind." Kit Marlowe, Robert Greene, and
the other fierce intellectual spirits of the time,
loved lace as they loved everything else that was

---

[1] The original picture was left as an heirloom long ago to the family of
J. M. Knapp, Esq., of Linford Hall, Bucks. My friend, the Rev. J.
Tarver, of Tyringham, who married into the Knapp family, wrote a poem
on the subject, with the title of *The Maids of Maids Morton*.

"passing brave." Edmund Spenser, author of
the *Faerie Queen*, appears in his best known
portrait in a collar trimmed with reticella of
beautiful design ; but most of Elizabeth's courtiers wore lace of geometric patterns which may
have been made in Devonshire.[1] Nobody was
happy unless his head looked like John the Baptist's on a charger.

Lace, indeed, had come to stay, but the trouble
was that the ladies could not properly see themselves in it, for they had on their toilette
tables nothing better than a sheet of polished
metal. But science, ever sympathetic to the sigh
of beauty, came promptly to the rescue, and presented the sex with what the poet George
Gascoigne called a " mirror of glas," that
"glistred bright" and showed " a seemly shewe,"[1]
which was well, for without a looking-glass what
even is lace !

Elizabeth's famous rival, Mary Queen of Scots,
was not only a wearer but also a designer of
lace. Moreover, she is said to have made lace
during the tedious years of her captivity ; and on
the fatal morning of 8th February, 1587, when
she appeared before the block, and so closed a
life made up of wild fits of delight and seasons
of unspeakable agony, she wore on her head " a

[1] See Chapter 6, Section 17.
[1] *The Steele Glas*, 1576.

dressing of lawn edged with bone lace," and a
" veil of lawn fastened to her cowl, bowed out
with wire and edged round about with bone lace."
Her resting-place is a cinque-cento tomb in
Westminster Abbey, and on her effigy is a laced
ruff. She too, scarlet as were her sins, is one
of the saints in the Lace-lover's Calendar.

The same year that Mary was executed Vin-
ciolo, the Venetian artist, published his Book of
Designs for Bone Lace, and doubtless its influence extended to England.

If the gallants and court beauties of Whitehall
decked themselves with reticella, Venice
Point, or the newly introduced laces of
Mechlin and Lille, the village beauties
of Cambridgeshire and Bedfordshire had recourse
to the cheap but showy lace, made locally no
doubt, which was offered for sale at the fairs
held in Cambridgeshire and elsewhere on St.
Etheldreda's[1] day (October 17th). What St.
Etheldreda's Lace (or Tawdry, as they called it ·
for short) was like we do not know—and we do
not even know whether it was a lace in the
modern acceptance of the term—but there are
many references to it in our old writers.

Mopsa, the shepherdess, in Shakespeare's
Winter Tale (Act IV., Scene 4) says : " You
promised me a tawdry lace and a pair of sweet

16. Tawdry Lace. 1590.

---

[1] St. Etheldreda died in 679, abbess of the convent at Ely.

gloves ; " and Amaryllis in Beaumont and Fletcher's *Faithful Shepherdess* (Act IV., Scene 1)
speaks of " The primrose chaplet, tawdry lace
and ring."

CHAPTER VI

FROM THE ACCESSION OF JAMES I. TO THE DEATH OF CROMWELL.

1603—1659.

Among those who revealed an enthusiasm for the beautiful Bucks lace was Anne of **17. Newport Pagnell, Olney, and Great Marlow.** Denmark (wife of James I.), upon whom it dawned that enthusiasm for anything that is beautiful, elevating, or provocative of thought, is the elixir of life—the new wine of the kingdom. This queen in 1603 purchased at Winchester and Basing both " Great Bone Lace " and " Little Bone Lace "—that is to say, wide and narrow point. A love for Art was beginning to spread through the country. In every great house there was a "Frippery"—a room set apart for the preservation of beautiful articles, including lace.

From the first all seems to have gone well in North Bucks; and the dealers of Newport Pagnell, not content with making a profit all the week, must needs do business on a Sunday; for we learn that in 1611 certain of them, " who continuallie travelled to sell bone lace on the Sabbath day," were presented at an ecclesiastical

Plate 8

POINT D' ANGLETERRE LAPPET.

Victoria and Albert Museum. See p. 49. *(By permission of the Authorities.)*

Plate 9

COLBERT.

*From the original by V. Mignard in the Collection of the Institute
at Paris.   See p. 16.*

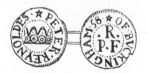

BUCKINGHAM LACE TOKEN,
showing strip of lace on the obverse.   See p. 57.

Lent by the Bucks Archæological Association.

visitation.[1] The prosperity of Newport Pagnell was shared by Olney (Ouldney, as Fuller and other writers spell it), Little Brickhill (then an assize town[2]) and Stony Stratford. As might be supposed, the Parish Registers of this part of Bucks contain many references to lace-makers, lace-men, lace-dealers and lace-buyers. The earliest in this category is the entry in the Ravenstone Register of the marriage of Roger Gadsden (24th January, 1636), who is later described as a "lace-maker;"[3] and there is an entry in the Bletchley Register under 1638 relative to William Stopp, "lace-buyer," but almost every parish could furnish instances.

In the south of Bucks things went not well, for on April 8th, 1623, a petition was addressed from Great Marlow to the High Sheriff of Bucks, representing the distress of the people from the "bone lace-making being much decayed." Then Sir Henry Borlase came forward and (in 1626) endowed the Free School at Great Marlow, where he provided for 24 boys to be taught reading and to "cast accounts," and for 24 girls "to knit, spin and make bone lace," but his efforts met with only partial success.

If Great Marlow suffered, it was not because lace was less worn, but because so many persons

---

[1] F. W. Bull : *History of Newport Pagnell.*

[2] Between 1561 and 1620 as many as 42 criminals were executed and buried here.

[3] At this period many men made lace.

imported from the Continent instead of sup-
porting the home industry. The ruff was still
patronised, but the Laced Collar, as might be
judged from the portraits of Henry, Prince of
Wales (James the First's son), Ralph Verney of
Claydon,[1] George Digby, Earl of Bristol, and
many other notabilities, was gradually supplanting
it. High boots lined with rich lace were also
worn in this reign, the tops being turned down
in order to display it.

The monumental effigies of the period, on
many of which lace is sculptured, show that the
taste for reticella and similar fabrics which prevailed in Elizabeth's day continued far into the
reign of James I. The geometric lace represented on the effigy of Lady Doddridge (1614)
in Exeter Cathedral, and on that to Lady Pole
in Colyton Church (1623) may have been made
in Devonshire.

The unbridled extravagance of the time under
the head of lace led the divines again and again
to thunder against it. The Rev. Henry Smith,
the pithiest preacher of the day, says in his
sermon, " The Triall of Vanitie,"[2] "And yet
there are more vanities in our apparrell, ruff
vpon[3] ruffe, lace vpon lace . . . as though
our apparrell were apparrelled vntil the woman.

---

[1] *Memoirs of the Verney Family*, 1892. Vol. i, p. 112.
[2] *Sermons*, 1618, pp. 158, 362.
[3] In the books of those days v's were often used for u's and u's for v's.

be not worth so much as her attire." He was no Puritan, he tells us, and therefore had nothing to say against lace in reason, but it grieved him to see gentlemen forced to "sell their lands" in order to "decke their wiues." Even the obtrusion of death did not stay the extravagance, and it was considered quite wonderful that the brilliant and versatile Sir Kenelm Digby, of Gayhurst,[1] whose dress was customarily as various as a rainbow, and who delighted in broad, rich and exotic laced collars and cuffs, attired himself, after the death in 1633 of his lady, in the dress of a "hermite," and never again wore either colour or lace.

Charles I., with the object of encouraging the English industry, brought in a law (1635) which strictly prohibited the importation of foreign "purles, cut works, and bone laces." An improvement at once took place in the local manufactures, and our goods were not only used at home but also to a considerable extent exported. The smuggling of lace from Flanders naturally followed, and, as we shall presently see, persons of all walks in life were again and again found to be engaging in it.

Under Cromwell the use of lace was discontinued among the middle and lower classes. The "quality," however, still used it, though sparingly. We hear

18. The Puritans and Lace.

[1] Bucks.

of a wonderful handkerchief consisting chiefly of broad point lace which had belonged to Cromwell's mother, and if many of the ladies were more given, as their enemies worded it, to "gossiping Scripture," than to decking their persons, nevertheless there were others who did not deny themselves "whisks" (lace gorgets), while their husbands thought it no sin to wear cuffs and bands. At the same time among the Puritans, absorbed as so many of them were in the study of "the History and the Mystery," that is to say of God's Word and God's dealings with themselves personally, the use of lace was as a rule discouraged, and it is worthy of note that the word "lace" does not once occur in the poems of Milton. If it be urged that the lady whom he chiefly celebrated could have had for the fabric no particular use, it must be pointed out that he also sang various modern ladies; moreover, the industries of Buckinghamshire and Cambridgeshire were as familiar to him as those of Eden.

Some of the Puritan beauties satisfied their consciences and at the same time gratified their taste for lace and embroidery by making these fabrics the medium for representing subjects connected with Scripture. As the satirists said, they wore "religious petticoats" and "holy embroidery."

Plate 10

OLD BUCKS POINT LACE.

(Lent by Mrs. W. W. Carlile.)

BUCKS POINT LACE.

(Lent by Miss Pope.)

Plate 11

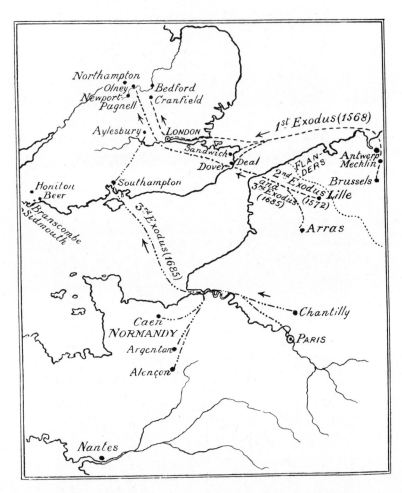

Map showing the principal routes taken by the Flemish and Huguenot
Emigrants in 1568, 1572, and 1685. In the last period a number of
the refugees went from Nantes and Bordeaux to Portsmouth.

CHAPTER VII

THE REIGN OF CHARLES II.

1660—1685

By the time of Charles II. Brussels Lace had undergone a remarkable alteration. The pattern became far more elabo-rate; the outline of the design and **19. Point d' Angleterre. 1660.** the veins of the leaves became raised—an effect achieved by twisting and plaiting, not by using a thicker thread; and a number of grounds were used, with the result of one of the most beautiful laces ever invented. It obtained the name of **Point d' Angleterre**[1] (English Point). In some varieties of this lace the openings left in the pattern were filled with *brides* (legs), whence this kind was called **Point d' Angleterre à Brides.** In both varieties fine needle-point fillings were often added.

Two theories have been put forth respecting the origin of this lace, and with a view to explaining its name.

1. That of Mrs. Palliser, Miss Alice Dryden, Miss M. Jourdain and others, who hold that it originated at Brussels—that it is, as a matter of

[1] See Plate 8.

fact, Brussels lace of the best period. They point out that in 1661 Charles II. issued a proclamation enforcing his father's Act which prohibited the entry of Continental lace; and allege not only that the merchants, finding themselves unable to bring their Brussels Lace to England openly, had recourse to smuggling; but also that, in order to protect themselves, they both sold it in this country and exported it into France as *Point d' Angleterre*.[1] Consequently, notwithstanding its name, none of it was ever made in England. In support of this theory, Mrs. Palliser quotes a memorandum by the Venetian Ambassador to the English Court in 1695, who states that the lace then in fashion in England was "that called English point, which you know is not made here but in Flanders, and only bears the name of English to distinguish it from the others."

2. The second theory, which is held by M. Seguin, Mrs. Neville Jackson and Mr. H. H. Armstrong of Olney, is that this lace originated in Devonshire where large quantities were made, and that the Brussels workers who made still larger quantities were only the copiers. They are of opinion that the name alone sufficiently proves that the lace was made in England. They argue further, that you might just as well contend that because the best Valenciennes lace was for long

[1] Ed. 1902, p. 117.

made at Ypres it was never made at Valenciennes, and they point out that it was the invariable custom in early times for a fabric to retain the name where it was first produced in quantity.

" It is quite time," says Mrs. Neville Jackson, " English people realised that one of the finest results of the lace industry which the world has ever seen, was an original English product, and that it owed only an occasional improvement in fine stitching to foreign influence.[1] . . Rodge of Devonshire obtained the Flemish secret of making the fine fillings and joins which give the finishing touch in rendering *Point d' Angleterre* one of the most perfect types of lace which have ever been invented. The chief portion of the finest *Point d' Angleterre* was made in England. The Honiton lace of to-day is but the exquisite *Point d' Angleterre* of the Restoration period in a debased condition."[2] Mr. Armstrong, who supports this view, considers that the ladder work alone which appears so frequently both in the Honiton fabrics and in *Point d' Angleterre* is sufficient evidence that *Point d' Angleterre* was made in Devonshire.

Furthermore, it is held by those who accept the second theory that the statement of the Venetian Ambassador carries very little weight, since his knowledge was derived only from hearsay—there

---

[1] *A History of Hand-made Lace*, p. 154, pub. in 1900.

[2] This was written in 1900. Since that date great improvements have been made in Honiton Lace.

being no evidence that he ever set foot in Devonshire.

In the courts of Louis XIV. and Louis XV.,
in the period, that is to say, of hoops and
powder, *Point d' Angleterre* was in high favour,
but it is mentioned in almost every book that
touches upon the fashions of that time. That
salacious gentleman, M. Jacques Casanova, writing
of the year 1760 and describing his adventures in
the inn of the Sword at Zurich, where he pretended to be a butler in order to get into con-
versation with a pretty lady, says : " I had tucked
my ruffles, which were of superb English Point
(Point d' Angleterre à l' aiguille) inside my sleeves,
but a bit of my cravat, which was of the same
lace, peeped through my button-hole. When I
handed her her plate she noticed it. ' Wait,
wait, a minute!' she said, ' What beautiful lace
you wear!' "

Of the dressy persons in Charles the Second's
time none has obtained more notice
than Samuel Pepys. As his famous
"Diary" shows, he regarded lace as a
necessity. So pleased is he on 8th October, 1662,
with his "scallop" (lace collar or band[1] with
scalloped edges) that cost £3, that he straightway
went and ordered another at the same price.
On "Lord's Day," October 19th, he writes :
"Put on my first new lace band; and so neat

20. Samuel
Pepys.
1662.

---

[1] A band-box was originally a box to hold bands (lace collars).

it is that I am resolved my great expense shall
be lace bands."

But although Pepys was never the man to
deny himself in lace, he was apt (alas!) to fall
into an economical mood when his wife was concerned. "My wife and I," he says on one occasion, "fell out about my not being willing to have
her gowne laced. . . At this she flounced away
in a manner I never saw her, nor which I could
ever endure." She even went so far as to say that
she "would go and buy a new one and lace it and
make me pay for it." Indeed, poor man! her
tantrums "vexed" him "cruelly."

Mrs. Pepys, however, was outdone by Mrs.
Loveit, in Etheridge's *Sir Fopling Flutter*, who, in
a fit of love and jealousy, broke "a dozen or two
of fans," tore "half a score points[1] in pieces,"
and destroyed "hoods and knots without number."

The Huguenot lace-makers, even though they
were out of reach of their French
enemies, were by no means exempt
from persecution. The nation had
warmly welcomed Charles II. and was
on the way to enshrining him in her large heart,
but she soon discovered that the temple was
too big for the god. As we have already noticed,
most of the immigrants had joined themselves
to the English Nonconformists, whose manner of

**21. The
Persecutions
of the reign
of Charles II.
1670—1672.**

---

[1] Pieces of lace.

worship their own closely resembled. In the reign of Charles II., however, Act after Act of Parliament bore upon the Nonconformists and their Huguenot friends with cruel severity; and the jails were filled with men against whom nothing could be alleged except that they were resolved to worship God in their own fashion. In the Lambeth MSS. (Tenison), "An Account of the Conventicles in Lincoln Diocese, 1669," we find the following notice of Olney and neighbourhood: " Parishes and Conventicles in them: Olney 2, at the house of Widow Tears ;[1] Newton Blossomville in private houses." As regards sect, &c., those at Olney are called Anabaptists, and their number was "about 200." Their quality is not described, but among their "Heads or Teachers" were " Mr. Gibbs, Mr. Breeden, and James Rogers, Lace-buyers "—this Mr. Gibbs being the Rev. John Gibbs who, after his ejectment, in 1660, from the benefice of Newport Pagnell, founded the Dissenting causes at both Newport and Olney, where he lived by dealing in lace, as a greater than he had lived by tentmaking.

The number at Newton Blossomville is put at fifty or sixty, who are described as " meane people, but such as say they value not His Majesty's clemency one pin "—which is just what

---

[1] Evidently the " Joan Teare widow " whose burial is recorded in Olney Church Register as having taken place 8th July, 1672.

a lace-maker, having so much to do with pins, was very likely to say. It was a glorious age for the bigot, the sycophant and the informer. Pretty nearly every man with a conscience was either in momentary expectation of arrest, in hiding or in prison.

John Bunyan at this time was spinning out of his holy soul, and in the very heart of the lace country, his *Pilgrim's Progress*, but the iron Puritan prejudice against lace still prevailed. Neither Christiana, nor Mercy, nor the " young woman whose name was Dull," nor anybody else, male or female, in the book either made lace, bought lace, or even mentioned lace. Yet there must have been plenty of " tawdry " on the stalls of Vanity Fair, and we may fairly assume that my Lord Fair-speech wore a lace collar round his oily throat, and Lady Feigning's daughter a laced petticoat about her mincing feet.

But the threat constantly impending of fine or imprisonment for religion's sake was not the only hardship the lace-makers had to endure. They were daily ham-

22. Lace
Tokens.
1648—1679.

pered in their business transactions owing to the shortage of small change. Half-pence and far-things were nowhere to be had in any convenient number. This hardship, however, was not confined to the lace-makers. The whole kingdom suffered, and then some enterpriser hit on the expedient of making his own small change. The idea was copied, and in a few years every prominent tradesman had his private mint. In the *Gentleman's Magazine* for 1757 is a description of the coining apparatus with which, though it was quite a simple affair, in a very short time many hundreds of half-pence or farthings could be coined. Among the tradesmen who issued these tokens were not only the lace-buyers, but also the grocers, mercers, bakers, rope-makers and others. The token of James Brierly, of Olney, who, as a deed[1] bearing his name shows, was a lace-buyer, has on the obverse, " James Brierly, B. I. M.; " and on the reverse, " Of Olney, 1658," and a pair of scales. As regards the " B. I. M," B stands for Brierly, I for his own Christian name, James, and M for his wife's Christian name, it being the invariable custom for the token to bear the wife's initials as well as the husband's. The scales show that he joined to lace-buying some other occupation. Apparently he was a baker as well. He died in 1670.[2] The James Brierly referred to under date 1677 in the Journal of George Fox, founder of the Society of Friends, was his son.

A still more interesting token, however, is that

[1] Preserved in the Cowper Museum, Olney : Conveyance of property on 24 Feb., 1650, by Richard Babbington of Turvey to James Brierly, lace-buyer, of Olney.

[2] The date of his burial as shown in the Olney Church Register was 28 July, 1670.

of Peter Reynoldes, of Buckingham, as it is adorned with a representation of the emblem of his trade—a piece of lace. Moreover, as his name proves, he was of Huguenot descent. On the obverse is, " Peter Reynoldes " and a strip of lace ; on the reverse, " Of Bvckingham, 58, P. F. R." (See Plate 9.)

Another Buckingham token of a similar character has on the obverse, " Iohn Rennals, 1668," with a strip of lace, and the initials, " I. E. R ; " on the reverse, " Of Bvckingham, his halfepenny."

Two lace tokens hail from St. Neots, Huntingdonshire, their peculiarity being a representation of a pillow used by two women, one on each side of it.

O. The overseers of. Their halfe peny.
R. The Towne of St. Eeds.[1] Two women, seated, making
                         lace.

O. The overseers of. Their halfe peny.
R. The Towne of St. Neots. Two women, seated, making
                         lace.[2]

The ladies of Charles's court wore laced caps, laced aprons, laced gloves, and petticoats " laced with rich lace at the bottom."[3] Colbertine[4] and other coarser kinds of lace they spoke of

23. At the Sign of the Laced Shoe, 1679. Green Lace.

---

[1] Old name of St. Neots.
[2] See *Trade Tokens, 17th Century*, by Wm. Boyne, revised by G. C. Williamson, 1889.
[3] Pepys.
[4] An open lace with a square ground. It took its name from its manufacturer, M. Colbert, Superintendent of the French Royal Lace Manufacturers. See Chapter 2, Section 8.

only with disdain and a toss of the head. In
the *London Gazette*, 1677, Jan. 28—31, appears the
advertisement : " Stolen from the Vicarage house
of Amersham in Buckinghamshire an apron of
needlework lace, the middle being net work."
The lax court beauties wheedled laced gloves out
of their royal lover ; similar fripperies were the
perquisite of the judge at the maiden assize ;
while the fop gave himself airs in the park or the
public garden in gloves " well fringed, which
reached to his elbow." John Verney, of Claydon,
on the occasion of his wedding, 9th June, 1680,
sent "a payre of Green fringed Gloves" for his
brother, and " white and collourd Lace Gloves "
for his sister.[1]

As we have seen, the courtiers of the reign of
James I. and Charles I. wore high top boots lined
with rich lace. The ladies were not slow to
imitate them, and by the time of Charles II.
every kind of foot-gear with pretensions had lace
somewhere about it. In the possession of Mr. T.
Watson Greig of Glencarse is a beautiful laced
shoe that belonged to a Miss Langley, who lived
at this period. Made of natural silk (and therefore
of a pale yellow colour) it is most tastefully
embroidered, and it is trimmed with lace " of an
intricate pattern and delicate as a spider's web."[2]

---

[1] *Memoirs of the Verney Family*, 1892, Vol. IV., p. 250.
[2] There is a large coloured photograph of it in the book of *Illustrations of Collections of Ladies' Old-Fashioned Shoes*, by T. Watson
Greig of Glencarse. For our illustration we are indebted to the kindness
of the Committee of the Northampton Public Library.

(See Plate 6.)   Shoe ties that went under the
name of "roses" and "riband roses" edged with
lace were also coquetries of the period.

In the 17th and 18th Centuries nearly all the
tradesmen had wooden shop signs projecting in
front of their places of business, or signs carved
in stone let into the front of their houses, and the
lace-dealers probably, both in the Midlands and
in London, displayed sign-boards or carvings
indicative of their calling.   Among milliners' signs
in London in the early 17th Century were "The
Fan," "The Crowned Fan," "The Hood and
Scarf Shope, Cornhill," and the "The Blue
Boddice, in the Long Walk near Christ Church
Hospital."   The lady of that period wore laced
trimmed tabs on her bodice and a laced scarf,
and she carried a lace trimmed folding fan.

A shop in Chancery Lane, "The Laced Shoe,"
is mentioned in an advertisement in the *London
Gazette*, July 31 to August 4, 1679.   The Mar-
chioness of Newcastle, in *Sociable Letters* (1664)
speaks (nose in the air) of a "Mrs. P. I.," previously a lady of fashion, who, having become "a
sanctified soul," left off curling her hair, and
regarded "laced shoes and galoshoes" as "steps
to pride," and fans and ribbons and the like as
"Temptations of Satan."[1]

The peculiarity of these shoes which were supposed to work so much havoc in the male heart, is

[1] *Sociable Letters*, 1st edit., p. 103.

that so many of them were green or edged with green lace. In James the First's time red was supposed to be the provocative colour. Thomas Wright, the psychologist,[1] indeed, had it from physicians, that "red colours moved and influenced the blood." Opinion, however, changed; and the passion for green in the shoe continued to the time of the *Tatler*. Stéele, in No. 143 of that periodical, reads quite a sermon on the perils of looking at green lace, and goes so far as to declare, in his arch way, that even the sight of it in a shoemaker's window created "irregular Thoughts and Desires in the youth of this nation," and he considered that "slippers with green lace and blue heels" were equally inflammatory. These slippers were also called pantofles. Burton (in *Anatomy of Melancholy*, 1621) says oddly, "It was Judith's pantofles that ravished the eyes of Holofernes."[2] Sappho's sandals of "rich Lydian work" played havoc with many a Greek heart. Evidently the only safe course, when a pretty lady comes along with embroidered or laced shoe-gear, is to look another way.

Nell Gwyn, as the unpaid bills found after her death[3] reveal, affected "scarlet satin shoes with silver lace." In all this extravagance the servant wenches, as Defoe tells us, imitated their mis-

[1] Writing in 1601.
[2] See *Judith* x. 4, where the original is rendered, correctly, of course, "sandals."
[3] In 1687.

tresses. When Joan comes up from the country
she has simple tastes and is satisfied with " neats
leathern shoes," but she has been scarcely a week
in town before this honest foot-gear is exchanged
" for laced ones with high heels,"[1] and she
indulges in other extravagances to match ; and,
if expostulated with, " whip she is off " to some
situation where she can " prink up " without fear
of censure. It was hard indeed to distinguish the
servant from the mistress. " I remember," adds
Defoe, " I was once put very much to the blush,
being at a friend's house, and by him required to
salute the ladies, I kissed the chamber-jade into
the bargain, for she was as well dressed as the
best. But I was soon undeceived by a general
titter, which gave me the utmost concern; nor can
I believe myself the only person who has made
such a mistake." What a predicament for a
punctilious gentleman to find himself in !

In the reign of Charles II., too, lace handkerchiefs were the fashion. " Lost," reads an advertisement of 1672, "a lawn pocket handkercher
with a broad hem, laced round with a fine Point
lace about four fingers broad."[2] When the
emotional heroine of an old novel, The Garden of
Love,[3] shed tears " which trickled down her
sorrowful cheeks," one might suppose that the

[1] Everybody's Business is Nobody's Business, 1725.
[2] London Gazette, Dec. 5—9, 1672.
[3] P. 58.

next step would be to sop them up with what she called her " pocket handkercher." Not at all, for we are informed that she then (out of respect, one supposes, for its edging of Point lace) " immediately dried them, with fanning wind in her face to enliven her spirits." But handkerchiefs, laced or plain, did have their uses, for if an attractive young lady chanced to leave the casement of her window open, one of her admirers would be sure to fling in a knotted handkerchief full of sweetmeats.

But not only were gloves, shoes, and handkerchiefs set off with lace, garters were also bewitchingly adorned; and in order that the graces of the last should not be hidden from an unhappy public, the lady very compassionately arranged that the garter should have "long fluttering ends of ribbon "[1] which allowed the lace on it to peep out beneath her petticoat.[2] Where there's a will there's a way.

---

[1] See Ben Jonson : *The Devil is an Ass.*
[2] The petticoat was, of course, in those days an outside garment.

CHAPTER VIII

THE THIRD EXODUS

Reign of James II. (See Map, Plate 11.)

1685—1689

As we have seen, Henry IV. of France signed in 1598 the Edict of Nantes which gave freedom of religion to the Huguenots. For long the Jesuits had plotted and schemed in order to lead Louis XIV. to persecute the Huguenots. They partially attained their ends as early as 1682, and at last on 22nd October, 1685, they succeeded in inducing him to revoke the Edict of Nantes.[1] But it pleased God to bring great good out of the evil, for tens of thousands of persons, many of whom were skilled lace-makers, flocked from Burgundy and Normandy into England, most of the lace-makers finding their way to the lace towns and villages of Bucks, Beds and Northants. The sufferings of these poor people were frightful. Some fled by land and, by a miracle as it were, escaping the vigilance of the dragoons and police, crossed the frontier into Germany and the Low Countries. Others escaped by sea, putting out

24. The Revocation of the Edict of Nantes. 1685.

---

[1] See *The Huguenots*, by Samuel Smiles, p. 183.

from Havre, Nantes, La Rochelle, and Bordeaux
in trading ships, shallops, fishing smacks, open
boats—" any wretched werry." The masters of
merchant vessels hid them under bales of goods,
in heaps of coals, or in empty casks where they
had only the bung-hole to breathe through. Some
of the girls and women disfigured their faces with
dyes, and feigned sickness, dumbness and even
insanity. Some disguised themselves as lacqueys.
Some died in the passage; others were landed
with wounded skins, but with whole and merry
consciences, at Southampton, Dartmouth and
Plymouth. Many of their Catholic fellow-country-
men pitied their fate and helped them to escape,
but at great risks to themselves, for any man who
was caught succouring these unhappy people was
sent to the galleys, and any woman was shaved
and imprisoned. The Huguenot churches were
demolished; their pastors when taken were immediately executed, their flocks were harried and
hunted like wild beasts. But faith upheld them,
that wondrous power—" stronger than any hellebore "[1]—which deprives the prison of its solitari-
ness, the stake of its horrors.

One woman, who carried with her a little
casket of jewels—her sole fortune—no sooner
reached the British shore than she threw herself
down and passionately kissed the ground, exclaim-

[1] Samuel Ward, the Puritan divine. The roots of hellebore were considered effectual against melancholy and madness.

Plate 12

MECHLIN PILLOW LACE.   See p. 15.

Victoria and Albert Museum.   *(By permission of the Authorities.)*

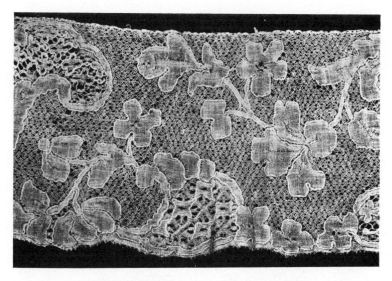

MECHLIN LACE, MADE AT CHESHAM, BUCKS.

The broad pattern was found on the pillow of Mrs. Sutthery, who died in 1814.   See p. 74.

(Lent by Mrs. Howe of Chesham.)

Plate 13

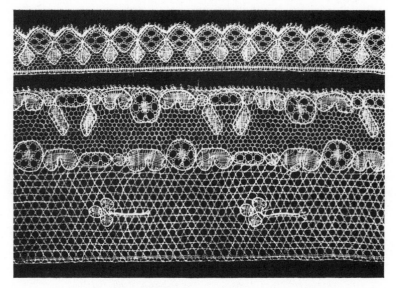

NORTHAMPTONSHIRE POINT LACES.

Upper : THE DUKE'S GARTER. Made at East Haddon.

Lower : REVOLUTION LACE. See p. 212.

Headside : Point Ground. Footside : Wire Ground (Kat Stitch).

This lace seems to have been first made in England after the French Revolution of 1789.

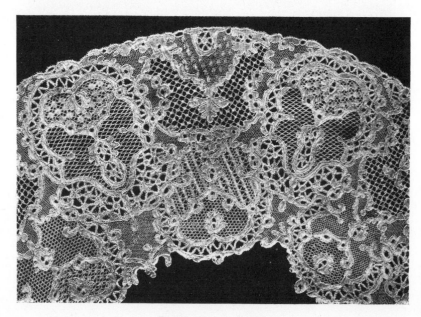

PART OF A COPE.

(Lent by Miss Pope.)

ing : " Have I at last attained my wishes ? Gracious God, I thank Thee for this deliverance from a tyranny exercised over my conscience, and for placing me where Thou alone art to reign over it by Thy Word, till I shall finally lay down my head upon this beloved earth ! " What a compliment to her adopted country !

Most of the emigrants, however, came ashore hungering and in rags. The English people crowded round them with indignant and pitying hearts. They gave them a cheery welcome, received them into their dwellings and handsomely relieved their wants. The clergy in many towns made collections for them ; for example under date 16 Feb., 1682, we find in the register of Clifton Reynes near Olney, " collected for the French Protestants £2 10 0," and another collection for the same purpose was made in 1686.

By their skill, their intelligence, and their industry the emigrants richly repaid this country for her hospitality. There was scarcely a branch of trade but at once felt the beneficial effects of this large influx of experienced workers. Speaking of the lace industry in reference to this exodus Defoe[1] observes that the people " are wonderfully exercised and improved within these few years past."

The Revocation of the Edict of Nantes was the making not only of a number of English towns

[1] *Tour*, 1724—27.

but also of Berlin and other German cities, for the skilled workmen who quitted France carried with them into the neighbouring countries their trade secrets as well as their money. " What can I do to show my gratitude to you ? " said on one occasion Louis XV. to Frederick the Great. " Promulgate a second Revocation of the Edict of Nantes," was the arch reply.

If the reign of Charles II. was the age of the lace collar, that of James II. was the **25. The Lace Cravat and the Fontange.** age of the lace cravat. (See Plate 9.) Discarding their own hair, men had taken to flowing wigs with long curls that completely hid the greater part of the collar, which, in consequence, gave place to the cravat. James himself led the fashion. Sir Edmund Verney,[1] on receiving some lace made at Claydon (Bucks) by the daughter of one of his tenants, at once ordered it to be made into a cravat of the latest pattern. " The Bonny Cravat " is, or was, the sign of an inn at Woodchurch, Tenterden, Kent, and the old song, " Jenny, come tie my bonny cravat," was sung on festive occasions.

While the gentleman's lace collar shrank into the narrow cravat, the ladies' lace cap, which had flourished particularly in the reign of Charles II., took upon itself new proportions. The change had its origin in a pretty incident. The frail, but

[1] *Memoirs of the Verney Family*, Vol. IV., p. 213.

beautiful, Duchesse de Fontanges,[1] when out hunting one day with Louis XIV. and his court, discovering that her hair was in disorder, hastily tied it above her head with a ribbon. She looked so charming in this impromptu coiffure, that her royal lover begged her to continue to wear her hair so arranged The ladies of the court followed suit; but one thing led to another. Instead of leaving "well" alone, the ladies took to massing their hair in curls over a wire frame; lace was added to the ribbon, and lace to lace, and shooting up and shooting up, the confection became at last the enormous and unbecoming Fontange. If a lady, wearing a Fontange twelve inches high, met another with a similar head-dress a couple of inches higher, she fell into the mood of Job and lamented the day wherein she was born.

This wonderful confection — this Tower of Babel—appears in the portraits by Sir Godfrey Kneller and other artists of the reign of James II. The only persons it really suited were that monarch's ugly mistresses, whom he took to, according to his brother Charles, by way of penance. Them no head-dress could injure.

Roxana, the heroine of Defoe's story of that title, wore upon her head "a suit of lace worth two hundred pounds"—"bone lace," as we judge

[1] Marie Angélique Scoraille de Roussillé, Duchesse de Fontanges. Born 1661, died 1681.

from the *Spectator*, No. 98,[1] being meant. The nobleman, her admirer, said he liked to see "a fine laced head" and "everything suitable." In the number of the *Spectator* just cited Addison (it was the year 1711) observed amusingly of the Fontange, or commode, as latterly it was called : "There is not so variable a thing in nature as a Lady's Head-dress. About ten years ago it shot up to a very great height, insomuch that the Female Part of our Species were much taller than the Men. The women were of such an enormous Stature, that we appeared as Grass-hoppers before them." The fashion of wearing the Fontange also spread to Germany, and Lady M. W. Montagu, writing home[2] from that country, observes : "The person is so much lost between head-dress and petticoat" that it would be well if the ladies had written on their backs for the information of travellers : "This is a woman."

[1] 22 June, 1711.
[2] 17 Nov., 1716.

CHAPTER IX

BUCKS POINT

As we have already said, the laces made in
Bucks, Beds, and Northants, immedi-
26. Bucks ately after the arrival of the Flemish
Point firmly
established. and Huguenot refugees, were mainly
1685.
Old Flemish[1] (produced by workers
from Mechlin) and Lille. Mrs. Palliser, whose
History of Lace appeared in 1875, tells us that she
received a number of the Old Flemish patterns
from Mrs. Bell of Newport Pagnell, who could
trace them as far back as 1780; and she describes
these patterns as wavy and graceful, the ground
being well executed.[2]

She further says that the next in antiquity is a
lace of Flemish design with the fine Brussels
ground, and observes that many of the earlier
patterns appear to have been run or worked in
with the needle on the net.

These remarks are interesting, for they show
first, that the earliest laces made by the Continental settlers were Old Flemish; and secondly,
that these laces continued to be made for a time

---

[1] All Old Flemish laces were, previous to 1665, called Malines (Mechlin)
by the French.
[2] P. 384.

in Buckinghamshire after the inception—and indeed after the firm establishment—of Bucks Point. Now comes the deeply interesting question: When was Bucks Point first made? It is adapted, as we know, from the laces of Lille and Mechlin. As we have already observed, Lille as a continental lace is mentioned as early as 1582, and Mechlin about 1630. Assuming (as is probable) that these laces were then in general demand, we may place the inception of Lille at considerably earlier than 1582, and of Mechlin at considerably earlier than 1630. Indeed, we may safely assume that Lille was made before the Second Exodus (1572), and Mechlin as early as the reign of our Queen Elizabeth. Bucks Point is any English-made lace with the Lille ground, and the Lille or Mechlin pattern. Like other history, that of Bucks Point emerges out of the mist of tradition. Some years ago, an old woman at Shutlanger, Northants, was busy upon a piece of the very beautiful Bucks Point, which is called Queen Elizabeth Lace (see Plate 7), and she informed Mrs. Harrison (wife of the Rev. J. B. Harrison of Paulerspury) that according to tradition it was made for Queen Elizabeth during one of her visits to the county. Examination of our illustration will show that it is a lace with a Lille ground (the mesh being of two sizes) sprinkled with *dots (plaits, leadworks* or *points d'esprit* as they are called), and that it has a Mechlin pattern,

honeycomb fillings and an almost straight edge.
The three facts educible are, (1) that the pattern
is very old ; (2) that it bears resemblances to the
patterns of the earliest known Mechlin laces ; (3)
that the lace was spoken of in the early 19th century as Elizabethan lace.

The Bucks Point Stocking fronts which figure
on Plate 7 may also have been from an Elizabethan parchment. From tradition and conjecture
we pass to history and actual knowledge. Whether
the " Great Bone Lace " and " Little Bone
Lace " purchased by Anne of Denmark at Winchester in 1603[1] was or was not Bucks Point
cannot be decided, but Mr. George Smith of
Olney, who is a lace-designer and the successor
of a lace-designer, possesses an acorn-patterned
parchment, prepared for a flounce, which certainly dates from the 17th Century (Plate 17).
It was given in 1857 to Mr. Smith by an Olney
woman who was then eighty, and it had belonged
to her grandmother.

As will be noticed from our illustration, the
Acorn Flounce,[2] instead of exhibiting the crude-

[1] See Chapter 6, Section 17.

[2] The flounce seems to have come in with William III. and Mary, when
the ladies, in Addison's words, were " flounced and furbelowed from
head to foot." *Spectator*, No. 129. Addison is writing in 1711 of a lady
who was at least ten years behind-hand in her dress ; that is, in the mode
of William III.
    The flounce indeed engaged the ladies' minds by night as well as by
day, for says Pope :

" Nay, oft, in dreams, invention we bestow
To change a flounce or add a furbelow."
Rape of the Lock, 1711.

ness that might be looked for in the infancy of an industry, is of a most elaborate design. It is magnificent in style and accurate in workmanship. If its grandeur is noticeable, so also is its simplicity. Moreover, it is just the design one would expect in a Jacobite, Show-your-oak Period. Apparently, an Englishman designed it. The Huguenot workers who came over from the Continent in 1685 may have used it. This parchment must be one of the earliest Bucks Point specimens in existence.

The next piece of evidence is a draught of very lovely pattern used, according to Mr. Smith about 1700, that is, in the reign of William III. The rose of England is united with a row of conventional Dutch tulips. (See Plate 16.) Instead of showing your oak it became the fashion to flaunt your tulip; and the lace-makers, who were Orange to a woman, were most happy to comply. Miss Burrowes, of Maids Morton, tells us that many of the Bucks Point designs used in her neighbourhood are the same as those of the time of William III. and Anne, and the Acorn and the Tulip patterns (see Plate 14) have always been favourites. There is indeed almost as much history in a yard of Buckinghamshire Lace—even if made only last week—as in a venerable Buckinghamshire Church. It is possible then that Bucks Point was recognised as a distinct lace under Queen Elizabeth, it is probable that it was made to some extent in the reign of James I., and it is certain that it was firmly established in the reigns of James II. and William III.

Mr. A. A. Carnes, of Bedford, has a Lace-maker's ledger dated 1778 with patterns of the period, which are evidently the patterns referred to in the various entries, pinned into it. The grounds of those attached to the earlier entries are either Point or Honeycomb, and a few pages later we come upon other grounds, including Wire, Chain-stitch, Four-pins-and-plaits, and Chain-and-plaits. Sometimes Wire, Honeycomb, Plait and Chain-stitch are all in one pattern.

This ledger is evidence that the industry was in 1778 not in its infancy, as some have alleged, but in its maturity. It may be noted in passing that one way of telling whether a lace is old or not is to notice the gimp, the sheen or polish on which is far more distinct in old lace than in later specimens.

I have been thus careful in marshalling these facts because Mr. John Ramsay M'Culloch, in his *Dictionary of Commerce* (1832),[1] makes the absurd statement that Bucks Point was introduced in 1778—a statement that has been followed by many others who have written on the subject of Lace.

I said that Bucks Point is any lace made in England with the Lille ground and the Lille or

[1] Mr. M'Culloch died in 1864.

Mechlin pattern. In Bedfordshire and Buckinghamshire fine and very beautiful lace, of which the design was entirely Mechlin, was made until about 1700, but gradually the workers discarded it in favour of the Lille. Among our illustrations (see Plate 12) is a specimen of Mechlin, made at Chesham in Bucks, by Mrs. George Sutthery,[1] seven yards of which were found on her lace pillow after her death in 1814. It has the familiar Mechlin scroll work and quatre-foil ornaments.

Northamptonshire seems to have favoured the Lille from the first, while Buckinghamshire preferred the Lille ground (sprinkled with square dots) and the Mechlin pattern. Consequently, the Bedfordshire and Northamptonshire laces were straight in the edge and had more gimp, and were stiffer in pattern than the Buckinghamshire variety, the designs of which have more floral and scroll work as well as more cloth-work ; and these characteristics of the different counties prevailed until about 1850, when, as we shall see, the introduction of new floral designs from Paris into Bedfordshire considerably altered the character of the Bedfordshire fabric. Even to-day, however, as regards Point Lace, the characteristics above mentioned mark to some extent the various counties.[2]

---

[1] Mrs. Sutthery, who was born in 1750, was grandmother of the late Rev. Wm. Sutthery of Clifton Reynes, Bucks (1828—1895).

[2] To put matters concisely, and to save the reader from turning back,

As the ground of Bucks Point is like that of Lille, it is made of two threads only, and these simply crossed, not plaited at their junction ; consequently (as in the case of Lille), if the threads at crossing are drawn tightly the mesh looks square, but as a rule they are left loose, producing a hexagonal appearance.

The firmer and stronger kinds of Bucks Point are reminiscent of Arras Lace, which, as already stated, differed from that of Lille only in texture. The Mechlin influence in Bucks Point is often seen (1) in its dainty, flowing patterns of sprays and flowers, each outlined with gimp; (2) in the roses and other flowers worked into the ground along with, or instead of, the square plaits ; and (3) in the fact that the various shaped " openings " in the pattern are sometimes found filled with a smaller mesh, and occasionally with a larger mesh.

The Lille influence in Bucks Point is often seen

the following are the salient characteristics of the Lille and Mechlin Laces :—

Lille ground.—The sides of the mesh are formed by twisting two threads round each other. It is a square mesh, but as generally worked it looks hexagonal. It is "the finest, lightest, most transparent of grounds." Nobody can mistake it.

Mechlin ground.—The mesh, which is hexagonal, consists of four twisted and two plaited sides, the plaited sides being shorter than those of Brussels.

Lille designs have more gimp than Mechlin, and they are simpler and stiffer—more formal.

Mechlin designs have more floral and scroll-work, and more cloth-work than Lille.

Lille Lace generally had a straight edge.

(1) in the fact that the net (with its square dots) is all on the foot-side of the pattern (whereas in Mechlin the net approaches the border, and the pattern occurs at intervals), and (2) in the fact that it often has no cloth-work—only gimp.

Bucks Point, as we have already more than once said, is any English-made lace with the Lille ground, and the Lille or Mechlin pattern. Sometimes the whole of the lace, with the exception of the pattern, consists of point net, the meshes of which are all of one size; but more frequently, while most of the foot-side is point net, the fillings— that is to say, the spaces formed by the pattern— are point net of larger mesh, wire ground, honey-comb, mayflower[1] (that is, cloth-work buds sur-rounded with honeycomb), or some other fancy. Again, the head-side may be point net and the foot-side wire ground, or the head-side honeycomb and the foot-side point net; and there are other arrangements.

27. The Grounds and Fillings.

The fillings in Bucks Point are charming beyond description. Instead of spending myself in at-tempting to convey in mere words some idea of their beauty, I will ask the reader to turn to the many plates in which they are represented. All honour to the designers of Bucks, Beds, and North-ants, to whom we are indebted for these lovely

[1] This filling bears some resemblance to the French *Oeil de perdrix* (Partridge's Eye).

lattices through which, by the seeing eye, some
glimpses may be discerned of the artist's heaven ;
and for the dainty ladders and stairways which
enable us to reach it. They are oriental and un-
English, just as the goldfinch with its rich, its vivid
colours is oriental and un-English; and yet that
gorgeous bird is very much at home in a British
hedgerow. Although we show many beautiful
fillings, it is probable that careful examination of
old parchments would bring others to light.

We have already spoken of dots, leadworks, or
points d' esprit, in the net ground. Diamonds of
half-stitch (as for example, in some of the specimens in the Foddy collection in the Northampton
Museum) and other ornaments also occur.

Now and again one comes across eccentricities
in the way of Midland lace. Mrs. Wilkinson of
Northampton, for example, showed me a piece,
made on her own pillow, which consisted of net
with square meshes ; and lace, of which the entire
net is wire ground or honeycomb, has occasionally
been made to suit the caprice of some whimsical
patron.

Most of the old writers speak of Olney as being
the centre of the Bucks Point Lace industry.
Thomas Fuller, as we have noticed, speaks as early
as 1640 about much bone lace being made about
" Ouldney." Defoe who made his Tours (as I
show in my *Life of Daniel Defoe*) in 1684 and published his account of them in 1724, refers to the

same industry in connection with "Ouldney," and
Lysons (1806—1822) tells us that the lace manufacture was then carried on to a great extent in the
town and neighbourhood, veils and other lace of
the finer sorts being made.

Of all the laces made in England none can compare with the beautifully designed and
delicate Bucks Point. Fine as a mist,
and exquisite beyond dreams, it has
for generations adorned the ivory neck and the
finely chiselled arm of British beauty. Dresses
have been trimmed with it, hats adorned with it,
handkerchiefs deeply bordered with it. To count-
less other purposes it has been devoted. The
choicer and finer kinds spun out of the soul of the
Bucks workers are handed down from one generation to another as heirlooms. Some proud owners
have said, "We would rather have it than
diamonds."

28. Names of Bucks Point Laces.

On many of the favourite patterns the workers
have affectionately bestowed names, some of which
have interesting associations. To the *Acorn* and
the *Tulip* (Plate 14) we have already referred.
Another wide lace is the *Bell* (Plate 42). The
Duke's Garter reminds us of the one and only
Duke to whom it could refer—him of Buckingham and Chandos, at the time Stowe was in
its glory, and emperors, kings, and statesmen were
his guests; and in honour of whom could the
Queen's Garter have been made if not of that

Queen whom he there entertained so splendidly—
Queen Victoria!

What is the *Great Running River* with its per-
petual meanderings but the cool, silver Ouse with
the snow-white *Swan* on its bosom! What is the
Little Running River but the laughing, babbling
Lovat! And where else would we look for the
Water Lily,[1] perfect in beauty! The *Seven Diamonds* are surely the seven wives, " all maidens,"
of John Carroll,[2] the irreproachable Olney Bluebeard.

Buckinghamshire and honey are inseparable.
The lace-makers who made the Honeycomb
ground made also the *Beehive* lace (Plate 42) and,
as we shall see, when the honey was drained from
the combs, the residue became their favourite
drink—metheglin. *Pretty Dick* sings in the hedgerows, *Lovers' Knots*[3] are carved on trees; and the
lovers walk among the *Barley*—George or Jacob
with *Lavinia, Matilda, Agnes* and the rest of the
village belles—the talk being naturally of the *Ring*
(Plate 41)[4] which George will give to Lavinia and
which perhaps, and probably in imagination only,
is to have a *Pearl*[5] or a *Diamond* in it; while some-

---

[1] Mrs. Atkins of Paulerspury was, at the time I called in May, 1917,
making a lace in which the water lily was repeated.

[2] He died 21 July, 1704. The names of two of his wives, Frances and
Anne, occur in the parish register.

[3] The Lovers' Knot is a Northants name.

[4] There is the *Little Ring* and the *Big Ring*.

[5] The Pearl is the narrowest of laces, " consisting merely of turn-pin
and foot-pin." Ladies use it to edge their netting.

times the fancy extends even to a *Diamond and Chain* (Plate 37), or to the *Watch*[1] which Lavinia will give to George. On their wedding day the *Wedding Bells* (Plate 42) will ring, and then George and Lavinia will settle down in a picturesque thatched cottage situated in a wood or in some sequestered village on a by-road, with the pretty name of Newton Blossomville, Weston Underwood, Lillingstone Dayrell, Maids Morton, Moreton Pinkeney or Clifton Reynes—to mention a few out of many. Their garden will be sweet with the smell of the *Primrose,* the *Rose* (Plate 41) and the *Honeysuckle,* rich with the purple of the *Pansy,*[2] and gorgeous with the red of the *Tulip* (Plate 14) and the orange of the *Marigold.* It will have a patty-pan bed for *Carnations* (Plate 14), a corner for *Solomon's Seal,* and a rustic arch for *Convolvulus.* On Sundays they will attend the picturesque village church or the neat and unpretentious village chapel, and the preacher will tell them to walk, not in the *Zigzag* road (Plate 49) that leads to destruction, but in the *Narrow Way*[3] that leads to life eternal, and he will speak of the *Crown* (Plate 49) that awaits them at the journey's end. As years go on a little family will gather about them, and the children will roam in the field to gather the *Daisy* and the *Cornflower,* or to chase the

[1][2] "Old designs pricked on horn parchment."—Miss Burrowes.

[3] The *Narrow Way* and the *Wide Way* are varieties of the *Running River.*

Plate 14

CARNATION LACE.   See p. 80.

WIDE TULIP.   See p. 80.

Plate 15

BUCKS POINT. Made at Akeley. Width 5¾ inches.

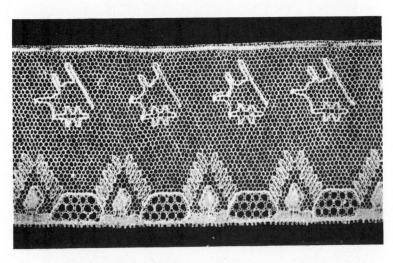

BUCKS POINT. Made at Akeley. Width 2¾ inches.

Butterfly, or raid the spinney in search of a *Bunch of Nuts*.[1] If the weather is wet they will play at home with the *Kitten*,[2] which rubs against them and purrs softly, the *Ball*, the *Ninepin*, or the *Sea Shell* (Plate 37), while the grandmother watches them admiringly from the chimney corner through *Spectacles* with circular eye-pieces. In their hat they will wear a feather from the *Peacock's Tail* (Plate 5), a gift from the gardener at the Hall.

For supper George and Lavinia have *Cucumber and Onions*, a dish of which George partakes too freely, with the result that he has a terrible nightmare in which a *Cat's Face* glares at him. Of course they keep a pig, and their affection for it leads them to call one pattern the *Hog's Nose;* and on the Lace-makers' Holiday, Tanders Day, of which we shall in a subsequent chapter speak, nothing tended so much to make them gay as the notes of the *Fiddle*.[3] It will be observed that the lace-makers have embodied their joys, but none of their sorrows, in the names of the laces. Their attitude to the sorrows may be gauged by the remark made to me by Hannah Perkins, a deaf and almost blind old lady of Weston Underwood, whose lace-making days were done. "Ah," she said, "if we had no sorrows down here we should

---

[1] This is a South Bucks name. The pattern, three circles arranged pyramid fashion, differs little from the Northants *True Lovers' Knot*.

[2] Sometimes called *Fanny*.

[3] An insertion.

have" (and she pointed upward) "no joys up
there;" and "up there" the good soul has since
gone. But to return to the laces and their names.
One is *Gretchen.* Who was she? Did she find
her way here in one of the early Exoduses or is she
a modern importation? And *Aimé?* Did she
come over in one of those beer barrels that we
spoke of in an early chapter, with her mouth glued
to the bung-hole! And was *Noyen* her native
place? And who was *Patience,* if she was not
some demure Puritan girl who put on lace when
her mother was not looking? But perhaps she
stepped out of the "Pilgrim's Progress." The
Fan [1] carries us into the 18th century, and *Dinah* [2]
to the days when (in 1851) English girls dropped
hot tears over the moving pages of "Uncle Tom's
Cabin." Then there were narrow insertions called
the *Plait,* the *Single Button Hole,* and the *Double
Button Hole.* The *Twink* was a narrow lace which
"the men made." They preferred it "because"
(lazy creatures!) "they could soon do a cut off."

Other patterns were the *Prince of Wales's
Feathers,* the narrow *Lady Denbigh* (made some
seventy years ago), the *Rose, Thistle, and Sham-
rock,* [3] also called *Emblem Lace,* the *Spider,* the
Fuchsia, the *Ivy Leaf,* the *Kidney Bean,* the
Acorn and Thistle, the *Anchor,* the *Ivy Leaf,* the

[1] There is also *The Fan and Diamond.*
[2] This lace is said to have been named after a Paulerspury worker,
Dinah Lucas.
[3] For description of draught see Chapter 15, Section 64.

Kidney Pattern, and the *Spot* (in five widths), the narrowest of which had one plait in the net ground, and the widest five plaits.[1] But the most delightful name of all is surely the *Old Woman of Cosgrove*—Cosgrove being the Northants village (near Stony Stratford) where, it seems, "the moon changes in a barn." The named parchment of this lace was found by Mr. A. A. Carnes among the collection of the late Mr. Coombs of Bedford. Who the old woman of Cosgrove was, or why the lace was so named, is unknown. Was she some centenarian, or some Cosgrove oddity? Is there a connection between her and Barbara, wife of William Bradshawe (ob. 1595), to whose memory there is a venerable brass in Cosgrove Church? History is mute.

Another charming name for a lace was the *Box of Knowledge*.[2] Who would not possess it? *Fremantle* is, of course, the family name of Lord Cottesloe. The ancient pattern called the *Wheatear and Cornflower* (Plate 49) is still made by some workers in the Winslow district.

To the "Bone Lace" industry in the 18th and early 19th centuries there is much reference in Book and Newspaper. Defoe, writing in 1726, describes the lace "of the tradesman's wife as having been procured from Stony Stratford," and

---

[1] Mrs. Howson of Olney made many of these laces. Her little granddaughter makes the *Spot*.

[2] A pattern of it belongs to Mr. A. A. Carnes. It is marked "Box of Knowligee."

he tells us that great business was done in baby lace, and edgings mostly used in trimming babies' caps. Owen in *Magna Britannia* (1720—31) says that more lace is thought to be made in Newport Pagnell than in any other town in England. A few years later Olney again became the leading town in the trade. Towcester was for long a centre, much lace being made at the neighbouring villages of Green's Norton and Silverstone. At Abthorpe[1] flounces and sectional pieces for covering parasols were made.

Laces of various kinds were made in the 17th century at Malmesbury and other towns in North Wilts. Downton, five miles from Salisbury, produced, and

29. Wilts, Dorset, Suffolk and Ripon Lace.

still to some extent produces, a lace with a net (locally called *bar-work*) which is similar to Bucks Point, and the Kat Stitch finds favour with the workers. Lace was also made at Blandford, Lyme Regis, Sherborne, and other Dorsetshire towns.

In the Victoria and Albert Museum are some specimens of Suffolk lace. They are similar to Bucks Point, the honeycomb being a favourite stitch. At Ripon, in Yorkshire, a lace derived from Lille, and therefore bearing relationship to Bucks Point, used to be made, but the industry has long been extinct.

[1] Abthorpe, as its old inn, "The Stocking Frame," still bears witness, was once a weaving village.

CHAPTER X

REIGNS OF WILLIAM III. AND ANNE

1688—1714

On 15th November, 1688, William III. landed at Torbay and rescued England from the tyranny of James II. His ablest _{30. Steinkirk and Ruffles.} and most trusted officers and great numbers of his soldiers were Huguenots, and so the people of England received an invaluable reward for their kindness to the poor refugees during the previous decade.

Changes in government were soon followed by changes in fashion. To the lace cravat succeeded another neckcloth, the "Steinkirk," an outcome of the battle of that name which took place 3rd August, 1692. The French officers, being suddenly ordered into action, and having no time to arrange their cravats in accordance with the prescribed custom of the age, knotted them hastily, and drew them through a button-hole. A passing necessity became a permanent fashion— with ladies as well as gentlemen, and not only in France but in England and other countries. The mountain in labour brought forth a mouse; this battle of the Titans produced a necktie! It is curious that the Steinkirk should have become so popular in England, seeing that at this battle the English were beaten, though not more curious than that the ladies should have adopted the Fontange—the head-dress of the mistress of a king whom they detested. The Steinkirk was often of lace (Blandford[1] Point at £30 a yard being a favourite wear), though it was often made of other materials, and we hear of a Steinkirk edged with lace of an inflammatory green! When the Steinkirk was not passed through the button-hole, it was fastened by large oval-shaped brooches of topaz or other stones.[2] In either case, however, the one thing necessary was to " arrange it with a graceful carelessness," without which it would not have been a Steinkirk, while its wearer would have been pronounced a South Sea Islander. In short, the ladies and gentlemen of this country had to look as though they had just been rushed off to battle.

Another Act for rendering more effectual the laws for preventing the importation of foreign bone laces was passed in 1698, and owing to that and to William's own steady patronage of the home industry, the lace trade in this country entered upon a new period of prosperity. Thanks to the craze for steinkirk, fontange, lace tuckers

[1] In Dorset.

[2] Many of these brooches have been preserved. Ladies of to-day, who sometimes wear them, may not know for what purpose they were first made.

and double sleeves, the makers were kept constantly busy.

Under Queen Anne the Acts which prevented
the importation of Flanders lace were repealed,
but the introduction of French lace was still forbidden. Towards the end of her reign "weeping
ruffles" and laced jabots (shirt frills) became the
mode. The ruffles were called "weeping" because,
owing to the breadth of the lace, they fell over
the hands. In weeping ruffles the beaux of the
day swaggered along the Mall; in weeping ruffles
the High Fliers drank, with bugloss in their wine,
to the King over the water.

None was more given to these fopperies than
Lord Bolingbroke, but in the rest of his attire he
was so dilatory that Queen Anne once said to
him, "I suppose you will some day come to court
in your nightcap."

But lace was worn on everything and everywhere. The lady of the period could not possibly
wait till she rose in a morning before putting it on.
She must needs have it in bed, and it became the
vogue for her to receive fashionable visitors before
dressing.[1] On opening those eyes "which must
eclipse the day," Belinda, having pushed aside
the curtains of her handsomely carved four-poster,
would knock with her high-heeled green shoe
(green again!) to summon her maid. The feature

---

[1] A custom copied from the French ladies, most of whom had their
petit lever, as it was called.

of the toilette that ensued was " a pretended
negligence "—as became a Steinkirkish period.
When visitors arrived the curtains, which had been
closed again, were once more drawn aside, this
time by the maid, when the goddess, who
" breathed cinnamon " and who was supposed
only at that moment to have opened those eyes
that " must eclipse the day," was perceived
reclining in a sea of billowy lace, with her
shoulder resting on a " small laced pillow."
Addison in the *Spectator*, No. 45, speaks of the
custom only to condemn it, and Pope in the *Rape
of the Lock* gives it a passing glance.

To stem the tide of extravagance the cry once
more rose for " Moderation." Arbuthnot repre-
sents " John Bull's Mother " (as in his *History of
John Bull*[1] he calls the Church of England) as
avoiding both the extravagance of the Cavalier
ladies and the plainness of the Puritan sister-
hood. If on her hands " she wore no flaunting
ruffles," neither was her head pressed by a " high
crowned hat." In short, she is represented as
standing for the Golden Mean.

It was quite time indeed to urge moderation,
for the rage for " weeping ruffles " and " laced
jabots," far from confining itself to the court and
the card room, had worked down to the raffish
tradesman and the " pretty valet," who was often
better dressed than his master. The kings and

---

[1] 1712.

queens in Mrs. Salmon's Waxwork Exhibition[1]
leered at one another in lace. Even some of the
Quakeresses were not proof against its fascina-
tions. Among the friends of G. A. Bellamy,
the actress, whose autobiography[2] appeared in
1785, was "a Wet Quaker," that is, one who
wore "ribands, gauzes, and laces."

In the early days of Lace-making, while the
Pattern Book was made for the expert,
the sampler (and the word sampler
means, of course, a pattern) was finding
its way into the nursery and the schoolroom. The
samplers from the time of Charles I. to that of
William III. were worked on strips of linen a
yard long, but in the time of Queen Anne they
began to assume the shape with which we are
most familiar. The early samplers, though consisting chiefly of embroidery patterns, also display
specimens of cut and drawn work, with needle-
point lace fillings in the style of reticella.
Specimens, dated respectively 1643 and 1696,[3]
and a third,[4] with a decorative alphabet of remarkable beauty worked in needle-point lace, are preserved in the Victoria and Albert Museum, South
Kensington.

31.
Samplers.

---

[1] Near Temple Bar.
[2] See Vol. 1, p. 48.
[3] See *Catalogue of Samplers*, issued by the Museum Authorities,
Plate 2.
[4] See Ditto, Plate 5. This catalogue, priced only at sixpence, is a
delightful work, and reflects great credit on the compiler, Mr. P. G.
Trendell.

With the alteration in shape the cut-work and lace fillings gradually disappeared, and in place of them we are presented with that delightful world which is inhabited by Adam and Eve, squirrels, peacocks, mermaids with green hair performing their toilette in public, court beauties in red hooped petticoats who are about as tall again as the saffron houses which they inhabit, blackbirds perched on trees which they could easily carry away in their beaks, all pleasantly mingled with dovecots, windmills, the alphabet from A to ampersand, and a verse from the Book of Proverbs—all done by some demure little maiden "aged seven years;" a world indeed that will ever be dear to lovers of the incongruous and the impossible. Who would not at any time during the four years of war have gladly taken a cottage in one of those idyllic, rococo gardens!

CHAPTER XI

SMUGGLING

It was the custom of the Buckinghamshire Lace-buyers, or Lace-manufacturers as they often styled themselves, to go once a week to the London Lace Markets which were held at the George Inn,[1] Aldersgate Street, and the Bull and Mouth, in St. Martin's by Aldersgate. Having sold their goods to the London milliners, they returned with a stock of thread and silk, which they gave out to their work-women to be made up according to orders. Lace Markets were also held at Newport Pagnell every Wednesday; at the Nagg's Head, Thame, once a month ; and at other towns in Buckinghamshire and the neighbouring counties, lace-buyers from London being the principal purchasers.

A Decision which forced the lace-manufacturers to take out licenses as petty chapmen or hawkers caused in the year 1717 great dissatisfaction. Those living at Chipping Wycombe (High Wycombe as it is now styled) led by Ferdinando

[1] Lieut. J. L. Coales of Newport Pagnell has a letter written from Fenny Stratford, in 1765, to Mr. Wm. Attkins, Lace Merchant, The George Inn, in Aldersgate Street, London.

Shrimpton of Penn, who had been eight times Mayor of Chipping Wycombe, petitioned against it, but with what success is not stated.

The Lace Fan had at this period a great vogue. Fans trimmed with lace were used as early as the time of Elizabeth, but by the end of the reign of Charles I. the whole of the leaf[1] was often made of lace. The 18th century, however, was pre-eminently the age of the fan. Watteau[2], Pater[3] and Boucher,[4] the famous French artists, all made beautiful fans; and sometimes we meet with a lace frame containing gauze medallions on which some unknown artist had painted a pretty design. For the "sticks" wood, ivory, mother of pearl, silver, and even gold was used, and the periodicals of the time (particularly the *Spectator*) are crowded with references to this pretty toy, and to the havoc it occasioned in the masculine heart.

When workhouses were first instituted the inmates were for the most part employed in spinning, but about 1720 they exchanged the wheel for the pillow. The old Levy and other Parish Books[5] of Olney contain numerous references to the lace made by the inmates of the Workhouse, which stood on the site now occupied by Victoria ˙Row. Every piece of lace was sealed at the end

33. Lacemaking in the Workhouses. 1720-1820.

---

[1] The lace before it is mounted.
[2] Died 1721.   [3] Died 1736.   [4] Died 1770.
[5] The books for the years 1746, 1768, 1782, 1812, 1818, and 1819, are preserved in the Cowper and Newton Museum, Olney.

while it was on the pillow in order to prevent anyone from stealing a portion, and it was sold
periodically for the benefit of the parish—the sum
produced varying from £28 to £32 a year. Among
the Regulations were the following :

"That if anyone in the Workhouse shall convey,
take or steal either . . . lace or anything
belonging to the Workhouse . . . they shall
be punished as the law directs, with the utmost
severity."

" That if any person shall presume to cut off
the seal affixed to the end of their lace, they shall
be severely punished."

Some items respecting Lace-making at Aylesbury Workhouse have also been preserved. Thus
in 1784 the overseers entered in their accounts:
" 2 cloths for lace pillows and paid 4d to four girls
for cutting off; " and on another occasion Mary
Slade received " 3s. 7d. to set up lace-making."
In 1743 the value of the bone lace made by the
children in the Workhouses of the city of
Dublin amounted to £160.

Moll Flanders,[1] light o' love and pickpocket,
occasionally honoured with her attention the country round the three
Brickhills in Bucks :

34. **Moll
Flanders.
The Coffin
Trick.**

> " There stand three Brickhills all of a row—
>   Great Brickhill, Little Brickhill, and Brickhill of
>   the Bow."

[1] Defoe's novel appeared in 1722.

When she was married at Little Brickhill to her fifth husband, the bank clerk (she was very wasteful with husbands), "finding it was a lace-making town," she gave to her bridesmaid "a good suit of knots," and to the girl's mother "a piece of bone lace for a head" (a fontange), and while she was at the inn there she heard that the coaches had been "robbed at Dunstable Hill, besides some of the lace-merchants that always travel that way had been visited too." But lace being a commodity in great demand, it was often carried off, not only by highwaymen, but also by pickpockets. Moll herself, after she became an "artist," as she prettily calls it, "made a venture or two among the lace folks," and once carried off "a parcel of bone lace worth nearly £20;" but her greatest prize was when she secured three hundred pounds worth of Flanders lace, though on that occasion, aware that this variety of lace was "prohibited," she made a virtue of her peccadillo, and divided the spoil with the Custom House officer.

Moll, however, was in this line of business but a dull jade compared with numbers of persons far higher in the social scale—men and women of title—who made, by smuggling, profits of many thousands of pounds. The favourite method was the corpse trick. Somebody, it was alleged, had died on the Continent or at sea. The body was duly landed in a coffin, which was covered with

a pall and carried, followed by a procession of
mourners in cloaks and hat-bands, to the nearest
churchyard, where it was met by a snuffling,
bewigged clergyman, reading the usual " I am the
Resurrection and the Life." The coffin was
lowered, and the words, " Earth to earth," were
drowned in sobs which proceeded from faces
buried in pocket handkerchiefs. It was a scene
that would have melted the heart of a millstone.
At midnight, needless to say, that grave was
re-visited by the broken-hearted mourners. In
most instances of this kind there was no corpse
at all, but even when there was a corpse care was
taken that there should be room for plenty of
lace as well. When the body of Bishop Atterbury,
who died in France, February 22nd, 1732, was
conveyed to England for burial in Westminster
Abbey, the High Sheriff of Westminster found
£6,000 worth of French lace secreted in the coffin.

As time went on, however, owing to the vigilance
of the Custom House officers, the trick became
dangerous. Perhaps on some occasion there was
too lavish a display of cambric and crape, or the
sobs may have been unnaturally loud. In any
case, the word went round that all coffins brought
in from sea were to be opened, with the result of a
sudden fall in the Continental death rate. When
the body of the Duke of Devonshire was, on the
3rd of October, 1764, brought over from France
where he died, the Custom House officers, not-

withstanding the indignant remonstrances of the family, not only opened and searched the coffin, but poked the corpse with a stick in order to see whether it was what it pretended to be, or so much Vraie Valenciennes.

That people were married in lace is only what might be expected. Nearly all the

35. Marrying, Hanging, and Burying in Lace. laces worn by the court at the nuptials (1736) of Frederick, Prince of Wales (son of George II.), were of English manufacture. The modern reader may be startled to learn that the bride wore a " night-gown " of superb lace. But in the early 18th century it was the fashion for women to wear in the streets a night-gown, night-rail, or bedgown, as it was variously called, over the usual dress—a custom which, as may be supposed, afforded abundant food for the satirists. " On Easter Day, 22nd April, 1764," says Dr. Samuel Johnson, " I went to church [St. Clement Danes, in the Strand]. I gave a shilling; and seeing a poor girl at the sacrament[1] in a bed-gown, gave her privately a crown, though," he amusingly adds, "I saw *Hart's Hymns* in her hand."

In 1750 was founded, with a view to encourage the home manufacture of lace, the Society of Anti-Gallicans, who held quarterly meetings and distributed prizes for the best work. At one of

---

[1] Of course, the Sacrament—"The Lord's Supper"—was in those days taken in the evening. The term "bed-gown" also occurs in Hayley's play, *The Two Connoisseurs*.

Plate 16

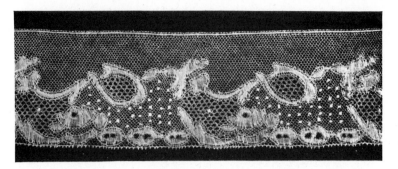

BUCKS POINT. Made at Great Horwood. Width 3 inches.

ROSE AND TULIP. See p. 72.

Draught of a very lovely pattern of Bucks Point Lace used about 1700 in Olney and neighbourhood.

Wherever the pattern is left blank it is whole stitch, as for example, in the outer petals and the innermost petals of the rose. The middle petals of the rose are half-stitch. They are linked together with honeycomb. The sepals of the tulip are honeycomb, the petals half-stitch. The ink lines show where the gimp is to go.

(Lent by Mr. George Smith, Olney.)

Plate 17

PARCHMENT OF FLOUNCE FOR A DRESS. See p. 71.

BUCKS POINT ACORN PATTERN. Date 1700, or earlier.

One of the oldest parchments of Bucks Point in existence. It was given to its present possessor, Mr. George Smith, of Olney, in 1862 by an Olney lace-maker, who was then about 80. It belonged to her grandmother.

Acorn cups, half-stitch; acorns, whole stitch; tiny fruits, 6 pins of whole stitch; circular "buds" in the ground, 8 pins of whole stitch. The ink lines show where the gimp is to go.

BLACK SILK LACE (Bucks Point). Made near Olney.

See pp. 211 & 229.

the earliest meetings, in 1752, the first prize to the
maker of the best piece of English bone lace was
awarded to Mr. William Marriott of Newport
Pagnell. In 1761 a pair of fine lace ruffles, the
output of Messrs. Milward and Company, at Newport Pagnell, was presented to George III.

The lace worn by many persons was a serious
inconvenience to them, but they used to say then,
as we say now, that you might as well be out of
the world as out of the fashion. It mattered not
how the body was incommoded provided the mind
was serene. Moreover, people were martyrs to
lace not only in the daytime but also at night.
Lord Charles Somerset, for instance, when visiting
at Wynyard's, the seat of the Earl of London-
derry, complained of not having had a wink of
sleep " through sleeping in ' cambric sheets,' the
Brussels Lace with which the pillows were trimmed tickling his face."[1]

To be kept from sleeping by lace was bad
enough, but to be killed by it was worse. The
infant daughter of the last Duke and Duchess of
Chandos was at its christening, in 1778, so loaded
with lace that it collapsed. The Archbishop of
Canterbury, who officiated, complimented it, as he
handed it back to the nurse, on being the quietest
baby he had ever held, which was probably the
truth, seeing that it was dead.

For an adult, however—to die in lace was a

[1] *Creevy Papers*, 1768—1838.

privilege.   From the time that James II., an exile
in France, had breathed his last in a "laced night-
cap," no good Jacobite peacefully gave up the
ghost unless he was similarly adorned.[1]

"Gentlemen of the road," as highwaymen
called themselves, liked to be hanged in lace.
Nor did they stand alone.   Their taste was also
shared by Lord Ferrers.   This nobleman, who
had been condemned to be hanged at Tyburn for
the murder of his land-steward, chose from his
wardrobe on the fatal morning (May 5th, 1760) a
splendid white suit, silver embroidered, and edged
with rich lace, saying, " I was married in these
clothes, and I will die in them."   And he did.

But people not only liked to be married in lace,
bedded in lace, and executed in lace, they also
liked to be buried in lace.   A notable example is
that of Anne Oldfield, the beautiful actress, who,
when asked whether the material was to be
woollen, made reply, in Pope's classic para-
phrase :

> " No, let a charming chintz and Brussels lace
> Wrap my cold limbs and shade my lifeless face ;
> One would not, sure, be frightful when one's dead.
> And, Betty, give this cheek a little red."

Her wishes were respected, and she was buried
beneath the monument of Congreve in Westminster Abbey, " in a very fine Brussels lace-head,

---

[1] Cf., " His night-cap bordered round with lace."
Swift's *Strephon and Chloe.*

a holland shift, and double ruffles of the same
lace."

The fashion, however, soon went out. The
Lace Apron, which had been popular from the
time of Elizabeth was also doomed. Beau Nash
so detested it, that he gave orders that anyone
who appeared at the Assembly Room, Bath, so
attired should be turned out. One day the
Duchess of Queensbury ventured in wearing an
apron of rich point which cost two hundred
guineas. Without hesitation Nash stripped it
from her, and tossed it on to one of the hinder
benches among the waiting-women, with the
remark, " None but abigails wear white aprons."
This sally is said to have given the fashion its
quietus.

About 1790, the workers in South Bucks took
up the making of **Black Silk Lace,**
with the view of humouring a fashion   36. The
which had come over from the conti-   Amersham
nent.[1] The centres of the industry   Veil and
                                        the Olney
were Amersham and Great Marlow,   Flounce.
                                        1790—1870.
which obtained a reputation for their veils. In
the Bucks County Museum, at Aylesbury, is
exhibited a filmy and very beautiful veil of black
silk (the gift of Lady Smyth), which was made at
Princes Risborough about 1836.

In the north of the county the lace continued

---

[1] There was an institution in Westminster for teaching girls how to
make black silk lace as early as 1775. It seems to have been both bobbin
and needle.

to be chiefly of the white variety, particularly at Olney. In the beginning of the 19th century, however, we find it producing Point Ground black flounces. They were used chiefly for trimming white silk evening dresses. The white silk dress with the black Olney flouncing, which "was fine as a hair," was a striking feature in Early Victorian levees, and at other important functions. (See Plate 17.) The industry declined in the middle of the 19th century, but revived after the Franco-German War.

The *Militia Rolls*, which are lists of men chosen to serve for three or five years, as the case might be, contain, as would be expected, numerous references to persons connected with the Lace Trade. The following names occur in the Rolls of North Bucks,[1] and it will be noticed that, as in earlier days, not only women but also men made lace.

OLNEY.

1785	Jaimes Cooper.	Lace-maker.
1788	Peter Perkins.	Lace-buyer.
1788	William Sample.	Lace-man.
1788	Nathaniel Hine.	Lace-maker.

NEWPORT PAGNELL.

1785	Walter Beaty, Junr.	Lace-man.

BRAYFIELD.

1779	Thomas Sparke.	Bobbin-maker.

[1] In the possession of Lieut. J. L. Coales of Newport Pagnell.

Plate 18

PORTION OF A FLOUNCE OF PILLOW MADE LACE.
(Bucks Point.)   Bucks, First Half of 19th Century.
Victoria and Albert Museum (13771).   (*By permission of the Authorities.*)
Property of Baroness Kinloss.

Plate 19

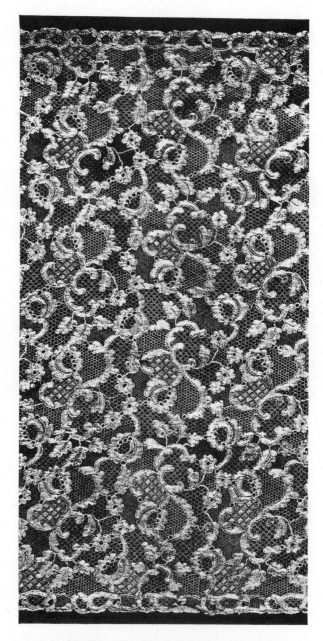

SCARF OF PILLOW MADE LACE.
First Half, 19th Century.
Victoria and Albert Museum.   (*By permission of the Authorities.*)
Property of Miss Best, Acton, Cheshire.

EMBERTON.

1779   Charles Cooper.   Lace-maker.

LAVENDON.

1785   George Osborne.   Lace-man.

MOULSOE.

1788   Charles Greenwood.   Lace-maker.

BROUGHTON.

1788   John Salisbury.   Lace-maker.

NORTH CRAWLEY.

1803   James Cobb.   Lace-maker.
        William Brewer.   Lace-buyer.

HANSLOPE.

1803   George Hancock.   Lace-maker.

STONY STRATFORD.

1807   Edward Lever.   Pin-maker.

CHAPTER XII

THE LACE SCHOOLS

Of the manners and customs of Laceland at this period we have abundance of trustworthy information. The children were taught lace-making at a lace school kept in some large room of a cottage, there being generally from twenty to thirty pupils, whose ages varied from 5 to 15. We might see them seated in several rows on four-legged stools, while in front of them are their pillows, furnished with bobbins and pins, and supported partly by the knee and partly by "the lady," as they called the three-legged pillow-horse. In some schools instead of each child having a separate "lady," a form was provided to support the pillows, and the children "sot" facing it on each side. They were very neatly dressed, with bare neck and arms, so that they could be slapped the more easily. Their hair was in plaits, lest a stray hair should fall and get worked up with the lace, and they were never allowed to touch their hair—the one great object being to keep the lace spotlessly clean. In full view of them sat, with a cane on her lap, the Argus-eyed mistress.

37. "The Pea" and "The Nine-pin."

Many mothers taught their little ones the rudi-
ments of lace-making at home, chiefly because at
the schools all the lace made the first year became
the perquisite of the teacher—the "dilling"[1] being
nearly always favoured in this way. Consequently,
although a number of children were sent to the
school at the age of five, most entered at six.
The beginners — those who had not received
instruction at home—were set to quite a narrow
edging—the *Pea*, the *Ninepin*, the *Town Trot*, or
the *Spider*. From these they would pass to the
Kidney Bean, the *Plaited Star*,[2] the *Diamond and
Chain*, or the *Double Ring*. The third step would
be the *Spectacles*, the *Old Trot*, which consisted of
eight plaits in a head, or the *Running River*. They
were also taught how to "halse" the bobbins,
that is, to wind the thread round them properly.

The children at first felt, to use their own
expression, very "unkid"[3] (and persons have been
heard to say, "I'd pity a dog that was unkid"),
for the work was puzzling and the teacher with
her lynx-like eyes and her "long, thin, yellow
fingers," who could "read lace like a book," was
frightfully strict, especially when she was riled.
But there was a little respite when the good
woman went out to get her "baver."[4] One

[1] The youngest child, who always came in for a little extra indulgence.
[2] At Nash, Bucks, for example.
[3] A Bucks word, meaning utterly miserable. Thus Olney people speak
of "unkid weather."
[4] Refreshment between breakfast and dinner. The word is sometimes
spelt "bever," but in North Bucks it is always pronounced "baver."
"We must have weer baver" being a common expression.

worker, recalling the old days, said to me, " When I was five, my mother took me to the lace school, and gave the teacher a shilling. She learnt me for an hour, smacked my head six times, and rubbed my nose on the pin-heads." It must be admitted that the poor child had more than value for her money. The boys were " spunky "[1] and gave the teacher continual trouble. They preferred to be " hommocksing "[2] over fields, or sitting on the side of brook or path and " scolching "[3] in the bank.

There were prizes, however, as well as penalties. If a child had been diligent, the mistress would, at the end of the year, present her with a bobbin (perhaps inscribed with her name) or a pair of pattens with iron rings, a gift which the dirty state of the old roads made very acceptable. The advice given in respect to Point Lace by a good Lavendon worker to the young people was :

> " Do your stitch,
> Stick your pin,
> And do your stitch about it."

That is to say, you should, after sticking your pin, do a stitch without making a pin. Unless this advice is followed, the work becomes limp and will not last. Some mistresses had the interests of the children really at heart.

[1] Mettlesome.
[2] This word is in common use in North Bucks.
[3] Sometimes spelt coalch. In Bucks pronounced " scolch."

At a school at Wootton, Beds, for example, the girls were required to read a few verses of the Bible every morning before beginning to work. At Elstow (Beds) the charge was 2d. a week for girls and 4d. for boys. The boys (as in Buckinghamshire) hated the work, and were " obstroperous,"[1] consequently the extra twopence was well earned. Another disadvantage as regards boys was, from the teacher's point of view, that as their necks and shoulders were covered up by their smocks, and their heads were too hard, there was nothing to "smack." It is possible, according to Ovid, to turn girls into boys; but when in Bedfordshire they tried to turn boys into girls, there was endless trouble. One villain, goaded by a stroke from the cane, ran out of school and dropped his pillow down the well—that classic well on Elstow Green from which John Bunyan had drunk; and another, similarly provoked, threw the whole of his apparatus into the duck pond. A third ran away to sea.

In the middle of a field called Dunsty, at Stoke Goldington, is an old ash tree, under which in summertime the girls and boys used to sit and work. They had to empty so many bobbins a day; and it is remembered that the boys, in order to lessen their labours, used to wind the thread round the bole of the tree. Of course, the trick was discovered; but boys never think of the future.

[1] Obstreperous.

At the Lace School at Spratton (Northants) the girls had to stick ten pins in a minute, or 600 in an hour; and if at the end of the day they were five pins short, they had to work for another hour. If little Mary Muskett dropped her pins, or tall Ann Warren "glined" out of "winder" at some hobbledehoy who leered at her when passing, a similar penalty followed. When a girl fell short of pins, she would go round the room singing:

> "Polly or Betsy, a pin for the poor!
> Give me a pin and I'll ask for no more."

There were within living memory three lace schools at Turvey, Beds, the position of one of them being indicated by a row of cottages in Nell's Lane,[1] called "The Lace Cottages." In front of them is a raised pathway, accompanied by a wooden rail and approached by stone steps. On this eminence a bevy of girls might have been seen any summer day busy with their pillows and bobbins.

Among the plans to incite the children to industry, one was to arrange them in two rows, in order to see which company could place "five score pins" in the shorter time. "The Five Score Breakings," as it was called, created great

[1] Named after the old Nell of the Tinker of Turvey. Nell's Well is nearly opposite the cottages. The Sign-board of the Tinker of Turvey, which shows all the figures referred to in the rhyme, is preserved in the Reading Room at Turvey. The rhyme runs:

> "The Tinker of Turvey, his dog, and his staff,
> Old Nell with her Budget, would make a man laugh."

emulation. "All hollered out" what pins they had stuck in. Two girls acted as "counters," and the side that was victorious called out triumphantly, "Fewest!" Usually, however, they counted to themselves every pin they stuck, and at every fiftieth pin they would call out the time, each endeavouring to out-do the other; but sometimes, instead of competing with one another, they raced the big hour-glass, which usually stood on the middle of the mantle-shelf. The children earned 6d. a day, and were paid at the end of every month.

In the summer-time, when the windows could be open, or when, still better, the children could sit out of doors, all went pretty well; but in winter-time their lot was a hard one. In Normandy, as we noticed, the lace-makers, in order to avoid the danger of having their work darkened by the smoke and dust from a fire, used to work over a cow shed. In Buckinghamshire the difficulty was met by the use of a **Fire Pot,** or **Dicky Pot** as it was sometimes called. These pots, which were of rough brown ware, used to be filled every morning, at the cost of a farthing, with hot wood ashes, obtained from the nearest baker's. A pot so filled would keep hot half a day or longer. When it began to cool, the insertion among the embers of the nozzle of a pair of bellows, followed by a few puffs, would revive the heat.

38. The Fire Pot.

These pots were used not only in the lace schools, but also by the older girls and the women in their own homes; but the practice of keeping them very close to their feet was not without inconveniences. Sometimes there would be a cry of "I smell burn! Polly Nurseaw, is it you?" and Mrs. Nurseaw would hurriedly put down her pillow in order to attend to a smouldering petticoat. Notwithstanding its drawbacks, however, the fire pot was regarded almost with affection. Anyhow, it was better than a Normandy cow; and on a Sunday it was carried to church or chapel, as the case might be. The Prayer Book, the pattens, and the fire pot, never failed in winter time on Sundays to make journeys together to the Parish Church, as did *Davis's Hymn Book*,[1] the pattens, and the fire pot to the village Chapel —except when their owners were down with "seventh day ague."[2]

The fire pots used in the south of Bucks were called *Hot Pots* or *Chad Pots*. Unlike those of North Bucks, which were plain, those of the south had a number of little holes near the rim. The "High Buck" people[3] ridiculed their southern neighbours for giving themselves the trouble to make holes that served no purpose; but no

[1] Much used in Northants in the 18th century. It was compiled by that good old fire-brand, Richard Davis, of Rothwell (1658—1714).

[2] A Buckinghamshire expression to account for the desire to stay at home on Sundays.

[3] People of North Bucks. Cowper uses this expression in one of his letters.

Plate 20

SCARF OF PILLOW MADE LACE.
First Half, 19th Century.
Victoria and Albert Museum.   *(By permission of the Authorities.)*
Property of Mrs. Bousfield.

Plate 21

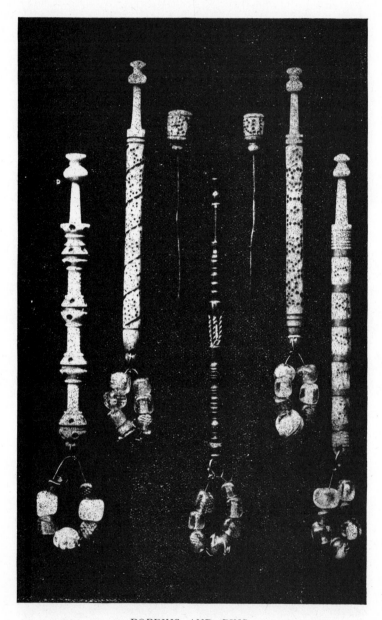

BOBBINS AND PINS.

Belonging to Mrs. Taylor, Huntspill Court, Bridgwater.

BOBBINS: 1. Bobbin from Paulerspury, Northants. 2. With cryptic inscription- TOB : TL : JS : EH : YB : KI : SLG : WL : DEARS : YEAR. From Paulerspury, Northants. 3. Brass "Window" Bobbin. 4. Frances Parrit, 1834. From Bedfordshire. 5. Lydia. The bands are of pewter.

PINS (from Bedfordshire): Inscribed respectively Thomas and Ruth.

southerner was ever convinced that the ashes in a chad pot could be kept in a glow without these superfluous holes. Most of the fire pots were undecorated, but others, made in "slip ware," that is, clay ornamented with colour, were extremely quaint looking. The well-to-do people in North-ants went so far as to use brass fire pots, per-forated round the rim; which, however, they filled with hot charcoal instead of wood ashes.

So indispensable were the fire pots that the terms, "Sitting over your pillow," and "Sitting over the fire pot," were regarded as synonymous. In Olney to this very day, when a person looks sallow and melancholy, as one does after being shut up for hours in a stuffy room, people say, "You look as if you had been sitting over a dicky pot all day." It is not surprising that there appeared in the *Gentleman's Magazine* for 1785 "An Essay on the Cause and Prevention of Deformity among the Lace-makers of Bucks, &c.," in which improved ventilation, among other remedies, was advocated.

To return to the lace schools, when the day's work was done, every child covered her pillow, turned her four-legged stool upside down, placed the pillow in it, and then ran off with a joyous shout. Saturday was usually a half-holiday. What a relief, after a week's work of ten or twelve hours a day, to be absolutely free for a few hours; to be able to hunt for violets in the hedgerows, or roam the ridings,[1] racks,[2] and slades[3] of Yardley Chase in search of primroses and wind-flowers!—to exchange the lace tell for the sough of the wind in the sycamores.

Some of the boys—for, like it or not, lace they had to make—did not lose their dexterity even when they had become men, and had exchanged the bobbin for the plough. One worker told me that when she was a little girl, and had to do so many heads of lace a day, sometimes when she was gone to bed, her father, after a hard day's work in the fields, would act Robin Goodfellow, and in the morning she would find four or five heads done for her. William Adams[4] of Stoke Goldington used every evening, after working in the fields all day, to do a yard of *Pretty Dick.* In our illustration, an Olney Lace School (Plate 35), will be noticed among those at work an old man—Joseph Huckle—who had made lace when quite a little child.[5]

In the winter evenings the women and children used to sit and work round what was **39. All Round the Candle Stool.** called a **Candle=stool** or **Candle= block,** a rather tall three or four-legged stool, the top or *Hole-board* of which had three, four, five or six holes in a circle near the edge, and one hole in the middle. In the

---

[1] Main roads in a wood.   [2] Roads through a wood.   [3] Dells.
[4] He married Charlotte Warren, one of the three famous lace-making sisters mentioned in Chapter 16, Section 65.
[5] He is still living (1919).

centre hole was a long stick—the *Nozzle*, with a socket for a tallow candle at the top and peg holes[1] through the sides, enabling it to be raised or lowered at will. In the other holes were *cups* (wooden sockets) which held inverted and securely corked flasks of " snow water; " while to prevent the flask from jarring against the cup, a circular *Flask Cushion*[2] made of rush was sometimes used. These flasks focused the light from the candle[3] on to the pillows, after the fashion of a burning glass. Hanging round the stools were *hutches* or baskets of plaited straw or rush in which the flasks could be preserved when not in use, and the indispensable snuffers were not far away. Often there were three circles of workers round the candle-stool—whence the terms First, Second, and Third Lights ; and the stools were sometimes on different levels, those nearest the flasks being the highest. On a shelf at no great distance from the candle-stool would be seen the *Tinder-box*, which was usually circular and of tin. At the bottom was the tinder (burnt rag), and above the tinder was a circular cover on which rested the flints and the iron striker. In the lid of the box was a candle holder. In order to get a light, a spark had to be struck so that it fell on to the tinder. A slip of wood tipped with sulphur having been

[1] Some nozzles had notches and a wire check.
[2] Miss Haynes, of the Arcade, Bedford, has one.
[3] " Eights " were generally used ; that is, eight to the pound.

applied to the spark, the candle could be lighted.
Mr. J. S. Elliott of Bewdley has another object
that was sometimes seen in the workers' cottages
—a *Lace-dyeing Bottle.*

For the drawing of patterns and the pricking of
parchments the designer requires, not
only an artistic eye, but also skill and
great patience. For five centuries this
work has occupied many men of taste, genius and
singleness of mind. Wonderful patterns were
brought over from the Continent by the refugees
of 1568, 1572 and 1685, and many patterns
executed in England by our own designers are
marvels of beauty.

40. The
Parchments.

From the 17th century those made in Olney
were, as we have seen (Chapter 9), both original
and delicate, but the names of the early
designers are lost, unless among them were the
Mr. Gibbs, Mr. Breeden and James Rogers (see
page 54) referred to in 1669, the two Brierlys
of a later date (see page 56), Thomas Osborne,
" Lace-dealer," buried June 6th, 1763,[1] Thomas
Abbott, " Lace-buyer," buried October 22nd,
1765,[2] Peter Perkins, mentioned as a " Lace-
buyer "[3] in 1788, and William Sample as a
" Lace-man "[4] in the same year.

The late 18th century and the early 19th have
been called the Golden Age of Parchment Design-

Plate 22

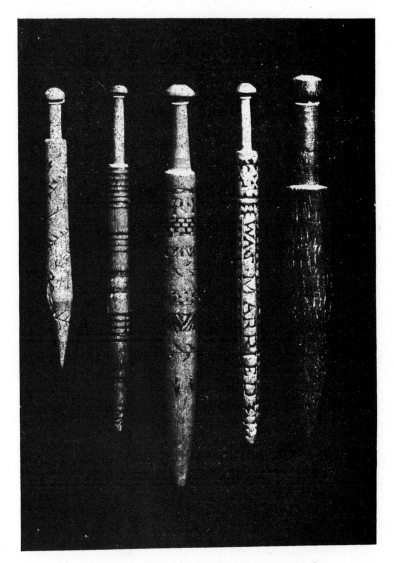

WILTS AND DEVON BOBBINS.   See p. 176.

1. Old carved Downton (Wilts) Bobbin.   2. Old Honiton Bobbin from Branscombe, with red and black rings.   3. Old Honiton gimp Bobbin from Beer. Lettered in red at top—M ! S ✚ R ✚. The ornamental work below is black and red alternately.   4. Old Honiton Bobbin from Beer. J A ✚ E was married May 12, 1878.   5. Old Downton gimp Bobbin.

Plate 23

Mrs. Unwin's Bobbin-winder on chair: Tinder
Box, with lid removed, on chair; Candle-stool,
with flasks and hutches (rush bags); Pattens
and Fire Pot.

*By permission of the Trustees, Cowper and Newton
Museum, Olney.*

THE LACE-MAKER'S GREAT CANDLESTICK.
Described on p. 196.
Preserved in the Museum, Aylesbury.

ing, and of the Olney designers of that period two
stand out as men of exceptional ability and
enthusiasm—John Millward[1] of Olney, and a Mr.
Harbert, whose parchments date from 1820, and
who seems to have lived first at Olney, where
the family had property until a few years ago, and
afterwards at Woburn Sands. The Harberts are
mentioned 70 times in the Olney Church Register.
Some of the members of the family spelt the
name Herbert.

The Millwards, who were a family of Lace-
buyers and Designers, seem to have come from
Newport Pagnell, where a designer of that name
was carrying on business in 1761, but our knowledge of them, and indeed of all the early
designers, is unfortunately nebulous. They are
first heard of in Olney on October 31st, 1780,
when William, son of John and Elizabeth Millard
(as the name is also spelt) was christened. This
"William Millard" may have been the father
of the John Millward already mentioned, who
designed many signed draughts dating from 1822
to 1850. Of Millward we shall have more to say
later. He is the Byron of the Lace world. He
was a tall, thin, sharp-featured man with a long
pendulous nose. Like Byron he had a club foot,
and it may be said of him too that he became
famous in a night.

[1] "Millward's," or as it is generally called, "Millard's Entry," a narrow
passage leading from the middle of High Street to East Street, took its
name from his house, which adjoined it.

The work of Mr. Millward was continued by
Mr. George Smith, who from 1870 has made very
many tasteful designs. The trade at Newport
Pagnell was for long in the hands of Mr. William
Ayers,[1] and the principal dealer at High
Wycombe was Mr. Gilbert, at one time mayor
of the town.

To Rennals, 1668, and Reynoldes, 1658, of
Buckingham as Lace-dealers we referred on
page 57; and in the *Verney Memoirs* there is a
reference to one Hartley, a lace-buyer of Buckingham, but whether any of these were designers or
not is not stated. The most distinguished designer
of Buckingham was Mr. E. Godfroy, usually
known as " the Black Man," because he was the
first to introduce black silk among the workers to
be made into lace; and he is probably the " black
man " riding " on a white horse " of one of the
lace-tells which we shall give in a subsequent
Chapter.[2]

Leaving Caen, in Normandy, he settled in
Buckingham about 1840; and ten years later
he introduced into the district first the Maltese[3]
and subsequently the Yak[4] laces, and he exhibited at the Exhibitions of 1851 and 1862,
where he won gold medals. Mr. J. Raftery joined

[1] Mr. Ayers supplied the chapter on "The Lace Trade" in Mr. F. W.
Bull's *History of Newport Pagnell.*
[2] See Chapter 14.
[3] See Chapter 16, Section 67.
[4] See Chapter 16, Section 70.

him in his business in 1871, and subsequently succeeded him.

The Abrahams were also a distinguished family of lace designers. William Abraham,[1] who resided at Stony Stratford, and afterwards, I believe, at Emberton, worked chiefly for Mr. Joseph Foddy, who, in partnership with Mr. Kightley, traded as a lace-buyer in Abingdon Street, Northampton; and his kinsmen, Samuel and George Abraham, lived at Kempston, near Bedford.

Much of the work of these designers is beyond criticism, and our indebtedness to their originality, fecundity, and versatility has never been sufficiently acknowledged. The patterns elaborated by them are their most jewelled thoughts stereotyped in parchment, just as the work of an inspired author is the expression of his inmost soul imparted, as Blake would put it, "fearfully and tremblingly" to the printed page. They did great things, for their thoughts were hitched to the stars. In moments of ecstasy, say the old philosophers, the soul divests itself of the body. In the finest of lace, as in a precious book, we seem to come into contact with the detached soul of a great personality.

The first business of the designer is to make and prick the pattern on cardboard, and to ink the lines where the gimp is to go. This is called

[1] Information supplied by his grand-daughter, Mrs. C. Randall, Northampton.

the *draught*. Over the draught is placed a piece of
transparent sheepskin[1] or calf-skin parchment
which is, in its turn, pricked and inked. Without
the inking the workers would, of course, be unable
to trace the design. We said "transparent parchment" for some is cloudy, owing to the action of
the weather at the time it was prepared, and therefore quite unfit for the purpose. The old *prickers*
were of brass and quaintly fashioned — being
indeed themselves little works of art, but a
common needle fixed in a bobbin has often
served.

The parchment, which is generally fourteen
inches long, is called a *down*, and when the lace-
maker has done a down she has to "set up," that
is, to move the lace back to the top of the parchment—a proceeding that requires both skill and
care. In Buckinghamshire, however, some workers
used, instead of the one parchment, two *eaches*,[2]
which, like the parchments, were generally fourteen inches in length, but there were "long
eaches" and "short eaches," just as there were
long and short parchments. By allowing one
"each" to follow the other the lace-maker can go
quite round the pillow and so avoid the operation

---

[1] Nowadays, for the making of Maltese and Torchon Laces, cardboard
is often used instead of parchment, the "legs" as well as "the gimps"
being inked.

[2] I have spelt the word "each" because it is so pronounced, rhyming
with speech, but it is also spelt "eche," "eke," and "etch." We say,
"I must try to eke it out." See also Chapter 14.

of "setting up"—hence the expression, "Each your parchment."[1]

Shakespeare uses very beautifully this archaic and quaint word, bidding us (*Pericles*, Act III.), as life is so short, to lengthen it by giving rein to our imaginative powers :

> " Be attent,
> And time that is so briefly spent,
> With your fine fancies quaintly[2] each."

That he had often watched the lace-makers at their pillows is quite certain. A single parchment that went all round the pillow was occasionally used.

Old parchments were generally provided with linen ends in order that they could more easily be secured to the pillow, and these linen ends were also called "eaches"[3]—hence the expression, "Sew your eaches on."

In all old laces the pattern is quickly repeated. In the mid-Victorian period a taste for "enormous heads" prevailed, and as a result the lace lost its daintiness. Of recent years a return has been made to the small heads.

Parchment used to be manufactured at Olney by a family named Grace.[4] For long it was made

---

[1] Which means, put the " each " after your parchment. It also means, as will be seen a few lines further on, " Fix your parchment to the pillow by means of the linen ' each.' "

[2] Skilfully, ingeniously.

[3] Thus the word " each " meant (1) a parchment that succeeded another parchment ; (2) the linen bands at the end of a parchment. In short, anything that extends anything else is an " each."

[4] First mentioned in the Church Register 1809. The widow of George Grace died at Newton Blossomville about 1914.

by Mr. William Cowley at Newport Pagnell, and
the business is now continued by his son.

The old-fashioned pillows were almost round.
41. The Pillow, the Lady, and the Lace Chest. Then oval or bolster-shaped pillows,
with a hole at each end, came into
use; and in recent years the half-
pillow, which being flat-bottomed can
be used on an ordinary table, has here and there
found favour. In respect to the half-pillow, the
parchment being fixed on a smaller and revolving
pillow let into a well in the large pillow, the
worker is saved the trouble of "setting up" her
work again; but, of course, half-pillows cannot be
used for wide patterns. The workers scornfully
refer to these as "Drawing-room pillows. A new-
fashioned fad. No good to us." Oxfordshire
pillows differ from Bucks and Beds pillows in
being "more round, and not so flat and wide."

Lace pillows, "firm as a rock," could be purchased at Olney and a few other places. At
Aylesbury one family named Smith had the
monopoly of making them. They were covered
with Hessian canvas. On receiving the pillow, the
worker, having covered it with a *pillow cloth*, which
was usually of butcher blue, attached the parchment to it, pinning down the eaches (the linen
ends) with *corkings*. Then sitting down to her
bobbin-winder, with its wheel, spool, and blades,
she placed the thread round the pegs of the
blades, "hotched" an end of the thread on to the

head of a bobbin, held the spangle in the spool, and turned the wheel.

In the Cowper and Newton Museum at Olney is the bobbin winder used by Cowper's friend, Mrs. Unwin.[1] (See Plate 23.)

The bobbins being wound, the worker ties the threads of two of them together, and sticks in the parchment her first pin, in order to keep them in their place. She next takes another pair of bobbins and inserts her second pin, and so on. Over the front of the pillow cloth and under the bobbins she pins another cloth of stronger material called the *Worker*, which owing to the friction of the bobbins has from time to time to be renewed. The "Worker" also protects the parchment where the hands rest. In order to keep the lace on the pillow clean, she covers that portion of it from which the pins had gradually been removed with a home-spun linen or patchwork slip, called the *Draw* or *Drawter*. I have seen one with a date in bold figures—1807. Covering the whole, when the lace-maker is not at work, is the *hindcloth* or *hiller*. A pin-cushion at the top of the pillow, a pair of tiny scissors suspended by a chain, and a *bobbin bag* with two compartments— "Empty" and "Full"—hanging at the side, usually complete the equipment; but at Bozeat and some other places it was customary to fasten

[1] Many of the bobbin winders were home-made. Mr. H. H. Armstrong of Olney still makes them.

to the left of the pillow a *Flour bag*, containing
flour or starch to dry the hands of the worker.

At Stoke Goldington and other of the best
lace-making villages, however, it was considered a
shameful practice[1] to use flour or starch, either for
the hands or to whiten (" get up ") lace[2] that had
been soiled. If at the lace school a girl was
detected at this practice, a smart slap on the bare
arms or shoulder and " I'll give you ' get up ' "
was the customary sequel. The children were
told that the only way to keep their lace clean
was by drying their hands on a cloth kept for the
purpose. In the various accessories of the pillow
the workers took great pride.

Children had besides their big pillow a *Play
Pillow*; that is, a pillow of their very own, at
which they could work—doing such patterns as
the nine-pin[3]—at the end of their nine-hour day.
The money earned in this way they could spend
as they liked. Some devoted it to taking in a
child's magazine, for the lace-makers have always
been lovers of reading. Surely, however, the
play-pillow idea was a mistake. Such close
application must have been attended by ill results;
but most of us are the victims of our virtues.

The pillow was supported, as we have already
said, partly by the knee and partly by the three-

---

[1] Told me at Olney.

[2] Even in a photograph one can tell whether the lace has been "got
up." When it has been tampered with the cloth-work looks clogged.

[3] Nine pins to a head.

legged pillow horse. Of late years a bow has been added, enabling the horse to stand upright by itself, hence the terms *Single Horse* and *Bowed Horse*. Some of the bows are elaborately carved, and I have seen one with the initials, " B. H."— Bet Hinde, who once kept a lace-school at Olney. To one of the names for the pillow-horse, *The Lady*, we have already referred. Another name, *The Maid*,[1] occurs in John Askham's lines, " The Old Granddame," where we read :

> " There she will sit with her pillow
> Propt with a wooden maid."

A few years ago Mr. H. H. Armstrong of Olney invented a collapsible pillow-stand, the advantage of which is that it can, when not in use, be folded and put away.

In Askham's poem is a reference to another of the lace-maker's necessaries, " her brown, old-fashioned *yard-wand*," which was taken down on " Cutting-off Day."

In many homes there was one more appurtenance to the industry—the old *Lace Chest*, which had the appearance of an ordinary oak chest standing on a low table. The chest itself consisted of two parts : the upper, in which was placed the pillow when not in use, and the lower, which consisted of a drawer or drawers for holding the bobbins and patterns. A picture of a beauti-

---

[1] In *Judith and other Poems*, by John Askham, the Northamptonshire poet.

ful lace chest, carved with the initials, E. H., and
bearing the date 1702, is given in *Point and Pillow
Lace*, by "A. M. S." (Mary Sharp). As a passage
in Cowper's *Task* (IV., 400) indicates, the lace
chest was to be seen in even the humblest cottage
in North Bucks. Speaking of the trials of the
poor during a hard winter, the poet says :

> " All the care
> Ingenious parsimony takes but just
> Saves the small inventory, bed and stool,
> Skillet, and old carved chest from public sale."

The early brass pins made in England had a
globular head of fine twisted wire made
42. Pins. separately and secured to the shank by
compression from a falling block and
die. Consequently the heads often came off. It
was not until 1840 that the kind with solid heads
now universally in use appeared on the market.

The workers liked to use pins with red waxed
or beaded heads for the *Headside*[1] (or *Turnside*) of
the lace, and gold wax or green beaded pins for
the *Footside*. Sometimes, however, for these purposes they used pins on which were threaded six
or more tiny beads of blue and white or red and
white placed alternately. In North Bucks these
pins are called *Limicks*, in South Bucks *Bugles*, in
Beds *King Pins*, and like the other coloured pins
they added greatly to the beauty of the pillow.
In making limicks, after the beads had been

---

[1] Also called *Dykeside* if the lace has dykes.

threaded on a pin, the head of another pin (often removed, I am sorry to say, by the teeth) was threaded to prevent the beads from dropping off, so for every limick that was made one pin was wasted. As the heads of modern pins are not removable, limicks cannot now be made. Other pins were ornamented with the seeds of goose-grass—*Burheads* as they are called, which were put on over the head of the pin ; not pushed up from the point. Mrs. F. Taylor of Huntspell Court, Bridgwater, has the great curiosity of two pins with bone heads, inscribed respectively, in the usual dotted fashion common to bobbins, with the names Ruth and Thomas. They were purchased twenty years ago near Brackley, Northants. (See Plate 21.)

The Olney workers, in order to time themselves, used to stick in a specially ornamented pin called the *Striver*, and they would notice how long it took before that pin was worked out again.

The Bucks Point Laces are sometimes made of Pure Irish Linen, which is sold in skeins, Number 250 being in most **43. Thread.** demand, though the finer Number 300 and the coarser Number 200 also find their way to the pillow.

Many workers use ordinary Lace Thread (which is, of course, cotton), sometimes called *Gassed Thread*, from the fact that it is drawn at a slow but regular pace through a flame of gas in order to deprive it of all film. A two ounce packet contains four "parcels," and each parcel a specified number of "slips." In the case of the extremely fine "14 slip thread" there are 14 slips, in the case of the "12 slip thread" 12 slips, and so on down to "3 slip," which is the coarsest in use.[1]

It may here be mentioned that the processes of the Olney method of washing lace are: (1) Stitch it round a bottle covered with flannel; (2) Place it in soapy water and gently smooth it with the hand; (3) Put the bottle on a stick in the garden, and leave the lace to bleach and "hazel."[2]

What, it may be asked, was done with the babies while their mothers made lace? At Gawcott, near Buckingham, there was in each cottage a *Revolving Post*, with a wooden arm to which baby children were secured, so that they could run round and round, "and thus enjoy exercise without the possibility of making their escape."[3] At Olney in some cottages there were *Go-carts*, but most of the workers had recourse to the simple device of an *"Imprisoning Board"* at the door.

On the whole, the lace-maker's lot in the 18th and 19th centuries was a hard one. A year or two ago I overheard a child telling her troubles to her grandmother, an old lace-maker. "Get along with ye," was all the comfort she got, "ye don't know what troubles are!"

[1] For the thread used for Maltese and Torchon see Chapter 16.
[2] To dry and sweeten. This word is in common use in High Bucks.
[3] *Bucks Biographies*, by Lady Verney, p. 210.

CHAPTER XIII

THE BOBBINS. CATULLUS IN A SMOCK-FROCK

The Lace District of North Bucks, West Beds **44. Wooden** and South Northants, is pre-eminently **Bobbins.** the country of beautiful bobbins. It is but rarely that one meets with bobbins of super-lative merit in South Bucks or the other lace districts. Head, short neck,[1] long neck, shank and spangle—to every part has been devoted affec-tionate care. The materials chiefly used were wood and bone, while some few were also made of brass, silver, gold, pewter and even glass, and it is asserted that ivory has been used for the purpose.

The earliest bobbins—called *Dumps* or *Bob-tailed Bobbins*—were ordinarily of box-wood, quite small and without spangles; and they were used to make only the finest kinds of Bucks Point, the thread of which would have been broken by heavier or spangled bobbins. To these seem to have succeeded the wooden bobbin with spangles. Almost any close-grained wood was used. Plum

---

[1] The thread is first wound round the long neck and then three times, or more, round the short neck. Honiton Trolly Bobbins have also the two necks, but other Devonshire bobbins have only the one long neck. All weighted bobbins require the short neck as well as the long neck.

and damson found favour owing to their darkness,
and bobbins of box, ebony, rosewood, maple,
spindle-wood, yew, blackthorn, may, cherry, apple,
and oak are often seen. A branch from a favourite
tree was sometimes utilised in this way. Historical
trees, such as Gog, Magog and Cowper's Oak, all
situated within a few miles of Olney, have been
put under tribute. Of the wooden bobbins there
were many varieties. Thus there were *Bitted
Bobbins*, made of dark wood inlaid with wood of a
lighter colour, which lost their popularity owing to
the fact that the inlaid parts were apt to drop out;
Bedfordshire Tigers,[1] with circles of pewter let in ;
Bedfordshire Leopards,[2] with spots of pewter let in;
Butterfly Bobbins, so called from the shape of the
metal mountings ; *Old Maid Bobbins*, which were
plain and particularly slender, and *Mother-in-Babe
Bobbins*, in the hollowed shank of which a tiny
wooden bobbin rattles. Sometimes instead of a
tiny bobbin one finds beads or shot. *Quills* are
bobbins on which the whole of the gimp from a
skein is wound. They are never attached to the
pillow, but the gimp is wound from them on to
another bobbin called the *Trolly*, which was always
surrounded with loose pewter rings called *Gingles*.
The trollies used in Huntingdonshire were called
Bedfordshire Trailers. Quills and trollies were in
every cottage sixty years ago, and they are still

---

[1] [2] These are names given in Huntingdonshire to the bobbins of this
kind made at Bedford.

used in South Bucks. In the net ground of many Point Laces appear four small plaits. The bobbins which were used to make these were distinguished by having tin bands round them, and they were called *Tallies.* Sometimes one comes across bobbins partially burnt that were rescued from Lucy Gutteridge's Lace School[1] at the time of the Great Fire of Olney, June 26th, 1854, which destroyed all the North end of the town.

When Yak lace first came in, enormous bobbins were used. These early *Yak Bobbins* were seven inches long and their heads were some four inches in circumference; but as time went on, smaller and more slender bobbins were made, until five and a half inches became the standard length.

Gold Lace Bobbins of a still later period were of plain wood and about four inches long. Like the Yak bobbins they were ugly. A variety of the gold lace bobbin is the *Cow and Calf Bobbin*, or *Jack in the Box*, the lower part of which pulls out or unscrews, and releases a miniature bobbin, also of wood. Sometimes on a tawny wooden bobbin one finds carved a girl's or a boy's name, or a date, but the material is, of course, one that does not readily lend itself to any kind of lettering.

The Rev. A. J. Roberts, Vicar of Harting, has a bobbin inscribed "Wakes Oak," made by James

[1] Nos. 86 and 88 High Street occupy the site.

Compton of Deanshanger, from the famous oak tree in Whittlebury Forest which was traditionally connected with Hereward the Wake, the last of the Saxon princes. The tree was burned down by schoolboys from Trinity School, Old Stratford, near Stony Stratford, in 1866. A Renhold bobbin inscribed (G P—F H August 26th 1813) probably commemorates an engagement or a wedding ; another from the same village is lettered " Jesus weepd." A Northampton bobbin has the single word " Glory," and two Turweston bobbins are inscribed respectively, "L. K. 1844" and "M.A.G. Ag. 18. Ro." [1]

Charming as are some of the wooden bobbins, it is only when we come to the Bone variety that we find the bobbin in all its glory. With the bone bobbin invention ran riot and ingenuity capped ingenuity.

45. Bone Bobbins.

The French blood in the people of North Bucks and the surrounding districts revealed itself in ten thousand artistic devices ; for these people are, as a whole, more imaginative, more poetical, fonder of colour and altogether more artistic in their ideas than those of the other districts.

And yet the Huguenots did not influence in the same way every locality in which they settled. The bobbins of the Aylesbury and Thame district, for example, are squat in form, plain to a wonder, and they have no spangles ; yet they are called,

[1] Perhaps short for " Robert."

Plate 24

The late Miss JANE MORRIS of Shelton, Beds.

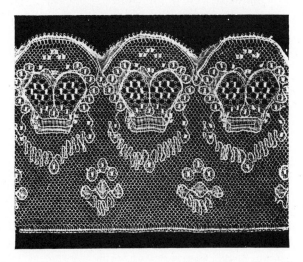

Lace made by Miss JANE MORRIS for Queen Mary's Coronation.

Plate 25

" REGENCY POINT " LACE (1810—1820). See p. 219.

Made near Brackley, Northants, where it was known by the above name.
The grounds in the pattern are Honeycomb with plaits and Cord Ground. The net is, of course, Point.

(Lent by Mrs. Taylor, Huntspill Court, Bridgwater.)

1. REAL VALENCIENNES. Made by a Northampton Lace-maker.
2. BLONDE LACE. Made in Bucks. See pp. 20 & 227.
3. BUCKS POINT WITH HONEYCOMB FILLINGS.

strangely enough, " Huguenots." These " Huguenot " bobbins are only 3½ inches long. The *Huguenot Trollies*, which are the same size, have loose pewter rings round them like the North Bucks trollies.

To return to the North Bucks bobbins. You pick up one of these delicate little works of art and recognise that it is a perfect poem. To describe it adequately is impossible. One rarely finds two alike. The most ingenious is the *Mother-in-Babe*, now often called the *Church Window Bobbin*. The shank is hollowed into compartments, similar to those in the wooden variety, but, thanks to the good humour of the material, with an infinitely better result, and in each compartment is a miniature bobbin. The wooden bobbin could rarely boast of more than four windows but twelve windows are not unusual in the bone variety. Instead of miniature bobbins one sometimes sees beads, shot or balls of bone. Then there are *Wire Beaded Bobbins* twined about with wire on which had been threaded tiny green and red beads, and *Birdcage Bobbins* with compartments containing coloured beads surrounded with fine wire netting. I have also seen a bone bobbin ornamented with gold and set with rubies and turquoises. There are bobbins which challenged the green of the emerald or the blue of old Limoges. There are scarlet bobbins, mole brown bobbins, jade green bobbins, dull blue bobbins, and white bobbins with green, red or blue rings. Those made by Jesse Compton and his son James of Deanshanger were stained with logwood chips and cudbear. Jesse used for inscriptions chrome yellow and green, James principally ver- milion and dark blue. Toll was taken of the rainbow, the goldfinch, the butterfly. Metal and glass have been brought to bear upon them in almost every conceivable way. What a riot of colour! They baffle description.

Bobbins are also found made entirely of brass, silver, iron and pewter. The lower part of an Olney brass bobbin unscrews, releasing a baby bobbin, and the lower part of the baby unscrews, releasing a still smaller " baby." Some buffalo- horn, ivory and wire bobbins made at Mysore, India, have also drifted to England.

But with all the ingenuity and taste bestowed upon these various inventions, there is one other kind of bobbin which in human interest sur- passes them all. That is the bone *Mottoed* or *Inscribed Bobbin.* Of these there are two varieties. In the one the inscription is punched in straight lines, in the other it is punched spirally, the latter being by far the more attractive. Not all inscribed bobbins are beautiful. In many of the straight lined variety the lettering is most carelessly done, for there were ignoramuses and blunderers in the bobbin making, as in every other craft. The best of the spiral bobbins, however, are worthy of the highest praise. As a rule the inscription begins at the bottom, and the letters, always in capitals, are alternately of red or blue dots. Many of these inscriptions are memorials of births, marriages and deaths. Love inscriptions are numerous. Sometimes one meets with texts of Scripture, lines from a song or a moral sentence. Hangings, suicides, transportations, elections, and historical events are also commemorated. Sets of two, three, four and even twelve bobbins are met with.

The bobbins were almost all made locally. Mr. Abbot of Bedford was a well known manufacturer, and his name may often be seen stamped on the shank. His speciality was the wooden *Butterfly Bobbin*, and other kinds inlaid with pewter. The bobbin having been prepared in the lathe was placed in a stone mould, and another mould was placed over it. A mixture of lead and pewter was let in by means of the runners, and when the bobbin was released, a pair of scissors removed the projections. He also made bone bobbins. The shaping was done in a lathe, and the open work was cut with a fine circular saw. Names and mottoes were dotted in with a little drill. The colouring of the bands, dots, etc., was effected by dropping the bobbin into dye (generally red, blue or green) and then submitting it once more to the lathe in order to remove the colour where it was not wanted. Sometimes in bobbins that were not inscribed the

46. The Bobbin Maker.

whole would be left coloured except the rings and the neck which were made to resume their original state. This was the Bedford method.

The Northants method must have been rather different, for the Rev. A. J. Roberts, after referring "to the marvellous longevity of colour in the bobbins," observes : " The colours used were vermilion, ultramarine, and occasionally chrome yellow. They were bought in the powder form and mixed to the consistency required with the best gum arabic. The composition was applied with a crow quill and worked into the little indentations (made by the drill) with a kind of twirling motion. Enough was left in the little drilled spots to fill the hole but not sufficient to allow running. The bobbins were then inserted in a board in which they were left standing in a vertical position until the colours were quite dry and hard." Mr. Roberts also points out that many of the inscriptions on the bobbins are coincident with the cult of the valentine (1860—1880) as the wordings even when unaccompanied by dates sufficiently show.

People have often wondered how baby bobbins were got through the windows. Bone, however, is more flexible when it is fresh, but if the manufacturer found that his bobbin was not sufficiently pliable he used to place it in hot water, after which the baby would squeeze through without demur. Bobbins were also made by George Lumbis of

Reynold, David Haskins of Leighton Buzzard, William Pridmore of Elstow, Nat Woods of Olney, Richard Adams of Stoke Goldington, and Paul Neal of Hanslope. At Cranfield were two bobbin makers, William Brown (Bobbin Brown, as he was called) and Arthur Wright, whose father ("Master Wright") made pillow-horses, winders, &c., and went from cottage to cottage to "new-middle" the pillows. Brown's lettering is unmistakable, being spiral, bold and very neat. There were two famous bobbin makers at Deanshanger, Jesse Compton and his son James—already alluded to—(born 1824, died 1889), and four brothers named Saunders made bobbins at Waddesdon. Sir William Long of Kempston Grange had a number of beautiful bobbins made for his daughters.

Orders for bobbins, usually to commemorate christenings, marriages and deaths, were taken at shops in the Market Place, Aylesbury. At Elstow a man named Riseley went round with a stock in a little cart drawn by a dog. Many were bought at Fairs and "Village Feastes,"[1] especially at Northampton Mop (Saturday following October 11th), Bedford Fair (October 11th), Cherry Fair at Olney (June 29th), North Crawley Feast (October 11th or first Monday after that date), and Cranfield Feast (first Monday in July)—

[1] Old folks give this word two syllables.

the cost being anything "from a penny to fip-pence."[1]

At Renhold, Beds, in days gone by, when persons got married they would take a bone from the ham or other joint provided at the wedding feast, and get the bobbin maker to fashion from it a bobbin with a suitable inscription.

It is only now and then that one comes across a lace pillow sumptuously accoutred, that is, with its original fine bobbins. This is due to two causes. First, to the Northants custom of giving, when an old lace-maker died, a bobbin to each of her friends as a memento; and secondly, to the weakness of the lace-maker when assailed by the blandishments of the antique dealer and the collector. Most bobbins made during the last twenty years are ugly.

The spangles attached to the end of a bobbin consisted when perfect of nine beads, namely, two *Top Beads*, one on each side, which were ornamental; six beads (three on each side[2]) called *Square Cuts*, though they are not cut glass, and a large round *Bottom Bead*, sometimes called the *Paisley*, *Venetian*, *Indian* or *China Bead*, from the towns or countries whence many of them were procured. There were also *Pompadour Beads*[3] (flowered and figured), named

47. The Spangles.

[1] Fivepence.
[2] Usually a red " cut " between two whites on each side.
[3] Used at Buckingham.

after the mistress of Louis XV. The square cuts
were made in England by a "lapidary," the process being quite simple. Having been melted off
one at a time from a stick of glass, they were
twisted on a copper wire in order to form the hole,
and lastly pressed on the sides with a file which
produced at once the square shape and the
peculiar markings on the surface. The colours
were usually red or white, but pale blue, dark
blue, pale green, dark green, and amber coloured
beads are sometimes seen. These old square cuts
are not only far more beautiful than the modern
beads, they are also much more convenient,
because, not being smooth, they hold better in the
spool of the bobbin-winder.

The Bottom Bead was also made on a wire.
Some, which are opaque and look like enamelled
pot ware, are adorned with a coloured scroll ;
others are transparent, and decorated with an
infiltration of colour in a quaint little design.
The best of the English bottom beads had
special names. Thus one, the largest made, was
called *Kitty Fisher's Eyes*, a reference to the
beautiful 18th century actress.[1] Could any name
be more charming ! It is of a gray colour with
circular dents which are filled with white. In the
middle of each little patch of white, is a dot of
red or blue. These colours were added while the

---

[1] She became the second wife of John Norris of Hempsted Manor,
Benenden, Kent, sometime M.P. for Rye. She died in 1767. I have
seen the bead at Olney.

glass was soft. Other beads were of greenstone, jade, firestone, coral, amber or cornelian; others had a number of diamond facets on each of which was stamped a pattern. Many of them were made at Bedford.

Shells and coins were sometimes added to the spangles. I have seen one displaying a spade guinea with the name and portrait of George III., and *Bird-cage Spangles* are sometimes met with, the cage being composed of small beads threaded on wire.

What with its forest of pins, many of them brightly beaded; what with its bobbins of red, emerald green, orange and bistre, all differing in design, beauty and sheen; what with the play and vagaries of light on the spangled and glittering Venetians, cuts and pompadours, a proud pillow furnished with a broad, delicate and beautiful piece of Bucks Point was a sight to electrify. Only one globe known to the lace-makers was more gorgeous—the sun himself when his solid golden disk sank amid streamers of crimson, amber and malachite green, and doubled in the flooded Ouse.

Most workers had a Bobbin Box made of oak or mahogany, measuring some seven 48. The Bobbin Box. inches by four, and two deep. It had wire hinges and fastening hook, and was often the work of one of the men folk on a winter's evening. It had two compartments, a

small one for the small bobbins with long necks—
the *Quills*, as they were called—on which the
whole of the gimp from a skein was first wound ;
and a large one for the *Trollies*, to which part of
the gimp at a time was transferred from the quills.
A bobbin box at North Crawley has the date 1743
carved on the front, and one at Emberton, which
was in use about 1750, the initials "M. R." (Mary
Rogers).

Mrs. W. W. Carlile has a bobbin box measuring
14 inches by 6½ by 6½, with a sliding lid and two
holes at the back, which enabled it to be suspended
from the wall. In it was a book of patterns
inscribed "Sarah Hull, Wooton,[1] Jan., 1820." At
Moulsoe I saw a very large bobbin box with the
carving on the bottom, "M. C. 1700."

Many bobbins, as we said, have names or
inscriptions. Occasionally the same 49. **Inscrip-**
inscription is found on a number of **tion Bobbins.**
bobbins, though the spelling often differs. In the
following lists I have in such cases put what
seemed the most popular version. Often, by
mistake of the bobbin maker, a letter is repeated
or omitted or put in error for some other letter.
However, everything is here set down just as it
occurs, mistake or no mistake. It is not for us to
tamper with the county records.

If the name of the village is on the bobbin it is
put in Roman characters ; if it is not on the

[1] Near Northampton.

bobbin, the name of the village where it was seen or procured is put in italics.

In the case of the wooden bobbin one rarely meets with anything beyond a name or a date. On bone bobbins are hundreds of different inscriptions. A bobbin of this kind was a book in little, and the best inscriptions—those consisting of apophthegms and texts of Scripture — were intended to cheer, revive and warm the soul.

The simplest form of lettering consists of *Biblical names*, as Adam and Eve, Lot, King David, Esther, Daniel, Joel; and *English names* as Henry, Alfred, Emma. Often the names are misspelt—Feby (Phebe), Amealy (Amelia), Caravina (Caroline), Saran (Sarah Ann), Saly (Sally) Murcy (Mercy), the last named being a favourite at Cranfield, Beds. " Comfort," which has a Puritan sound, is also met with. Sometimes an adjective accompanies the name, as " Lovely Thomas," " Sweet William," " Dear Jacob," and sometimes we have both Christian and Surname:

> Mary Bless. *Cranfield, Beds.*
> Henery Cox. *Cranfield, Beds.*
> Nanny Lydown. *Newport Pagnell, Bucks.*
> Sarah Best. *Waddesdon, Bucks.*
> Susanna Spencer. *Edgecott, Bucks.*
> Tome Dood. *Wilstead, Beds.*

Nicknames occasionally appear :

> Quirk Nickles. *Olney, Bucks.*

The people mentioned in these lists have long been dead.

DATED BOBBINS.

Many bobbins have dates on them :

Lydia dear, 1798. *Gayhurst, Bucks.*
M. M., 1816. *Olney, Bucks.*
1819.
Ann Woolaston,[1] 1821. *Emberton, Bucks.*
Mary, 1822. *Stony Stratford, Bucks.*
Elizar Jufcut, 1833. *Stoke Goldington, Bucks.*
Timbrose[2] **Fells,** 1858. *Hanslope.*
Keblib[3] **Ranbow,** February 5, 1883.

PLACE BOBBINS.

Many bobbins have in addition to the name of a person, the name of a town or village :

BUCKS.
John Darby, North Crawley.
William Bennett, Waddesdon, Bucks.
Julie Wickens, Hanslope, Bucks.
Thomas West, Emberton.

BEDS.
Job Warrien, Millbank.
A present from Thomas Neal, Todonton.

NORTHANTS.
William Maples, Northampton.
Eli and Joseph Barrett, Norton.[4]
Thomas Robins, Hartwell.
Sarah Berrell, Bozet, haged 8.
Enoch Gardner, Bugbrook.

[1] She lived at Castle Ashby. [2] Apparently a mistake of the bobbin maker's for Ambrose. [3] Caleb, evidently. [4] Near Daventry. Many of the families mentioned on these pages are extinct.

Paul Gardner, Bugbrook.
Sarah Spencer, Whittlebury, died Sept. 11, 18—.
Thomas Garren, Whittlebury.
Ellen Kent, Silverstone, age 20.
Henery Eight, Roughton.[1]

HERTS.

Joseph Mason, Radwell.

NAME, PLACE AND DATE BOBBINS.

The following are examples of bobbins that give all three particulars, name, place and date.

BUCKS.

Thomas Lear, Maids Morton, 1843.[2]
John Osuald, Maids Morton, 1843.[3]
Jane Tarry, Olney, Bucks, 1844.
Allen Mills, Haversham Mill, 1844.
My cusan Samuel, Wickham,[4] 1840.
Mary Lane, Broughton ◇ 1860 ◁
Jemima King, Quainton, 1829.
Martha Bucknell, Hadwick [Hardwick], 1838.

BEDS.

William Knot, age 20, Toddington, 1854.
Isabel Jackman, Oakley, 1833.

NORTHANTS.

Elizabeth Lovesay, Syresham, 1850.
William Berrill, Bozeat, 1862.
Samuel Shirley, Pauler's Pury, 1846.

---

[1] Probably a mistake for Boughton, the great fair of which village begins on June 24.

[2][3] Miss K. Dickinson, St. Albans, has two bobbins thus inscribed, and she also has one "Martha Burnell, Hadwick, 1838," evidently the same as Martha Bucknell. This shows that it was the custom to have a number of bobbins inscribed with the same name, no doubt for presentation.

[4] High Wycombe.

Elizabeth Earl, Weson[1] by Wedon, 1841.
Sarah Prestige, Moreton[2] Pinkney, 1840.
John Varneu,[3] Silverstone, 1846.
Faby[4] Tarry, Yardley Hasting [s], 1859.

OXON.

Rebecca Harris, Bodicote, 1840. [2 miles S. of Banbury.]
Mary Ann Lines, Bicester, 1843.
Harriot Bunce, Stratton, 1840.   [Stratton Audley.]
Hannah Hearlwell, Horton,[5] 1832. [6 miles N.E. of Oxford.]
Joseph Bayliss, Souldern, 1842.
John Kirrby, Fritwell, 1832.

OCCUPATION BOBBINS.

Occasionally one comes across a bobbin that records a person's occupation.   Thus at Bozeat I found one with the inscription :

Thomas Barker, Brafield Green, Sweep ;

and I learnt that this was made for a chimney sweep, who odd to say was also a lace-maker, and lived at Brayfield on the Green, near Northampton.   Now and again one comes across inscriptions like the following :

Edward Markham made me this 1842.   *Oxford.*

MEMORIAL BOBBINS.

Many bobbins were made to commemorate births, marriages and deaths :

[1] Weston, near Weedon Lois.
[2] Often spelt Morton.
[3] Evidently an error for Varney.
[4] Phoebe.
[5] Horton-with-Studley.

Bucks.

Thomas Turnham, born 1760, died April 22, 1836, aged 76 yrs. *Waddesdon.*

William Simons,[1] born December 15, 1852. *Hanslope.*

Tryfena Mary Ann Elizabeth Claydon, 1864. *North Crawley.*

Beds.

Samuel Cox,[2] my dear Father, di. Nov. 18, 1863, age 53. *Stevington.*

Mary Cotton, Dear Grandmother, died Dec. 21, 1865.[3]

James Bellington,[4] my father, a. 52, died Nov. 25, 1855. *Cranfield.*

Grandmother Ingram. *Haynes.*

Joseph Lathall, died Feb. 7, 1875. *North Crawley.*

Mary Lancaster, my dear granemother, 1871. *Cranfield.*

Joseph Morris,[5] my dear father. *Elstow.*

Oxon.

Samuel Judkins, died 1866. *Fritwell.*

Sarah Aldridge, died July 9, 1838.

Hunts.

Ann Maria Lovell, died Sept. 27, 1858, age 75. *Eynesbury.*

GRAVE-RAIL BOBBINS.

Now and again one comes across a bobbin that reads more like a grave-rail or a tombstone:

Charles Brouncil, died May 12, 1843, aged 22 years, at Ash-wood in Kent. Lost from sight but still in mind.

This bobbin is at Hanslope where the Brownsell family resided.

---

[1] He was of Huguenot descent.

[2][3] These belong to Miss Sophia Cowley. Samuel Cox was her great-grandfather, Mary Cotton her great-great-grandmother.

[4] Father of Mrs. Caroline Cox, Cranfield.

[5] Father of Miss Morris and Mrs. Carroll of Elstow.

Occasionally we come across a bobbin commemorating a 21st birthday, as:

John Blakes, aged 21, Janry 19, 1837.

GIFT BOBBINS.

Of bobbins of this kind I have met with:

A Christmas Box.
A present for one I love.
A gift from Oliver Benson, 1871.
A present from Mary Eliza Betel, Ipscombe.[1]

ALPHABET BOBBINS.

These have all the letters of the Alphabet. The lettering is spiral and the characters are alternately blue and red.

FIRST DAWN OF LOVE.

Bobbins with inscriptions relative to the subject of love are, however, the most numerous of all; and, as we shall see, the authors sometimes break out into verse! It was, however, a very clownish Catullus that sang. The following are indicative of only the First Dawn of Affection:

john Rodd is a friend of mine. *Olney*.
Thomas Shakeshaft[2] a friend of mine.
Love give me thy ♡.
A trifle showe respect.

---

[1] There is no village in England with this name. The bobbin maker must have spelt the word incorrectly.
[2] Shakeshaft is a Weston Underwood name.

Love for Ginette. [Jeannette.]
Those who love me I will love. *Turweston, Northants.*
Give me a kiss for a token. *Thornborough, Bucks.*
I will keep this for my love's sake. *Oxford.*

ASPIRATION BOBBINS.

Occasionally the wording is that of an aspiration rather than of a well-founded hope.

May I have those in my arms that I love in my heart.
  Deanshanger, Northants.
A loving husband I long to find. *North Crawley, Bucks.*
I wish to wed the lad I love, 1842. *Olney.*
I wish to wed and love. *Oxford.*
I long to wed the lad I love. *Cranfield, Beds.*
I long to be a loving man's wife.
If you love me squeeze my hand and tell me. *Deanshanger.*
To love and live happy that is my desire. *Kempston, Beds.*
May I be happy and my love no it. *Oxford.*

"Love," says Dorothy Osborne[1] (afterwards Lady Temple), "is a terrible word, and I should blush to death if anything but a letter accused me on't."[2] The lace-makers of her county, however, were less bashful, as the following inscriptions on what I call Invitation Bobbins incontestably prove.

INVITATION BOBBINS.

Elizabethe wed me my love. *Winslow.*
Love come again.
Love cross my lips.

---

[1] Of Chicksands, Beds.
[2] *Letters*, p. 151.

Plate 26

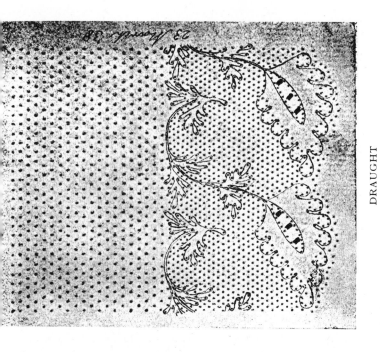
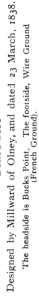

DRAUGHT

Designed by Millward of Olney, and dated 23 March, 1838.

The headside is Bucks Point. The footside, Wire Ground
(French Ground).

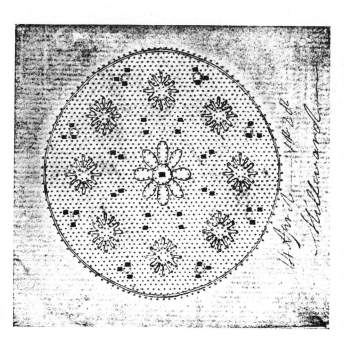

DRAUGHT OF ROUND (CROWN) FOR BABY'S CAP.

Date on Draught, 14 April, 1828.

Below is the autograph of the Designer, Millward of Olney.

See p. 217.

Plate 27

BUCKS POINT.   See p. 221.

Draught of the Lace that won the Gold Medal at
the Exhibition of 1851.

Designed by Mr. John Millward of Olney.

It was made in three widths. Mr. George Smith of Olney has the
widest, which is dated 12 Dec., 1850, and the narrowest, dated
22 Jan., 1851.

(Lent by Mr. George Smith, Olney.)

Love me, my dear.
Sit down, my love. *Kempston, Beds.*
Kiss me.
Kiss me, my love and be true. *Newport Pagnell, Bucks.*
Come and wed wed[1] with me my love.
Come love and live happy with me. *Milton Keynes, Bucks.*
Sweet love be mine and make me thine.
Love the giver.
Buy me a ring. *North Crawley, Bucks.*
Love me truley. *Cranfield.*
Marry me my own true love.
Marry me and love me dear. *Oxford.*

" Come home to me if you love me," was probably said some February evening·when Venus hung like a silver lamp in the twilight. Who at such a moment could resist !

CONSTANCY BOBBINS.

Many of the bobbins indicate that the lovers of Lace-land were for the most part constant to one another. Wherever their affection was set, it was fixed like eternity. Thus we have :

Be constant and true to me, my dear, and I will be your
    loving wife.
I love the still.
Absent maks the hart grow fonder. *Olney.*
A true lover's hart will never change. *Wolverton.*
Constant prove to me, my love. *Waddesdon, Bucks.*
I love my choice too well to change.
Prov my love constant.

[1] The words repeated by mistake of the bobbin maker. Many other mistakes of this careless personage will be noticed.

If you prove true I will love you. *Olney.*

To my dear I will prove true. *Oxford.*

I'll forever love the giver. *Weston Underwood, Bucks.*

I will wed with him who loves me dearly.

A true love is sweeter than honey.

> Except a trifel from a friend
> Whose love from you wil nevr end.

Love me for ever, my dear.

Love me constant. *Stevington, Beds.*

Love me and forsake all other.[1] *Fritwell, Oxon.*

Love me now and forsake me never. *Sherington.*

My boys if I am raged[2] my heart is true.

I'll vow to be true.

My dear love me or leave me alone. *Oxford.*

I love thee as the glad bird loves the freedom of its
    wings. *Deanshanger, Northants.*

My 💟 above the world, love. *Ravenstone, Bucks.*

Ofttimes my love I think on thee.

Let love abide till death divide.

Lads cannot love two lasses at once.

Lads never court to lasees at once.

> My mind is fixt I cannot rainge
> I love my choice too well to change.

> My mind is fixt, my heart doth beat,
> I love my love, He kisses sweet. *Eynesbury, Hunts.*

My fortune is with my love and me. *Weston Underwood.*

U love me as I love U.

Nothing but death shall part us too.

> We will love each other while we have breath
> Nothing shall part us save only death.
>   *Great Linford, Bucks.*

---

[1] Also with word "others," same village.
[2] Ragged.

The following is on a Gimp Bobbin, which is an
inch and a half in circumference:

> I will be constant true and just
> Unto the one that I love best.
> I. W.; W. T. 1838. *Ravenstone, Bucks.*

The initials stand for Isabel Warren and
William Tebbey—Mrs. Course's mother and
father.

A RIFT IN THE LUTE.

Alas! sometimes there was a rift in the lute.
Now and again the heart of the village lad did not
respond to eyes that sparkled when he approached;
now and again a giddy village maiden was given
to flirtation; sometimes eager ears listened for
footsteps at an appointed time and listened in
vain; often bitter tears were shed; and so we
have:

> Be kinb and true harted.
> It is hard to be slited by one as I love.[1]   *Emberton, Bucks.*
> Love don't be cruel.   *Stevington, Beds.*
> Don't vex me.
> Love is sharr to feel the smart.
> Lovs a sharp thorn.   *Emberton, Bucks.*
> Keep your temper, my dear.   *Milton Keynes, Bucks.*
> Forsake me not my lovely dear.   *Oxford.*
> Tis hard to love and not be loved again.

Often it is to be feared the cry went out from

---

[1] This inscription, with variations in the way of spelling, is met with in
almost every village.

some gentle maiden who did not deserve to suffer, " Oh my love, my love, you are breaking my heart." Even when proof was wanting that anything had gone wrong, the maiden as she shuffled her bobbins sometimes had misgivings, and black thoughts came and sat in a circle round her, otherwise she would not have expressed herself as follows :

> Love me or leave me alone. *North Crawley* and *Olney.*
> Love me or leave me.
> Forsake me not but love me as I love you.
> *Weston Underwood.*
> Forget me not, 1874. *Cranfield, Beds.*
> Keep your promise.
> Love dont be false. *Eynesbury, Hunts.*
> Let not malice reach my true love's ♡. *Emberton, Bucks.*
> Love me and no one else.

If George or Joseph suffered in any way, the sympathetic Mary Ann or Susan would have a bobbin inscribed :

> My hart hakes for you. *North Crawley, Bucks.*

Mr. J. S. Elliott has a bobbin which came from Bedfordshire, with the curious inscription :

> Da her. I love her but I'll never go nigh her no.

A girl may be almost everything that is engaging, but one unpleasant characteristic may mar the picture. We can sympathise with the love-lorn youth who had this inscription stamped on the bobbin, though we may regret that he in this way stereotyped his feelings, for I do not think we should be wronging him by the assumption that " Da " is an abbreviation for an expletive which, it is to be hoped, he was not in the habit of using.

ANNABEL LEE BOBBINS.

Sometimes, as in the case of Annabel Lee of Poe's beautiful poem, a kinsman interfered between the lovers. Hence we have :

> No father or mother shall part me and my love.

DECLARATION BOBBINS.

Often on the bobbin the maiden boldly inscribed the direction in which her passion lay :

> Tis you my dear I wish to wed.
> Richard Brooks is the lad 1 love. *Cranfield, Beds.*
> My dear George it is you that I love.
> I love U.
> I love you, my dear, that is true. *Fritwell, Oxon.*

And George or Richard would offer to Mary Ann or Jane a bobbin worded :

> The gift is small but love is all. *North Crawley.*
> *Fenny Stratford, Bucks.*

QUESTION BOBBINS.

> Who is your lover my darling ?
> Mother when shall I marry ?
> Do you ever think of me love ? *Oxford.*

BLIGHTED LOVE BOBBINS.

Sometimes a lover was false beyond hope, and instances of this kind had for outcome :

My love's been false to me and she has been my ruin.
I wonce loved them that ner loved me.   *Stoke Goldington, Bucks.*
Let no false lover gaine my hart.
My love as broken my poor heart.
Place no confidence in young men.
Young men are deceitfl.

When Lesbia was false Catullus suggested that a woman's promise might very well be engraved on wind or water, but in Bedfordshire faithlessness revealed itself chiefly in the sterner sex. Kempston in particular was prolific in cross-wounded[1] hearts.

My love is lost for ever.   *Kempston, Beds.*
Sweet is the love that meets return but
bitter when it meats a frown.   *Kempston.*

The following, to use a Bucks expression, is " sour as vargis."[2]

X U R and X U B and
XX U R to me.   *Kempston, Beds.*

On one bobbin that I have seen the initials of the culprit are given—and it is a lady!

Richard Cobb slited by one A. S.

Fortunately for the memory of " A. S." the name of the village is unknown.

Sometimes it is difficult to decide whether the allusion is to falseness on the part of a lover or to a temporary separation, as for example :

Tis hard to part from my sweetheart.   *Turweston.*

---

[1] One wound on the top of another crossways as it were.
[2] Verjuice.

SATISFIED LOVE.

Many of the bobbins, however, indicate that in the quiet tree-surrounded villages of Beds and Bucks the course of love ran as smoothly as the rivers in their level valleys. In the following, for example, there is an unruffled satisfaction :

> I love my love, he his true to me.
> I love my love, because my love loves me.
> Siting on a stile, Mary, happy as the day.[1] *Hanslope, Bucks.*
> The sight of my love fills my ♡ with joy. *Turweston.*
> Dont I love my Nance. *Kempston, Beds.*
> Hearts united must live contented.

The satisfaction and astonishment of Suky, a little, timid, mouse-like thing, glancing furtively at you from under her eyes—a girl who had never expected to have a lover—is embodied in the two words,

> Fancy me! *Fritwell, Oxon.*

WEDDED BLISS BOBBINS.

On hundreds of bobbins George promised to be true to Susan, and Susan to love George for ever. But was he? and did she? I regret to say that bobbins commemorative of wedded bliss are very scarce. It has been said that if courting could be continued after the wedding, the marriage state would be elysian. Of bobbins on which appear

---

[1] " I'm sittin' on the stile, Mary," is the first line of Lady Dufferin's song, "Lament of the Irish Emigrant," written in 1850.

both the husband's name and the wife's I have heard of the following :

> John Jones. Elizabeth Jones. 1836.
> Levi Meakens and Sarah Meakens.
> Newman Brier. Sophia Brier.

Who these good people were I do not know, but Meakins is an Olney name.

The next inscription leads us to picture the bobbin maker standing at the door of Nancy's thatched cottage and asking what she will have put on the new bobbin. Nancy, after being long lost in thought, biting all the while the hem of her pinafore, at last suggests, " Love is . . ," and hesitates. At last, with a flash of inspiration, she bursts out with, " Love." No better definition is possible, and a week later the bobbin maker duly delivers the pretty treasure, and on it in bright red and blue dots twining round the shining white is the inscription,

> Love is Love.

Perhaps it was the one brilliant remark she made in her life; but the most torpid are, in God-given moments, capable of great sayings.

LOVE IN A HURRY.

Sometimes Mary Ann was in a desperate hurry, with the result of

> **Marry me quick.** *Eynesbury, Hunts.*

Marry ma quick. *Moulsoe, Bucks.*
Marry me quick and love me for ever. *Newport Pagnell.*

Sometimes it was William who was in a hurry, as in :

Marry me quick and love me for ever.
To love and live happy is my desier, William Tebbey.[1]

Ravenstone.

" I wants a husband " *(Olney)* is very plain speaking, and seems to tell of one who was weary of waiting for " love's chemick gold."

THE SAILOR.

Pretty girls received more bobbins than their share. " An old woman," says Miss Isemonger, " who died not long ago and had been a beauty in her youth, had a wonderful collection of such offerings, from a wooden one, rudely carved with two names and a heart between them, to one most ingeniously wrought after the fashion of Japanese ivory work, in a series of three, one inside another," but she most prized a bobbin which was inscribed :

When this you see, remember me, and bear me in your
    mind
For all the world is naught to me as long as you are kind.

This is tattooed in red and blue. A tiny silver anchor and a bit of coral threaded among the beads of the spangle, suggest that the bobbin was

[1] Mrs. Course's father.

the gift of a sailor lad to his Buckinghamshire sweetheart. Was he faithful? Did they marry? Were they happy? The bobbin is silent.

Another bobbin, presumably made to commemorate the return of a sailor who had been given up for lost, is stamped:

Jack alive. *Lavendon, Bucks,*

the bottom bead being a foreign nut; and other bobbins whose spangles are adorned with Indian berries also bring us a whiff of the sea, and present us with pictures of this same Jack with his head in his hammock and his heart in some cosy Buckinghamshire or Bedfordshire cottage; and of Jane busy over her pillow, while an occasional sigh escapes her when she reflects on "what a sailor suffers." So it is not surprising that one of her bobbins is inscribed:

My love is at a distance but ever in my mind,

and another,

I long to see my love once more.

THE SOLDIER.

The request on another bobbin, " Dont list love " *(Lavendon)*, is not without pathos. John Clare, the Northants poet, has told[1] how, when the recruiting sergeant entered a village, strutting in lace and ribbons down the street before his men,

[1] *Village Minstrel,* LXVI. Published in 1821.

" the tuteling fife " and the " hoarse rap-tapping drum " accompanying them, the lads went almost mad with excitement and the girls were tempted to slight their old sweethearts. But one sturdy Lavendon lad hesitated, and one little Lavendon maiden, unmoved by the blandishments of the " dinkin "[1] soldiermen, or the rat-tat-tat of the drum, whispered, with a break in her voice and a tear in her eye, " Don't list, love ! "[2] Of course he yielded to the entreaty, and of course a kiss from a red little mouth, and two loving arms thrown round his neck were his delightful recompense. And what does this mean, " If you love me, come away " ? Here again we seem to see Lavinia balancing her charms against the recruiting sergeant's cockade. Or is she trying to lead Caleb out of bad company ?

PATHOS.

There is pathos, however, in not a few of the inscriptions. The following seems to have been uttered by way of reproof to some " cockered " child who had been behaving badly :

I had a mother once like you. *Kempston, Beds.*

After that, it is refreshing to read,

I love my mother ;

while

Dont cry for me

was probably a death-bed utterance.

[1] From dink, to dress out.
[2] Also occurs as " Love don't you list." *Stoke Goldington.*

NAUGHTY INSCRIPTIONS.

Then there are inscriptions which can only be described as naughty, as for example:

> Kis me quck my mome is comin. *Weston Underwood.*
> Kiss me quick my mother is coming. *Stoke Goldington.*

One would like to know more about the girl who unblushingly made this request, but perhaps she did blush when the bobbin maker, having executed her order, put the pretty bauble with its bright dots and gay spangles into her hands. What was her name? Was the spelling her own or the bobbin maker's? One would rather get a reply than learn the identity of the Man with the Iron Mask.

But if the preceding inscription is naughty, the following is worse still:

> Dont tell my mother. *North Crawley; Newport Pagnell; Cranfield, Beds.*

"I love the boys" *(Hanslope, Bucks)* is decidedly brazen, while "I do so love the lads" is even worse; and one can only shake the head sadly at the frontless girl who wrote:

> If I love the boys that is nothing to nobody.

We can excuse, however, the Ravenstone maiden who gave the order for

> If I love a lad in Eavenstone[1] that's nothing to nobody,

---

[1] The E for R, the first letter of the word, is a mistake no doubt of the bobbin maker.

for it is clear that her affections were set on only one lad ; and as all Ravenstone lads are good her choice must have been a happy one.

REFUSAL BOBBINS.

Sometimes Mary Ann would not have George at any price, and her refusal takes the following form :

> Too wise you are too wise you be
> I see you are too wise for me. *Kempston.*

An Oxfordshire maiden repels an admirer with the chilling information,

> No lodge here.

THE BOISTEROUS LOVER.

Sometimes in his excess of fondness the gentleman disarranged the lady's toilette, leading her to admonish him as follows :

> Kis me, court me hug me tite, dont crump my colr tonight. *Kempston, Beds.*

As she had made that collar of beautiful Bucks Point on the pillow with her own fingers, Joseph ought to have been more careful. It may have been this same Joseph who said,

> Well, my beauty, how I love the ;

but " Huddle me, cuddle me " (*North Crawley*), seems to have come from a lady.

Sometimes when in the presence of his sweetheart George in his excitement was more apt to bellow than to coo, whereupon Mary Ann, who was not at all deaf, and who, moreover, did not want all Cranfield to hear what was going on, made the observation :

Marry me quick and lowley speak.   *Cranfield, Beds.*

But in other villages also the undertone was preferred, as for example :

Whisper soft to me my lovely dear. *Stoke Goldington, Bucks.*

Fervent indeed must have been the emotions which inspired :

Squze me if I do Jene Johnson ;

or,

My lovely, my beauty, my sweetest honey,
No toung can expres how I do love thee.

My love is like a blooming rose.   *Moulsoe.*

" Spelling," says Stendhal, " is not genius." Neither is it devotion.

Sometimes this bovine method of courting not only crumpled Sare-Ann's collar, but set at defiance the most elementary rules of grammar; but when George's arm is round Sare-Ann's waist how can he be thinking of the regulations laid down by the excellent Lindley Murray and other equally approved precisians, especially as he never heard of them; and he exclaims, while the lady's cheeks are suffused with blushes :

My love you am the pride of my ♡ ;

and in order to accentuate the declaration he
has the same inscribed on a bobbin.

THE BASHFUL LOVER.

But if the attentions of some of the young
gentlemen were as eager and ungainly as those of
the hippopotamus or the mastodon, now and then
a lover was either obtuse or bashful—so difficult
is it, in a crooked world, to encounter the happy
mean. In the latter case the young lady had to
encourage him with such pointed admonitions as:

> Love dont be shy. *Oakley, Beds.*
> Kiss me quick, don't be shy.
> William kiss me quick and dont be shy
> For you love kissing, dear, as well as I.[1]

All of a sudden the timorous William becomes
bold as a lion. A sounding salute follows the
unequivocal invitation, and Eliza, hardly prepared
for so vigorous a response, has gently to reprove
him for sending her hat all North Crawley.[2]
Doubtless, however, Eliza was wise to offer the
invitation, and William sensible to accept it, for
does not the poet sing :

> " Gather ye rosebuds while ye may ! "

Kissing, whether performed " quick " or more

[1] Mrs. Ward, Manchester, has this bobbin.
[2] A saying in North Bucks. It refers to North Crawley brook, which
rises near Wharley Farm, Cranfield, runs north to Hardmead, west to
Chicheley, and south-west to Newport Pagnell, where it joins the still
crookeder Ouse. Another saying is, " Your parting is like Crawley
Brook "—that is, the parting of your hair.

deliberately, is now out of all question, for Eliza is under the turf and William, with bent back, "rheumatiz," and other troubles, hobbles, and only just hobbles, through the village street.

The following were also addressed to lovers who had shown themselves provokingly shy:

> Buy the ring. *North Crawley, Bucks.*
> Love buy the ring. *Olney; Stevington, Beds.*
> Love bye the ring. *Milton Keynes.*
> Kiss me quick and dont be shy. Love me till the day I die. *North Crawley.*

Sometimes "Dear William," too shy even to place his gift of a bobbin in the hands of "Sweet Kitty," would steal into her mother's cottage in the twilight, seizing an opportunity when nobody was at home, and attach surreptitiously on her pillow his pretty love token, inscribed:

> Take this small gift I freely give
> May God protect you while you live.[1]

Kitty, however, would be no shrewd Buckinghamshire girl if she did not guess who put it there. Her slon-black[2] eyes would sparkle with delight when she read the dotted epistle, and the chances are that she would order another bobbin to be made of the same pattern, with the wording:

> I will keep this for my love's sake;

or she would send one to William lettered, " A

---

[1] Miss Saunders of Worcester has one with " And the Lord " instead of " May God." It came from Olney.
[2] " Slon," Bucks for " sloe."

Plate 28

MALTESE HANDKERCHIEF BORDER.

Made by Mrs. W. Crowsley.

On the headside is the *Turnpin* or *Purl Edge* (consisting of tiny loops, called *Purls* or *Turnpins*). A series of *Legs* joins this edge to a strip of *Clothwork* (called the *Trail*). Next, in the corner scallop occurs the *Wheat-ear ornament*, each ear (Bedfordshire fashion) having square ends. Then comes a filling of Honeycomb, each filling being separated from the next by a patch of *Half-stitch*. In the middle of the Honeycomb Work in the scallop is a patch of Clothwork. A feature of the work is the *Raised Plait*.

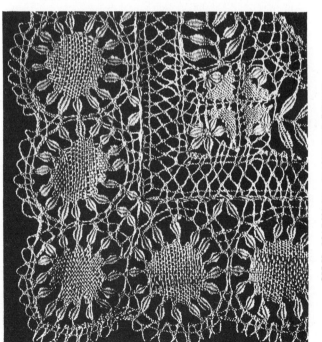

SILK MALTESE HANDKERCHIEF.

Made at Malta, 1917.

Maltese made at Malta differs from that made in Bucks and Beds in that it has (1) Maltese Cross; (2) "Wheat ears" with pointed ends; (3) No purl edge. It will also be noticed that it revels in plaits.

(*Lent by Miss W. Field, Olney.*)

Plate 29

BUCKS-MALTESE FAN. MADE AT OLNEY.

BUCKS-MALTESE FAN. MADE AT OLNEY.

small present for W. Robbins."[1] *Olney*. Another inscription of a similar nature is, " Keep this for my sake, my darling."

THE MEN PROPOSE.

We should, however, be wronging the girls of the Newport and Wymersley Hundreds[2] were we to assume that most of the courting was done by them. The following inscriptions indicate the voice of the stronger sex :

Let me fix the wedding day my dear.
When will youu fix the wedding day ?
Come love and be happy with me my dear. *Olney and Whitchurch, Bucks.*
Sweet love be mine. *Weston Underwood, Bucks.*
Meet me by moonlight alone;

and meet they would in front of the Shiel Hall,[3] at Walker's birge,[4] or by the spinney.

This ring is round. So is a shilling
I am ready when you are willing.
Love when will you marry me. *North Crawley.*
Love will you marry ?

Lavinia listens with reddened cheeks and lowered eyes; but there is only one word to suit the occasion, a very small one—and, of course, she says it.

[1] Robbins is an old Olney name. It occurs 33 times in the Parish Register, the last entry being in 1762.
[2] Formerly the counties were divided into Hundreds only. Newport Hundred is part of N. Bucks, Wymersley of E. Northants.
[3] A quaint Early Georgian building, formerly on Olney Market-place.
[4] A birge is a bridge over a brook. " Walker's" is on the Lavendon Road.

CRYPTIC INSCRIPTIONS.

Puzzle Bobbins.

It is convenient to a lover who has a window in his breast to be able to draw the curtains sometimes, hence there were puzzle bobbins on which the letters of each word were purposely arranged in wrong order, either from caprice or with the object of preventing a stranger from arriving at the meaning. Some may be in cypher and therefore unreadable without a key, but when the name of the village is known research sometimes furnishes the meaning. Of these I have met with twelve. Mr. J. S. Elliott of Bewdley has the following:

(1) YM RDAE I LEOV OUY SAS SRIBD OLVE SHEREIE[1];

which is to be read:

My dear I love you as birds love cherries.

Miss Agnes E. Ellis of Leicester has a bobbin inscribed:

(2) YM ·:· DREA ·:· FI ·:· UYO ·:· EVOL ·:· EM ·:· EMKA ·:· EM ·:· ROYU ·:· ERIBD ·:·

My dear, if you love me, make me your bride.

Mrs. Taylor of Huntspill Court, Bridgewater, has a bobbin which reads:

(3) W B I E L T L I O A Y M D W U O N O K L L O E N Y. 1844.

the letters being alternately red and black. This

---

[1] It will be noticed that in "sas" the bobbin maker has (probably by mistake) put a letter too much, and that in "shereie" he has left out a letter and put an "e" for a "c."

too, puzzling as it may seem at first view, really
presents very little difficulty. It is evident that
the bobbin maker intended the red letters to read
"William Dunkley," and the black to read "Betsy,
Wooton;" but in endeavouring to mystify others
he fell into error himself; for in one place he lost
the sequence of the letters—making part of
"William" go from red to black. He also put
an o instead of an s in Betsy. However it is
clear that the inscription is "William" (and)
"Betsy Dunkley, Wooton." The bobbin came
from Paulerspury (Northants), from which the
village of Wooton is six miles distant. Dunkley
was a common name at Wooton and the adjoining village of Collingtree. There was in 1894 a
William Dunkley at Paulerspury.

Mrs. Taylor has another which runs:

(4) MAHER SHALAL HASH BAZ WYHES,

which came from Olney.

By turning to Isaiah viii. 1—4 we seem to get a
clue. Possibly the inscription should be read,
"My father and my mother"—the letters in
WYHES being the initials of their names. Such
inscriptions as "John and Ann Lovel my father
and my mother" are common. But the H in the
middle of the word WYHES may be a mistake
of the bobbin maker's for K. The name WYKES
occurs 44 times in the Olney parish registers. If
so the inscription may commemorate some sudden
stroke of fortune, and may mean, "Haste to the

spoil, Wykes!" It may be remarked that most of the Olney lace-makers were deeply read in the Scriptures, and fully acquainted with the meaning of Scripture terms. The latter interpretation is more likely to be the correct one than the former.

A worker at Hanslope, Bucks, has a bobbin inscribed :

(5) IL ON AT DS EE MY LOVER.

As another bobbin on the same pillow is inscribed " Henry Deaton," I am inclined to think that Deaton is the hidden surname. If so, the inscription would read :

LE DEATON IS MY LOVER,

the L being a mistake of the bobbin maker's for H.

Mrs. Lambert of North Crawley has the following :

(6) M . DILY . M . BI . P . YO . F.A.T.R. LOVE ME.
OR . NOT . OR . LET . ME . ALONE. 1839.

The bobbin once belonged to Ann Wickens of Hanslope, and Dily was a Hanslope name.

The six preceding mysteries we have either entirely or partially unravelled, but the next six defy all attempts at interpretation.

One of them (on a Paulerspury bobbin which belongs to Mrs. Taylor of Bridgewater) runs :

(7) TOB : TL : JS : EH : YB : KI : SLG : WL : DEARS : YEAR.

Another was sent me by Miss Turnham, of

Plate 30

MALTESE COLLAR.   MADE AT OLNEY.

Plate 31

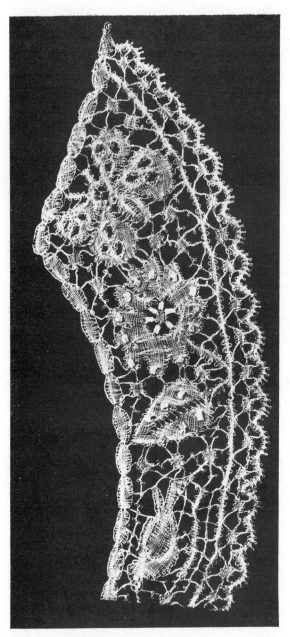

BIRD AND BUTTERFLY LACE. MADE NEAR OLNEY. See p. 225.

Waddesdon, Bucks. It is on a Waddesdon bobbin that belongs to a friend, and runs :

(8) MANUEL HINGFOR ABOBZIN IL SIN.

It is as terrifying as anything heard in a nightmare, and I doubt whether Daniel himself could
have furnished us with the interpretation. Certainly he who reads it deserves to be clothed in
scarlet.

The following is from Turvey, Beds :

(9) WT. MS. IV. AH. MR.

From Whittlebury, Northants, come three puzzle
bobbins. The inscriptions are :

(10) ·:· N : S : E : H : C : N : Q : A : R : F : F : P ·:·
T : N : O : L ; OL ·:· S ·:· E : I : H : I ·:· N ·:· P ·:· ♡ ·:· :···
(11) H . F . T . Y . L . M . A . I . L . Y . N . D . P . J . U . T . A.
F . Y . D . N . H . T . R . H . E . S . T . H . R . F . H .
(12) N . E : K : D : W : A : D : F : N : R : C : S : E : N : R : I : F :
R : O : A : R : R : D : L : O : L : W : W : P : O .

A worker at Stony Stratford, through whose
hands these bobbins passed, had a fourth puzzle
bobbin, from Whittlebury, but it is lost. For
none of these is there any clue. They are
probably miniature soul-histories, but the persons
concerned in them are dead, and the keys lost.[1]

HISTORICAL BOBBINS.

Some bobbins are memorials of famous events,
as :

---

[1] If any reader of this book can furnish other cryptic inscriptions on
bobbins, he would oblige by communicating with the author.

Jubilee of George III. 1810.
Waterloo. 1815.
Queen Victoria Crowned. 1838.
Alma. 1854.
War in Egypt, Tel el Kebir. 1882.

Others of famous persons:

John Bunyan. *Elstow; Oakley.*
Nelson. (Died in 1805.)
Queen Caroline. (Died in 1821.)
Queen Victoria.
John Wesley.

MURDER, SUICIDE AND TRANSPORTATION BOBBINS.

An old dame who kept a lace school at Lavendon, Bucks—Mary Freeman, or Polly Granny, as she was usually called—was in her way a sort of author. She composed mottoes for bobbins. But if Lace-land had its authors, it had also in the bobbin makers its journalists, whose one great aim naturally was to be topical, comprehending as they did that a bobbin referring to any event that was engaging public attention, was certain of a large circulation. Hence there were Murder, Suicide and Transportation Bobbins.

Of bobbins to commemorate hangings, suicides and transportations, I have met with or heard of seven, which are inscribed as follows:

HANGINGS.

(On Biddenham Gallows, Bromham Road, just outside Bedford.)
Matthias and William Lilley. 1829. *Elstow, Beds.*

(At Bedford Jail.)

Sarah Dazeley, hung 1843. *Lavendon, Bucks.*

Joseph Castle, hung 1860. *Ravenstone, Bucks; North Crawley, Bucks.*

William Worsley, hung 1868. *Weston Underwood; Oakley.*

William Bull, hung 1871. *Ampthill, Beds.*

SUICIDE.

Joseph West. *Cranfield.*

TRANSPORTATION.

Rannson Dillingum, Botany Bay. *Ampthill.*

It is not surprising that young people should have been so deeply interested in these events. A girl—a mere baby—would be told that if she worked well at her pillow she should go to see the hanging.

The trial and execution of Sarah Dazeley, who murdered her husband at Wrestlingworth, Beds, by administering arsenic, created at the time a tremendous sensation, owing partly to her youth (she was only 22), and partly to her personal attractions. From the fact that she was also suspected of having poisoned her first husband, and the rumour that she had expressed the intention of having seven husbands in seven years, people called her the Female Bluebeard. An old lace-maker,[1] who in her childhood had lived at Riseley (Beds), told me that she was only four when her father held her up in the crowd which had

---

[1] Mary Ann Cowley of Clapham. Two other persons now living witnessed this execution, Widow Dennis, Dame Alice Street, Bedford, and Ann Harding of Elstow.

assembled at noon in front of Bedford Jail on August 5th, 1843, to see Sarah Dazeley hanged. Immediately the prison bell began to toll, and the wretched woman, who was dressed in pink, appeared on the scaffold, "a terrific shriek" arose from the crowd. When the fatal moment came and the murderess disappeared, the child said to her father, " Why, dad, they've kicked the well lid up!"

Joseph Castle, who had murdered his wife at Luton, was brought to justice by the help of a bloodhound kept at the Luton police station. This event also created an extraordinary sensation, and the satisfaction that retribution had overtaken the murderer was so lively that "on the night of Castle's public execution (March 31st, 1860) the friends of his deceased wife held a ball," and every guest on departing was presented with a bobbin as a memento of the occasion.

William Worsley, who murdered William Bradbury at Luton, was executed at Bedford on March 31st, 1868. The fact that Worsley's was the last public execution in Bedford accounts for the popularity of the Worsley bobbin. In the words of an owner, " Everybody wanted them."[1]

William Bull, who murdered at Little Staughton an old woman named Sarah Marshall, was executed at Bedford, April 3rd, 1871. A bobbin

[1] I found one at Oakley (Beds), one at Bedford, one at Olney, and two at Weston Underwood.

inscribed with the name of his victim was also on sale.[1]

Bobbins were also made out of sympathy for the fate of two brothers, Matthias and William Lilley, who were executed on April 4th, 1829, for shooting at a gamekeeper named King in one of the Bromham Woods. According to the story, the Lilleys on meeting the gamekeeper told him that if he moved they would shoot. As he moved, they fired. At the trial the judge, who was inclined to leniency, suggested that the occurrence was an accident, but the gamekeeper stoutly persisted that it was a wilful attempt at murder. The Lilleys were taken in a cart from Bedford Jail and hanged on Biddenham Gallows, Bromham Road, just beyond the Bedford boundary. It is said that King never again enjoyed peace of mind, and that he could be seen for hours walking moodily backwards and forwards in his house. The outburst of popular indignation at these executions did much towards abolishing the death penalty for offences of the kind. King, who lived to be an old man, is buried at Bromham. When the mother of the Lilleys died in 1833 a stone was placed at her grave in Kempston Old Churchyard, and under her name appeared :

Matthias Lilley departed the 4th of April, 1829, aged 29 years.
William Lilley died at the age of 21.
Sons of the above.

[1] Dr. Lulham, Stonehouse, Glos., has one.

Matthias left a widow and one son, whose descendants are still numerous in Kempston and neighbourhood.

Some sixty years ago one Joseph West was for some misdemeanour put for the night in the Lockup which stood near the Cross Keys at Cranfield. Next morning he was found to have hanged himself " with a bootlace." Bobbins commemorative of the event were made, but I have never met with one.

As regards Rannson Dillingum, perhaps like " Thomas Brown, Jack Williams and Poor Joe " of one of the Lace Tells, he got "fourteen years" for poaching. It could scarcely have been sheep stealing, for that was a hanging affair.[1] In any case we seem to hear his mother crying to him as the " aged mother " in the old Bedfordshire song, " The Roving Blade,"[2] cried, while she tore " her old grey locks " :

> " Oh son, oh son, what have you done !
> You're going to Botany Bay."

Let us hope that he returned home in due course, shunned thenceforth " all evil company," and married, also in the words of the song, " a girl in Bedford town."

---

[1] The writer watched the funeral some thirty years ago at Elstow of a man who, in his youth, had been sentenced to death for sheep stealing, and reprieved.

[2] *Old Songs sung in Bedfordshire*, p. 16.

ELECTION BOBBINS.

Of Election Bobbins I have met with :

Vote for Osborne. *Lavendon, Bucks.*
Crawley for ever.
Althorpe for ever.
Vote for Althorpe. *Paulerspury, Northants.*
Gunning and Reform.
Chandos for ever.
Success to the Lace Pillow.

The first doubtless refers to John Osborn, M.P. for the County of Beds 1806—7 and 1818—20; the second probably to S. Crawley, who was returned for the same county with J. S. Whitbread in 1832; the third, fourth and fifth Northants bobbins refer to Lord Spencer and one of the Gunnings; the sixth, a Bucks bobbin, commemorates the Marquis of Chandos. The last seems also to have originated at an election time.

TEXT BOBBINS.

(Texts or adaptations of texts.)

Many bobbins were inscribed with passages of Scripture.

OLD TESTAMENT.

Remember thy Creatr[1] in the days of thy youth. Eccles. xii. 1.
Joy for ever. Psa. xvi. 11 (an adaptation of).
The Lord is my Shepherd. Psa. xxiii. 1.
God is good to you all. Psa. cxlv. 9[2] (an adaptation of). *Oakley, Beds.*

[1] Dr. Street of Cranfield has one with this word spelt " creater."
[2] " The Lord is good to all."

Those that seek Me arly shal find Me. Prov. viii. 17.

Prepare to meet thy God. Amos iv. 12. *Eynesbury, Hunts.*

Seek ye the Lord. Isaiah lv. 6.

Buy the truth and sell it not. M. A. G.[1] 1860. Prov. xxiii. 23. *Weston Underwood.*

Love mercy. Micah vi. 8.

Love truth. Zech. viii. 19 (" Love the truth ").

NEW TESTAMENT.

Do not steel. Mark x. 19; Luke xviii. 20. *Stoke Goldington.*

Repent and believe the gospel. Mark i. 15. *Emberton.*

Repent that you may be saved. Luke xiii. 3 (an adaptation of). *Deanshanger, Northants.*

Ye must be born again. John iii. 7. *Stevington, Beds.*

Jesus weept. John xi. 35. *Olney.*

Thou knowest that I love Thee. John xxi. 16.

God is love. 1 John iv. 8. *North Crawley.*

Christ Crucifie. 1 Cor. i. 23.

Fear God. 1 Peter ii. 17.

POETRY AND POPULAR SONG BOBBINS.

Some of the inscriptions are citations from poems, hymns or popular songs.

Jesus died for me. (Part of chorus of several hymns.)

O God of Jacob.[2] (Gimp bobbin.) *Olney.*

With all thy faults I love thee still. (Taken from Cowper's *Task,* Bk. i.: " England, with all thy faults, I love thee still.") *Milton Keynes, Bucks.*

O that will be joyful, when we meet to part no more. (Taken from T. Bibly's hymn, " Here we suffer grief and pain.")

---

[1] Mary Ann Gorman.

[2] A variation of the first words of Doddridge's hymn, " O God of Bethel, by whose hand," &c. This variation appears in several hymnals.

Plate 32

MEDALLIONS, OR MOTIFS.   See p. 232.
MALTESE MADE AT OLNEY.

Plate 33

CLUNY LACE. Made at Northampton.
See p. 227.

CLUNY LACE. Made at Northampton. See p. 227.
Star made of plaits with Rose Ground, sometimes called Double Rose.

Not for Joseth. [On some bobbins spelt correctly.]
Wait for the waggon. *Hanslope, Bucks.*
Nix me dolle [dolly]. (From a song in one of Ains-
worth's novels.)
Pop goes the wesel.
Slap bang hear we are again.

APOPHTHEGM BOBBINS.

Then, too, one meets with bobbins containing
apophthegms or moral sayings, as :

Time his short.[1] *Cranfield, Beds.*
Death's shore. [= Death is sure.]
Nothing venture nothing have.
Whear true love is planted it grows.
Never faint. *Kimbolton.*

PRAYER AND ADMONITION BOBBINS.

Bobbins with admonitory inscriptions are not
uncommon, as :

Do love the Lord. *Hanslope, Bucks.*
Bless my John.
Love Jesus whilst you are young. *Deanshanger, Northants.*
Remember Jesus Christ.
Marry not till 26.
God save the Queen. *Fritwell, Oxon.*
Honour the Queen.
I · M · P · R · O · V · E.
Seek salvation. *Deanshanger, Northants.*
Repentance is nedeful.

As long as I live in this world
Lord keep me from evil.

---

[1] Also met with in correct spelling. "The time is short" occurs in
1 Cor. vii. 29.

PIOUS UTTERANCES.

Jesus his a friend of mine.
Jesus is love. *Kempston.*
I do love dear Jesus. *Hanslope.*

THE VILLAGE WAG.

Every village had its wag, and his ponderous
wit sometimes expressed itself in bone.

Peep fool peep.   Peep at your brother
Did you ever see one fool peep at another. *Cranfield, Beds.*

Peep foole peep, din't you never see a bobin afor?
Shevington, Bucks.

SETS OF BOBBINS.

It was a frequent custom to make sets of bobbins—twos, threes, fours and even twelves.   At
North Crawley on the wedding morning the young
man used to give his betrothed a pair of mottoed
bone bobbins.   A worker of that village has a
pair inscribed :

(1) I'll buy the ring.
(2) A Present for Mistress Bride.

They were made by Samuel Wright of Cranfield,
and given by her father, Joseph Lathall,[1] to his
wife Isabella.

A pair of bobbins, made at Bedford, were in the
possession of another worker of North Crawley.
They read :

---

[1] He died Feb. 7th, 1875.

(1) When this you see remember me and bear me in your mind.
(2) Let all the world say what they will speak of me as U find.[1]

As an interesting set of three the following may be noted :

> (1) Faith Setchill, born June 10, 1831.
> (2) Hope Setchill, born June 10, 1831.
> (3) Charity Setchill, born June 10, 1831.

These were made for a Mrs. Setchill of Dean (Beds) to commemorate the birth of triplets.

A Hanslope lace-maker once possessed a set of four bobbins which were thus inscribed :

(1) Tis sweet to love but sweeter to be loved
(2) Again, but oh how bitter is that thought to love yet love in vain.
(3) There's none on earth that can conceive how bitter is that pain
(4) To be in love with those who don't love us again.

She showed me bobbin No. 1, and repeated from memory the inscriptions on the others, which had drifted elsewhere.

A set greatly sought after consists of Twelve Bobbins, each of which is inscribed with a clause of the Lord's Prayer. One of the bobbins from a set of this kind was seen at Wilshamstead, Beds.[2]

---

[1] A similar pair is inscribed :
> Bobbin No. 1 : Let all the world say what they
>   ,,   No. 2 : Will speak of me as you find.

[2] There are good collections of inscribed bobbins in the Cowper and Newton Museum at Olney, and in the museums at Aylesbury and Northampton. Mr. H. H. Armstrong of Olney also has a fine collection.

The bobbins of Devonshire are of two kinds :
"Honiton Lace Sticks" and "Trol-

50. Devon-shire and Wiltshire Bobbins. lies." (1) Honiton Lace Sticks, which are mostly of spindle or olive wood,[1] have pointed ends, which are necessary to the worker in manipulating the threads. Those used at Beer are highly decorative, exhibiting crosses, fishes, sea-weeds, anchors, ships with sails, and various other ornaments in red and black. The Branscombe bobbins have bolder designs, the more ancient sorts being dark owing to their having been burnt with aquafortis. (See Plate 22).

(2) Trollies. In Bucks a trolly is a bobbin used for gimp, but in Devonshire it means a bobbin used in the making of a special kind of lace, "Devonshire Trolly," which we shall speak of in Chapter 15, Section 60. As this is what we may call a "Finish as you go" lace, the bobbins have blunt ends, there being no necessity for a point. None of the Devon bobbins have spangles.

The bobbins of Downton (Wiltshire) resemble the Devon bobbins in being pointed and without spangles, and differ from them in being shorter and fatter. (See Plate 22.)

As regards the inscriptions on the Devonshire bobbins, some savour of the sea and others are religious, as might be expected of persons saturated, as were so many of the Devonshire people,

[1] A few are of mahogany.

Plate 34

LILLE PILLOW LACE FLOUNCE. Made in 1875.

Victoria and Albert Museum (18454).

(By permission of the Authorities.)

Plate 35

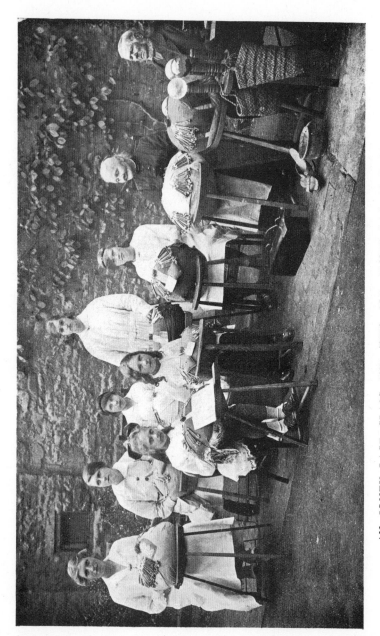

AN OLNEY LACE CLASS AND TWO OLD OLNEY LACE-MAKERS, 1918

with the Bible and John Flavel.[1] Several of the
inscriptions have a small heart at the beginning
and at the end. One has a large heart with the
words, " Forget me not," within it. Most have
fishes, ships or seaweed painted on them. On
St. Valentine's Day a boy would go to his
sweetheart's door and throw in a packet of lace
sticks of his own carving. If he did not throw
in the whole set of 24 (the number ordinarily used
on a Devonshire pillow) he was considered a
laggard in love.

Mrs. Roberts of Spratton has a Devonshire
bobbin (from Brent) with a double twisted inscription which begins from the top and runs :

> S. B. Wair two hearts in unian meet
> Sweet O sweet is that sensation.

Other Brent bobbins in her possession are
inscribed :

> 1803. A present from Thomas Darke. Susana Cox.
> S. P. 1826.

Miss M. Maidment of Ilford has a Devon
bobbin with a very long inscription :

> E. N. You have a true love on the main, for love he has
> venturd his life, but soon will return home again,
> and make you his own happy wive. P. G.

Others belonging to Miss Maidment are
inscribed :

---

[1] The great Devonshire preacher and author of many works, who died
in 1691.

Love and live. 1843.
Forget me not. Remember Lot's wife. (Spiral.)
Prepar to met God. (Spiral.)
For ever thine The girl I love. Forget me not. (Spiral.)
E. J. A. was married May 12, 1878.

I have also heard of :

> The ring is round and hath no end
> So is my love for you my friend ;

and,

> May God protect the sailor still
> From rocks and sands and every ill.

As will have been judged by the foregoing, most of the Devon bobbins smack of the ocean. In handling them we feel that we are continually in touch with " those that go down to the sea in ships, that do business in great waters."

CHAPTER XIV

THE LACE TELLS AND THE LACE-MAKERS' HOLIDAYS

The proficiency of the children at the Lace School was, as we have already 51. The Bucks Tells. noticed, estimated by the number of pins placed in an hour, and to assist themselves in the counting they used to chant in a sing-song voice the amount of work to be got over:

> 20 miles have I to go,
> 19 miles have I to go,
> 18 miles have I to go.

These and the more elaborate countings were called **Lace Tells.**

That the practice of singing songs at the pillow was common even in Shakspeare's day is evident from the remark of the Duke in *Twelfth Night:*[1]

> " O fellow, come, the song we had last night
> Mark it, Cesario, it is old and plain.
> The spinsters and the knitters in the sun,
> And the free[2] maids that weave their threads with bones
> Do use to sing it."

[1] Act II., Scene 4.
[2] Some persons have been puzzled by this word. If they had studied the Bucks and Beds Lace Tells they would have understood it. Of course it means "without care"; as in the Beds Tell, " Come, all you bold bachelors, jovial and free."

And then the clown breaks out into that pathetic and exquisite dirge beginning:

> " Come away, come away, Death ! "

Doubtless Shakspeare, who knew Buckinghamshire so well, founded these jewelled lines upon some uncouth ditty which he had actually heard sung at some Stony Stratford or Grendon Underwood pillow.

As might be expected the Buckinghamshire tells are similar in character to those with which Shakspeare[1] was evidently acquainted. Of artistry they are innocent, but coming from an impressionable people they abound in allusions to coffins, shrouds, corpses, bones, lightning flashes, sardonic laughter, hyena-like cries, and other lurid, gruesome, clammy or grizzly terrors :

> The ravens hoarse, the mandrake's hollow groan ;
> The shrieking owls which fly in the night alone.

The simplest of the tells took the bald Dialogue form :

> Knock, knock at your door. Who's there ? It's me. Come in. Does your little dog bite ? Yes. How many teeth has it ? Six ; seven next time ; eight when I call again.

Silence was then kept while eight pins were stuck

---

[1] He is said to have stayed at the Ship Inn, Grendon Underwood, and there to have picked up some of the humour of his *Midsummer Night's Dream*. Two Grendon men are immortalised in Dogberry and Vergis in *Much Ado about Nothing*. " Vergis " is a Bucks word meaning " verjuice." It is often pronounced " vargis."

into the pillow, this space of time being called a
" glum."[1] In the following bit of doggerel we are
hurried unceremoniously into another glum :

> Dingle, dangle, farthing candle,
> Put you in the stinking dog's hole.
> For thirty-one speak or look off for sixty-two.

Anyone who happened to look off her work or to
speak during the glum from thirty-one to sixty-two
received the imposition of another glum of thirty-
one pins. The cry of relief when the work was
done sometimes took the form of

> Tip and stitch turn over,
> Let it be hay or clover,
> My glum's done !

The great question ever in the mind of the
worker was, Would she get her work done before
dark ? for to be obliged to work by candle-light
except between Tanders[2] and Candlemas was the
bitterest of punishments ; hence the tell—one girl
singing the first couplet :

> 19 miles to the Isle of Wight,
> Shall I get there by candle light ?

and another in sing-song replying,

> Yes, if your fingers go lissom and light,
> You'll get there by candle light.

A scrap of village history sometimes wove itself

---

[1] That is, "A period of gloom."
[2] St. Andrew's Day, November 30th.

into these lace tells. One is the lurid story of a girl and a worthless lover. After playing with her affections he turned from her, and resolved to murder her. In order to get her into his power he requested her to meet him on a dark night under a certain tree. He and an accomplice arrived there before the appointed time, and at once set to work to dig the grave, being lighted by a lantern, which they tied to the tree, and the ghastly streaks of blue summer lightning. The girl approached the spot earlier than she was expected, and seeing from a point of vantage two men instead of one, her suspicions were aroused. The murkiness of the night added to her terrors. At the same moment " the Fox," as she called her faithless lover, while looking about to see whether anyone was near, happened to catch sight of her, and imagining that she was not alone, he gave the alarm to his companion, and they made off. She arrived home in safety, and she tells her tale in a couple of stanzas that are gruesome enough, if only they had been poetry, to have been taken from one of the plays of John Webster.

THE FOX.

19 miles as I sat high
Looking for one, and two passed by,
I saw them that never saw me—
I saw the lantern tied to a tree.

The boughs did bend and the leaves did shake
I saw the hole the Fox did make.

The Fox did look, the Fox did see[1]
I saw the hole to bury me.

This little song sung in the twilight, and ming-
ling with the distant hoot of the owl or the monotonous "Crake, crake, crake," of the corncrake,
would send a thrill through every heart. The
following tell also reveals the leaning of the Bucks
lace-makers towards the gruesome, the uncanny
and the truculent.

> Get to the field by one
> Gather the rod[2] by two
> Tie it up at three
> Send it home by four
> Make her work hard at five
> Give her her supper at six
> Send her to bed at seven
> Cover her up at eight
> Throw her down stairs at nine
> Break her neck at ten
> Get to the well-lid by eleven
> Stamp her in at twelve.
> How can I make the clock strike one,
> Unless you tell me how many you've done?

In the last two lines allusion is made to the
plan sometimes followed in the lace schools, and
already in these pages alluded to, of counting the
number of pins stuck and calling out at every fifty
or a hundred ; each girl endeavouring, in order to
show her dexterity, to be the first to call out.
Another tell (taken down at Weston Under-

---

[1] The word "that" is understood.
[2] To whip her with.

wood) is a variation of the venerable story of Hugh of Lincoln.

THE JEWESS MAIDEN.

There was a Jewess maiden, or so my story states,
Who beckoned to a little boy who peeped between her gates.
An apple so red, a plum so sweet, she gave him from her
  tree ;
She dazzled his eyes with a garry[1] gold ring that was so
  fair to see.
And when she got him in the gates she laughed, he knew
  not why,
And uttered many wicked words and told him he must die.
She laid him on the dresser board, no mercy then she
  showed,
But stabbed him with a knife and stabbed until the life-
  blood flowed.

In the version of the story sung at Haddenham (Bucks) some fifty years ago, children playing near the Jew's garden toss their balls over the wall and break the windows. The Jew's daughter, dressed " all in beautiful green," comes out and, with a cherry as red as his blood and a gay gold ring, entices one of the little boys into the garden. She takes him into the cellar, lays him on a dresser with a Prayer Book at his head and a Bible at his feet, and stabs him to death with a penknife.

Several other versions of this old libel on the Jewess maiden were sung in other parts of Lace-land,[2] but in every instance the " garry " or " gay "

---

[1] Gay.
[2] See also *Notes and Queries*, 4th Series, Vol. IV., p. 8.

gold ring and the dresser board are among the properties, and the final thrill is managed with some sort of knife.

At the end of another gruesome ditty which simply revels in coffins, corpses, skulls and worms that creep in and worms that creep out, the listener is supposed to ask,

Shall I be so when I am dead ?

and the answer comes in sepulchral tones :

Yes, you'll be so when you are dead ;

whereupon everyone would pretend great fear, and jerk out suddenly " Oh ! "

Along with the shudder, indeed, occasioned by the singing of these songs, was a certain amount of real enjoyment. If, however, the pressure became too great and the younger workers got " afeared," some twinkling eyed girl would strike up with, " Come lasses and lads." At once the tension would be relieved, and the ghosts, wizards, bones, corpses, worms and other properties, would be laid aside until next day, when they would be brought out once more to play their agreeable parts.

Another favourite way of counting was called " All round the Town,"—and in old times every village called itself, and was referred to in the Parish Register, as the Town. In this method every time you stuck in a pin you called out the name of some householder, until you had exhausted

the village. The penalty for those who could
not keep up was a terrible one, as became a com-
munity that had so insatiable an appetite for
horrors, for the conclusion of the tell was, " Them
as aint come are stamped on and drownded."

That the Bucks lace-makers, however, could
appreciate the pleasant as well as the morbid, is
evidenced by the following, which was sung at
Weston Underwood.

> A lad down at Olney looked over a wall,
> And saw nineteen little golden girls playing at ball.
> Golden girls, golden girls, will you be mine?
> You shall neither wash dishes nor wait on the swine.
> But sit on a cushion and sew a fine seam,
> Eat white bread and butter and strawberries and cream.

The " golden girls " were, of course, the gold-
headed pins that marked the footside of the lace.
The word " nineteen " runs in many of the tells,
that being the number at which counting often
commenced.

The following, too, has in it nothing of the
charnel-house.

> Up the street and down the street
>   With windows made of glass;
> Call at Mary Muskett's[1] door—
>   There's a pretty lass!
>
> With a posy in her bosom,
>   And a dimple in her chin;
> Come, all you lads and lasses,
>   And let this fair maid in.

[1] The name of any girl could be inserted.

Then there was " Round the Pot of Lavender,
John," and " The Ravens," and a tell that recorded " The Woes of Arabella," who died of a broken
heart; but of none of them have I been able to
obtain the words. All these belong to North
Bucks. Enquiry in the south of the county has
elicited the reply that nothing was there sung at
the pillow except the monotonous

Nineteen miles have I to go.

The Bedfordshire Tells are of an entirely different character from those of Bucking-
hamshire. They turned less on bones, **52. The Bedfordshire Tells.**
gibbets, and other horrors customarily
referred to under one's breath, than on the neat-
ness of the village lace-maker's appearance, the
wisdom of choosing one of these comely Bedfordshire girls " to be your sweet wife "[1], and the
anticipated joys of the approaching wedding;
moreover they are enlightened with an occasional
gleam of pawky humour. The following evidently
dates from the 18th century.

THE BEDFORDSHIRE FARMER.

In Bedfordshire lived a rich farmer, we hear;
A Bedfordshire maiden had lived there a year.
She started for home on a short holiday,
When a highwayman stopped her upon the highway.

[1] This is the tell that begins, "Come, all you bold bachelors, jovial and
free." It was sung at Wootton, Beds. I have heard a version of it at
Newton Blossomville, Bucks, and one still different at Cranfield, Beds.

> She screamed out with fright, she screamed out with fear,
> But help ('twas the Bedfordshire farmer) was near.
> The highwayman, hit by a blunderbuss, died ;
> And there soon was a wedding, and she was the bride.

No doubt more than one Bedfordshire maiden subsequently took a stroll on the highway on the off-chance of being stopped by a "gentleman of the road." But there is another version of the story, according to which, the girl not only screamed out, but stunned the highwayman with a serviceable stick, when another highwayman appeared, and it was this second gentleman who received the attentions of the Bedfordshire farmer. The denouement, however, was the same in both cases. Let us hope that the wedded pair lived harmoniously ; for that there was sad bickering in some Bedfordshire homes is from the following tell painfully evident.

THE OLD COUPLE.

> There was an old couple and they were poor,
> They lived in a house with only one door,
>   And poor old folks were they.
> And the poor old man said he wouldn't stay at home,
> And the poor old woman said she wouldn't sleep alone,
>   And poor old folks were they.
>
> And she said, " If you've got any love for me,
> You'd fetch me an apple from yonder tree."
>   And poor old folks were they.
> He fetched her an apple and laid it on the shelf,
> And said, " If you want any more, you can fetch them
>   yourself ! "
>   And poor old folks were they.

To judge by the next tell, it was the custom of Bedfordshire young women, when a man offended them to throw a turnip at him:

> Nineteen miles to Charing Cross,
> To see a Black Man ride on a white horse.
> The rogue was so saucy he wouldn't come down,
> To show me the road to the nearest town.
> I picked up a 'turmut' and cracked his old crown,
> And made him cry 'turmuts' all over the town.

On the whole we are inclined to sympathise with the "Black Man," whose punishment seems to have been out of all proportion to his offence. Who was he? Evidently, Mr. E. Godfroy the lace-buyer, with whom the lace-makers sometimes had differences; and a lampoon in the shape of a lace tell was their little revenge. Another rhyme of the neighbourhood refers to the same person and to a lady buyer.

> Behind in this meadow you'll find a dry land,
> Two beauties of Bedford, and there do they stand;
> He on the white horse and she on the gray,
> And so these two beauties go riding away.

The word "beauties" is evidently intended as sarcasm.

At Ickwell Green, near Northill, used to be sung an amusing song called "Hodge of the Mill and Buxom Nell," which describes how Hodge, who was given to flirtation, surrendered at discretion to the lady on learning that she was worth as much as "fifty shillings." "No Wife like a Lace-maker" comes from Wootton, "The Roving

Blade " from Bromham, " The Deserted Lover "
from Ravensden, and " Amen, said the Fool," a
sarcastic rhyme about various village characters,
nobody from the parson to the blacksmith being
perfect, was sung in many Bedfordshire lace
schools some fifty or sixty years ago.[1]

The following was used by the children in the
lace schools of Renhold.

> Needle pin, needle pin, stitch upon stitch,
> Work the old lady out of the ditch.
> If she is not out as soon as I,
> A rap on the knuckles shall come by and by.
> A horse to carry my lady about—
> Must not look off till 20 are out.

They then counted twenty pins, and if anyone
looked off before she had got through the twenty,
the others would call out :

> Hang her up for half an hour,
> Cut her down just like a flower.

The girl referred to would then put in another pin
and reply :

> I won't be hung for half an hour,
> I won't be cut down like a flower.

And who can blame her ?

The Northants Tells have none of the gruesome
features that characterize those of
Buckinghamshire, and they are less
hoydenish and more sentimental than

**53. The
Northants
Tells.**

---

[1] Some of these are printed in *Old Songs Sung in Bedfordshire,*
Beds Times Office.

those of Bedfordshire. The Northamptonshire maidens do not gloat over ghosts, corpses, black coffins and gibbets, nor do they throw turnips at the heads of inoffensive gentlemen who happen to be passing on horseback. They had no taste for dark parables. In the Northants tells, while admission is made of the hardships of existence, the future is looked forward to not without hope.

THE WEDDING DAY.

Nineteen long lines hanging over my door,
The faster I work it'll shorten my score.
But if I do play it'll stick to a stay;
So ho! little fingers, and twink it away,
For after to-morrow comes my wedding day.

My shoes are to borrow, my husband to seek,
So I cannot get married till after next week.
And after next week it will be all my care
To prink and to curl and to do up my hair.

Six pretty maidens, so neat and so clean,
Shall dance at my wedding next Monday morning.
Down in the kitchen the cook she will run,
And tell Mr. Bellman to ring the ting-tang.

There are twenty-two more lines.

The Northants girls were indeed more optimistic than their sisters in High Bucks and West Beds. They seemed to grasp that life consists not of hours as indicated by the clock, but of the hours in which one is cheerful. They had dropped into the habit of hanging bright pictures in their minds.

Another tell runs on " the cherry trees in blos-

som," the brown nuts that "hang so ripe," (for in
the lace world of Northants cherries blossom and
nuts ripen in the same month) ; and the prepara-
tion for a plum pudding which would take less than
half-an-hour. Then there is the "Song of the
Nutting Tree," which begins :

> I had a little nutting tree,
>   And nothing would it bear,
> But little silver nutmegs[1]
>   For Galligolden fair.

But who Galligolden was, and what she wanted
the silver nutmegs for, is not clear.

At Yardley Hastings they sang :

> Twenty pins have I to do,
> Let ways be ever so dirty.
> Never a penny in my purse,
> But farthings five and thirty.
>
> Betsy Bays and Polly Mays,
> They are two bonny lasses ;
> They built a bower upon the tower,
> And covered it with rushes.

I give this jingle as it was told me. It evidently
refers to the old custom of carrying rushes and
garlands to church on Rush-bearing Day—a custom
that is still observed in the North of England.
"Upon the tower" should probably be "within
the tower." Of course any names could be sub-
stituted for Betsy and Polly.

---

[1] *Notes and Queries*, 4th Series, Vol. II., p. 281. "Gilded Nutmegs"
are referred to in the verses that preface *Sociable Letters*, by the
Duchess of Newcastle, 1664 ; and in *Love's Labour Lost*, Act V., Scene
2, we hear of "A gilt nutmeg."

Plate 36

LACE SCHOOL AT CRANFIELD, BEDS, 1918.

(Photo by Mr. Alfred De Ath.)

See Note on the text.

Plate 37

OLD TORCHON.

Reduced from width of one inch and three-quarters.   The zigzag is filled with
spiders. Above and below it are triangles of whole stitch.

(Lent by Mrs. J. B. Harrison, formerly of Paulerspury.)

NORTHAMPTONSHIRE LACES.

No. 1. The Ear-ring (Mears Ashby).
  ,, 2. Sea Shell (Wollaston).
  ,, 3. Diamond and Chain (Olney).
  ,, 4. Point and Honeycomb (Brayfield-on-the-Green, nr. Denton).

The song of " Long Lanken," which, with its trimmings of corpse and gallows, might seem damaging to the theory of the sentimentality of the Northants tells, is really not a Northants song at all, having been imported from the Scottish border.

The tells of all three counties—Bucks, Beds and Northants—are influenced by the superstitions of the people; nor is this surprising, seeing that in every town and village there is some story of a supernatural character—of ghosts that stalk and gibber and wizards that peep and mutter. The Devil and Headless Horseman traditions of Olney, and the names " Great Goblin's Hole " and " Little Goblin's Hole," [1] of Turvey, would alone bear witness to the insatiable appetite of the lace-makers for the uncommon and the uncanny.

We are told that the effect of thirty or forty children's voices uniting in the sing-song of these tells would never be forgotten by anyone listening to them for the first time, and that the children found the singing of the tells a real aid to them in their work. It was a very pretty sight in a lace school of some 30 girls, some of them little more than babies, to see, as an old lace-maker puts it, "all the fingers and all the bobbins going." Singing at the pillow, too, was particularly helpful both to adults and children in dull weather—which, as

[1] These are both shown on the copy of the Ward Map which hangs in the Reading Room at Turvey.

an old Newport Pagnell lace-maker said, used to
" mommer "[1] her and make her feel as if she had
no " docity "[2] in her.

The custom is not confined to the English
Midlands. In Saxony where it also obtains, the
favourite songs are those of the " The Cuckoo
with thirty Wives and what each did," and " The
twelve Geese who stole oats."

The great holiday of the lace-makers was Tanders (St. Andrew's Day, Nov. 30th),
54. Catterns.
but in some parts of Northants, Bucks
and Beds, the leading festival was Catterns (St.
Catharine's[3] Day), Nov. 25th—St. Catharine being
the patron saint of the spinners, to whom the lace-
makers considered themselves related. As time
went on, Catharine the Saint became confused
with Katharine the Queen—that is to say,
Katharine of Aragon (wife of Henry the Eighth)
of Kat Stitch fame, who was born on Dec. 6th,—
old St. Catharine's Day.

In some of the towns and villages the bellman
used to go round before daybreak ringing his bell
and calling out :

> Rise, maids, rise !
> Bake your cattern pies.
> Bake enough, and bake no waste,
> And let the bellman have a taste.

[1] Make her feel stupid.

[2] Pronounced " dossity." The word really means " aptness to learn."
To have no docity = to be lifeless.

[3] St. Catharine of Alexandria, who was tortured on a wheel, and put to
death in 307 A.D.

As early as 1672 it was the custom to give the inmates of the workhouse at Aylesbury sums of money to keep Catterns Day. At Peterborough a number of the girls, attired in white, decorated with scarlet ribbons, and headed by the prettiest of their number who wore a crown and carried a sceptre, went the round of the city singing a ballad commencing :

Here comes Queen Katharine, fine as any queen.

At Kettering, Ampthill and other places, Cattern cakes—made of dough and caraway seeds—were sent about, and the evening was given up to singing, dancing and feasting; the principal dish being stuffed boiled rabbit "smothered with onion sauce." At Podington (N. W. Beds) they kept Cattern on old St. Catharine's Day "by wetting the candle-block," that is, taking tea together, and eating Cattern cakes. After dancing to the music of a fiddle they crowned their diversions by supping on a great apple pie.

The people of Wendover (Bucks) called Catterns "Candle Day," it being the first day on which they commenced to make lace by candle-light, and they celebrated it by eating "wigs," [1]— round, spongy gingerbread-like cakes, flavoured with caraway seed, which obtained their name from their thick rim which resembled the curl of

[1] In Lower Saxony a four-tailed loaf worked with must is called a *wegge*. It was a loaf in the form of two clubs joined together. *Notes and Queries*, 1862, 3rd Series, 387.

a Georgian wig; and drank "hot-pot," a liquor compounded of warm beer spiced with rum and thickened with beaten eggs. At the lace schools the girls and boys danced in a ring round the great lace-maker's candlestick (see Plate 23), singing:

Wallflowers, wallflowers, growing up so high,
All young maidens surely have to die;
Excepting Emma Caudrey, she's the best of all.
She can dance and she can skip,
And she can jump the candlestick.
Turn, turn, turn your face to the wall again.

The girl or boy mentioned turned so that he or she faced outward from the ring, and they continued to dance till all had turned, when the difficult feat of jumping the candlestick, lighted candle and all, was attempted. In other places, including West Suffolk, which was formerly a lace-making centre, the song was,

Jack, be nimble! Jack, be quick!
Jack, jump over the candlestick.

The name of any boy or girl was inserted in both the rhymes. The object it seems was to clear both the candlestick and candle without extinguishing the light. If the light was extinguished[1] ill luck was supposed to follow during the subsequent twelve months. One of these candlesticks, two feet two inches high, is preserved in the Museum at Aylesbury. As the lighted candle

---

[1] In parts of Ireland the object in the game was, and I think still is, to extinguish the flame with the tip of the toe without breaking the candle or overturning the candlestick.

would give at least another three inches, the feat
of leaping it was, at any rate for a girl, not an
easy one. The festivities finished by letting off
Catharine wheels, but all these customs died out
about 1890.

From the preceding it will be noticed that Catterns was observed chiefly in north
Northants and Beds ; in the greater   55. Tanders.
part of lace-land, however, the principal holiday
was Tanders (St. Andrew's Day), November 30th.
On that day at Olney people congregated in " one
another's housen."[1]   No-candy was made, frumenty—or, as it was generally called, "thrumety"[2]
eaten and rich metheglin[3] (made hot), with toast
floating at the top, was drunk.

The proprietors of the Honey House,[4] now
No. 24 High Street, were in the early 19th century
John and Mary Cobb,[5] who used to take out for

[1] The old plurals and preterites of Bucks are, I suppose, doomed.
"Housen" (for houses) is still heard in our villages, but an old lace-
maker, who explained to me how the children " sot " at work, corrected
herself—to my dismay—and said " sat."

[2] Wheat boiled in milk. Plums, nutmeg, cinnamon or sugar can be
added. If the wheat is boiled soft this is a splendid dish, and much
cheaper than the packeted foods sold by the grocers and used for porridge.
The reader should try it.

[3] Metheglin is made by washing the honeycomb ; mead, which resembles it, by dissolving honey in boiling water, flavouring it with spices, and
adding ground malt and a piece of toast dipped in yeast, and suffering
the whole to ferment.

[4] The front of the house has been re-built and the cellar filled up, but
the back of the house which included the Honey Room with its oak
ledges for the "coolers," wax press, and wire gauze ventilators is
unaltered. In the season, a tilted cart full of pails was sent out to the
villages to collect the honey, and in a good year two tons, beside wax,
would be brought in. The wax was run into moulds and sent to London,
and the bee-bread (refuse) was burnt.

[5] Their daughter Mary married James Hollingshead, whose son, George
Cobb Hollingshead, at the age of 93 gave me the above particulars.

the occasion a three days' licence; people from all the country round brought their pitchers and panshons[1] for the indispensable liquor ; and as much as two and a half hogsheads would be sold in a day. If on that occasion metheglin was not forthcoming the lace-makers considered that they had been bilked out of their due.

In the evening the old folks were bidden to go bed—for Tanders and Methuselah in his dotage did not mix well—and then the young folks indulged in bob-apple and other riotous games. For bob-apple the "blades" (which form a cross) were removed from the bobbin winder and suspended by a cord from the oak beam of the ceiling. On the pins of the blades were stuck alternately pieces of apple and short lengths of tallow candle. If, when blindfolded, you chanced to get a bite of the apple it was very amusing to you ; if, however, you happened on the candle, it was amusing chiefly to the spectators.

At Turvey (Beds) figs were eaten on that day, the fruit for many years having been a present from the late Mr. Charles Longuet Higgins, whose birthday happened to be on " Tanders."

At North Crawley and Cranfield was, and is still occasionally, made a Tanders Cake, the Cranfield recipe for which is: " Half pottle[2] dough,

---

[1] Vessels wider at the top than at the bottom.

[2] 3½lbs.—Brewer's yeast should be used. I hope every reader of this book will make a Tanders cake.

6 ozs. lard, 6 ozs. sugar, 1 oz. caraway seed." At
North Crawley they are more liberal with the
accessories, and insist on : " Half-quartern dough,
half-pound lard, half-pound sugar, and 2 ozs.
caraway seed." Bake for an hour and a half. In
those days (may they return !) people made their
own bread, using " brewer's yeast, flour, mashed
potatoes and a pinch of salt," and a portion of the
dough would be set aside for the Tanders cake.
It will be noticed that in these cakes, as well as in
the Cattern cakes and the wigs, the great indispensable was the caraway seeds. There was a
reason. The practice arose with the farmers, who
had the cakes made for their men, and the
caraway seeds, whether used on Catterns Day or
Tanders, were a reminder that the time for sowing
all autumn seed (wheat, oats, &c.) had passed by.
The custom of eating " thrumety " had the same
origin. As early as 1557 Thomas Tusser, the
Suffolk poet, had written :

> " Remember thou, therefore, though I do it not,
> The seed-cakes, the pasties and furmenty pot."

At Stoke Goldington on Tanders the people
made sweets called "Black Buttons." At Stevington they ate Tanders cake and drank hot elder-
berry wine. At Elstow the mistress of the Lace
School allowed the girls to invite their sweethearts
to spend the evening with them, and she used to
open the festivities by entering the room, carrying
in each hand, raised high, a fire pot filled with

metheglin, and crying, " Tan, my boys, Tan ! "
At Kimbolton on old St. Andrew's Day (December 11th) was held Tandrew Fair. At Spratton
(Northants) the children of the lace school used
to seize the opportunity, when the mistress left
the room, to lock her out. On her return they
would sing :

> Pardon, mistress, pardon, master,
>   Pardon for a pin ;
> If you won't give us a holiday,
>   We won't let you in.

After a brief display of counterfeited anger the
mistress yielded to their demands. At Bozeat
(Northants) the church bells used to be rung
at noon. Everywhere fiddles struck up and
ballads were sung, and as, according to an old
writer, " music and songs stir up the passions," a
good deal of boisterous love-making took place.

At Hanslope the frolics on Tanders Day often
exceeded the bounds of prudence. The lace-
makers, in order to lose nothing by their festivities,
used " to work the whole of the previous night,"
and the girls and their sweethearts observed the
great Day itself with all the abandon of young
and giddy spirits. On one occasion the lads, with
painted faces and wearing outrageous wigs, broke
unexpectedly into the midst of the tea drinkings.
Screams of terror ensued, chairs were overturned,
teacups upset, and, worst of all, amid the racket
and confusion, the candlesticks were toppled over

and their precious flasks smashed into a hundred pieces.

At Yardley Hastings the merry-making commenced at noon. At midnight the church bells were rung, and when the first sound was heard the company ceased from their games and sat down to tea and Tanders cake.

In some of the villages of Northants and Bucks "Thomas's" (St. Thomas's Day, Dec. 21), was also kept as a half holiday. In Warwickshire and the parts of North- ants adjoining, the old women, wearing **56. The Minor Holidays.** red cloaks, used to go "Thomasen," that is, begging from house to house, the gifts bestowed being called "Thomasers." At Stoke Goldington (Bucks) and Ecton (Northants) the children in the lace schools used to lock out the mistress and demand a holiday in the fashion that elsewhere was observed on Tanders Day.

At North Crawley (Bucks), Riseley (Beds) and other villages, Shrove Tuesday was also a half holiday. At North Crawley the Parish clerk always rang the Pancake Bell at eleven, and as soon as the sound, "Pan, pan," filtered down from the church tower the women, who had been wait- ing for it, ran, helter-skelter, out of their cottages to the belfry, each carrying a pancake and endeav- ouring to be the first to offer it to the clerk. But the first pancake was not necessarily the best. as owing to the hurry it was likely enough to be

" boltery." [1]   At Riseley the favourite game on this holiday was " Long Eche." [2]   Two girls stretched out a shawl and attempted to catch the others, who tried to run under it.   To the parchment called the Long Eche we have already referred.

Candlemas Day (Feb. 2) was a holiday at Hanslope (Bucks).   The scholars put the candlestools away at half-past four, "and they'd be lissom to do it."   At North Marston (Beds) the mistress of the household when evening drew near used to call out, " Candlemas, candleless."

At Cranfield the people kept in addition to Tanders, Nov. 5th and Feb. 14th, which they called *Candle-light Holidays*, because on the former they began to work by candle-light, and on the latter they ceased to use the candle.

Another custom which is apparently peculiar to Lace-land is that of eating figs on Palm or, as it is here more usually called, Fig Sunday.   Tons of figs are sold at Olney and the surrounding villages on the preceding Saturday.

May Day was kept as a holiday by the lace-makers in some villages.   At Fenstanton (Hunts) sweets and frumenty were made and eaten, and garlands taken from house to house while the children sang part of what is generally known as the Hitchin version [3] of the May Day song which

---

[1] A bolter is a lump of flour in a pancake not made properly.
[2] Pronounced "each."   See page 116.
[3] See *Book of Days*, Vol. 1, p. 578.

contains the verse :

> A branch of may we have brought you,
>   And at your door it stands ;
> It is but a sprout, but it's well budded out,
>   By the work of our Lord's hands.

At Mears Ashby (Northants) also May Day was the great holiday. The children carried a branch of may, on which were dolls dressed with lace, round the village, while they sang the version of the May song which commences :

> This morning is the first of May,
>   The prime time of the year.

In all the lace-making villages there was every five weeks *Cut-off Day*, when the lace was removed from the pillow and carried to the lace-buyer or his agent, who generally met the workers at the village inn.

The people round Bedford usually took it direct to the shop of Mr. Thomas Lester—the girls not without trepidation, for he was a terrible autocrat. In his shop was a drawer which was usually left open an inch or two, and if the lace was not done well, he would take a girl's hand and deliberately pinch her fingers in the drawer. If Sare-Ann was seen shortly after walking down Bedford High Street sucking her fingers, and anybody asked what was the matter, she usually had the discretion to say, " Oh, nothing ! " On the other hand, if her lace was done well she would be praised, and rewarded with the present of a bobbin dotted with the words, THOMAS LESTER.

At Buckingham Mr. Godfroy used to collect lace at the White Hart. A bell rang and the workers, 300 or 400 in number, were admitted one at a time, and paid partly in money and partly in tokens.

Of the Tokens used in the 17th century I have already spoken. At the close of the 18th century there was again a most inconvenient shortage of small change, and tradesmen once more began to issue tokens. Unlike the old tokens which were small and thin, the later tokens were the size and thickness of a present day florin. A well known example has on one side " Lace manufactury " with a representation of a woman seated under a tree making lace; on the other, PAY AT LEIGHTON BERKHAMSTED OR LONDON. 1794—and the figure of a sheep; on the edge, CHAMBERS LANGSTON HALL & CO.[1] Most of these are of copper, but Mr. Arthur Brown, of Stamford Hill, London, N., has one of silver.

57. 18th Century Lace Tokens.

Other tokens with the same Obverse have for Reverse, "PAYABLE AT JOHN ROOKS NORWICH X X X " or, "PAYABLE AT W. GOLDSMITHS BRAINTREE ESSEX." Another token is figured and lettered as follows :

Obverse. Woman seated under a tree making lace.
      Legend : LACE MANUFACTORY. 1795.
Reverse. On a scroll in indented letters : MUSLINS IRIS CLOTH HOSE &c.
      Legend : MOORE NO 116 GREAT PORTLAND STREET.
Edge diagonally milled, in some instances coarsely and in others finely.

[1] They were wholesale haberdashers at 46 Gutter Lane, London.

Of Chambers's tokens one ton were struck and of Moore's half a ton. Mr. S. H. Hamer, who supplied this information, says, " There were also a few struck which had an edge-reading not connected with the general design of the token, viz.: PAYABLE AT I. JORDANS DRAPER, GOSPORT."

CHAPTER XV

COWPER'S YON COTTAGER. BABY LACE

William Cowper is pre-eminently the Poet of
the Lace Pillow ; and his works and
those of his friend, the Rev. John
Newton, teem with references to the
lace industry. Newton came to Olney
in 1764, Cowper three years later. Newton
removed to London in 1780. Cowper removed to
Weston Underwood, a mile and a half from
Olney, in 1786, and left the neighbourhood ten
years later. From 1767 to 1772 Cowper and
Newton held prayer meetings, which were attended
chiefly by the lace-makers, on Sunday mornings at
the Great House, an old mansion that stood close
to the church, the service commencing at the
early hour of seven.

58. " Nothing
Dandled but
the Lace
Pillow."

Referring to these meetings in a letter written
long after (November 30th, 1793), Cowper says :
" Time was when on Sabbath mornings in winter
I rose before day, and by the light of a lanthorn
trudged with Mrs. Unwin, often through snow and
rain, to a prayer meeting at the Great House.
There I always found assembled forty or fifty
poor folks who preferred a glimpse of the light of

God's countenance and favour to the comforts of
a warm bed, or to any comforts that the world
could afford them; and there I have often myself
partaken that blessing with them."

The story is told of a little maiden who, know-
ing that she would have to do so many heads of
lace on the Monday morning, and wishing to take
time by the fore-lock, waited till her mother had
left the cottage for the prayer meeting, and then
whipped out her pillow and managed to get two
" heads " finished.   The mother, however, discovered what had been done, and next morning
she meted out punishment by saying to the mistress of the lace school, " You'll please make my
gal do two heads extry to-day."

Both Cowper and Newton looked after the
temporal as well as the spiritual needs of the
workers, whose condition in 1780 became so hard
that they and others sent a petition to the Lord of
the Manor, praying him to approach Parliament
in their behalf.   But comedy always mingles with
tragedy.   One prominent person would not sign
the petition because he did not think it grammati-
cal; and Cowper, who was one of the signatories,
commented, " Yet I think Priscian himself would
have pardoned the manner for the sake of the
matter."[1]   It was stated that " one thousand two
hundred lace-makers " in Olney alone had reason

[1] Wright's edition of the *Correspondence*, I., p. 207.   Letter of June
23rd, 1780.

enough while a certain bill that affected them was in agitation, " to look upon every loaf they bought as the last they should ever be able to earn."[1] Mr. Robert Smith[2] (created in 1797 Lord Carrington), who made Cowper his almoner, sent for four years in succession (1782—1785) large sums to be distributed in the town. Cowper, who calls him " our beneficent friend, Mr. Smith,"[3] adds, " How I love and honour that man. . . My bosom burns to immortalize him!"[4] And immortalize him he did in *Task*, IV., 428 :

> " I mean the man who, when the distant poor
> Need help, denies them nothing but his name."

When Samuel Rose in 1793 wrote to Cowper, who then resided at Weston Underwood, to ask whether there was any possibility of finding in Weston a nurse for his baby, Cowper replied, " Girls fit to be nurses, and worthy to be trusted with little William, are scarce, and especially scarce in this country where the lace pillow is the only thing they dandle."[5]

The originals of Cowper's poem, " The Flatting Mill" (1780) and the fragment commencing, " Methinks I see thee decently arrayed," are written on the Bill of a " Lace Manufacturer " named James Nicholls.[6]

---

[1] Wright's edition of the *Correspondence*, I., p. 210 ; II., 415.
[2] 1752—1838. [3] *Correspondence*, II., 25.
[4] *Correspondence*, II., 151.
[5] *Correspondence*, IV., 355.
[6] Several members of this family were lace-buyers, the last being Susannah Nichols who died in 1860. She was the widow of William Nichols, who died in 1840. They lived in High Street South, in a large house on which are sculptured cross keys and the date 1717.

Plate 38

BUCKS POINT.   Made at Spratton (Northants).

BUCKS POINT.   Made at Northampton.

Plate 39

WINSLOW LACE INDUSTRY.   See p. 12.

1. Lee Insertion for Furniture.   2. Lee Border.
3. Daisy Russian Insertion.   It can be had with coloured daisies.
4. Old Greek Pointed Lace.   For use on linen.

Few passages of poetry have been more frequently quoted than Cowper's lines on the lace-
maker and Voltaire.   (*Truth*, lines 317—336.)

> " Yon cottager who weaves at her own door,
>   Pillow and bobbins all her little store;
>   Content, though mean, and cheerful if not gay,
>   Shuffling her threads about the live-long day;
>   Just earns a scanty pittance, and at night
>   Lies down secure, her heart and pocket light."

Then follows the beautiful tribute to her, who

> " Just knows, and knows no more, her Bible true—
>   A truth the brilliant Frenchman never knew;
>   And in that charter reads with sparkling eyes
>   Her title to a treasure in the skies."

Among the well-known characters at Olney in
Cowper's time was one Elizabeth Robinson, a
" serving-maid " and lace-maker, whose sad story
is immortalized in the lines on " Crazy Kate ".
(*Task*, lines 534—556):

> " There often wanders one whom better days
>   Saw better clad, in cloak of satin trimmed
>   With lace, and hat in splendid ribband bound."

Her lover was a sailor, and when she heard " the
doleful tidings of his death " she " never smiled
again." Her reason left her, and she used to roam
all day long and sometimes all night in tattered
clothes on the roads by the water-courses and
in the fields and spinneys around Olney. Even
in this distressing state she could not forget her
pillow, for

> " She begs an idle pin from all she meets
> And hoards them in her sleeve."[1]

One of the romances of the lace trade is referred to by Cowper in his letters of March 29th and April 10th, 1786, which tell of a common sailor who, after fighting under Wolfe at Quebec (1759), came to Olney penniless, entered the lace business, amassed money, built a big house and, although he had so often swung in a hammock, afforded the whole town occasion for mirth by giving £20 for a bed. After a period of prosperity he put the bulk of his substance to hazard by sending a cargo of lace to America, and the venture failing, he was reduced almost to his former indigence.

Cowper's protegée, pretty Hannah Willson, was a lace-maker. Writing on April 14th, 1789, the poet says: " Her chief occupation at present in the daytime is to make black lace for a cloak, which she does, by the account of the judicious in those matters, exceedingly well." Later—on June 6th—he tells Lady Hesketh: " Mrs. Unwin will be obliged to thee also for a black summer cloak, *untrimmed*, because Hannah is making a trimming for it."

Among Cowper's acquaintances at this time was Thompson Pater, a lace-buyer at Weston Underwood, and great-grandfather of Walter Pater,

---

[1] As time went on she partially regained her reason. She died April 5th, 1821, aged 63, and there is a tombstone to her memory in the Baptist Graveyard at Olney.

author of *Marius the Epicurean*, and other works.
The old home of the Paters is still standing, and
there are several tombstones to members of the
family in the churchyard.[1] In 1840 Cowper's old
house at Olney, now the Cowper and Newton
Museum, was used as a lace school.[2]

What Cowper was to the lace-makers of North
Bucks another great poet, Percy Bysshe Shelley,
became twenty years later to the workers in the
south of the county. When Shelley in 1825
resided at Albion House, Marlow, and while the
fever in his soul was expressing itself in the
Revolt of Islam, he continually interested himself
in the condition of the workers, many of whom
were his pensioners. At this period Black Silk
Lace was largely made.

As a result of the French Revolution occurred a
Fourth Exodus of lace-makers into
England. (See Map, Plate 11.) As in **59. The Fourth**
the case of the First Exodus, the **Exodus, 1794.**
workers from one district flocked to **Revolution Lace.**
Cranfield and other Bedfordshire vil-
lages, and those of another to Devonshire. It was
chiefly the refugees from Valenciennes who found
their way to Cranfield. They brought with them
numbers of new patterns, and as a result Cranfield
became a centre of the parchment making industry

[1] See Wright's *Life of Walter Pater*, Vol. I., p. 9.
[2] It is referred to by Hugh Miller (who visited Olney, September 9th,
1845), in his *First Impressions of England*, pp. 274—303.

which flourished for over forty years, and the neighbourhood became famous for " English Valenciennes," which was "quite equal to the French variety."

Among the laces introduced by the refugees from Valenciennes was one called *Revolution Lace* (see Plate 13), which was in demand from 1789 to 1838. The pattern on the head-side was filled in with Point Ground, while there was Kat Stitch (Wire Ground, Six-pointed Star Ground or Hairpin Stitch) on the foot-side. It is still made in Northamptonshire. At this period Hanslope and Stony Stratford in Bucks and Towcester in Northants were great lace centres. At Hanslope 800 out of a population of 1275 were employed at the pillow, and £9,000 net profit was annually brought into the village.

While, however, the Valenciennes workers drifted to Cranfield, those from Normandy made their way to Devonshire, where they introduced the Trolly Lace industry. (See Map, Plate 11.) In Buckinghamshire, as we have seen, the word " Trolly " means gimp, and a lace of the most delicate texture could be correctly called Trolly Lace (though the term is not much used) if the pattern has a gimp outline. In Devonshire, on the other hand, the word Trolly, whatever its original signification, came to mean a lace made of coarse British thread, with heavy bobbins, and

60. Devonshire Trolly. 1789.

worked straight on—round and round the pillow.
This lace, which is unlike any other Devonshire
fabric, was made by old women at East Budleigh
(Devon) as late as 1896, and a few years ago
Thirteen-hole Trolly was obtainable in the villages
round Exmouth, but the industry is now practically extinct.

For many years attempts had been made to
produce lace by machinery, and towards
the end of the 18th century an inven- 61. Heath-
tion called the " Warp Machine " gave   coat's
an impetus to the idea.   Little pro-   Machine.
                                          1814.
gress, however, was made until 1809, when John
Heathcoat patented his Second Bobbin Machine,
which became the foundation of an enormous
industry.   The low prices at which machine lace
could be sold caused great consternation among
the Bucks workers.   " Nottingham Net " was followed by " Urling's Figured Imitations."   It was
in " Urling's Patent Lace " that Miss Stephens
sang, "And they're a' Noddin," and that
Madamoiselle Noblet danced.   Belgravia and
May Fair wore it on their " Cleopatra backs,"
and fashioned it as a mob under their sea-green
Leghorn bonnets.   A " colerette standing up and
finished by two rows of Urling's Patent Lace "
was considered irresistible, particularly if the
young lady carried a twisted gold chain from
which was suspended a circular eye-glass and
wore lemon coloured gloves.   In the park, in the

church, at Belzoni's Exhibition—everywhere in 1822—there was Urling's Patent Lace. Urling! Urling! Urling! The people of Buckinghamshire were goaded to madness.

The one question they asked of any candidate for Parliament was whether he would fight tooth and nail in behalf of Bobbin Work. At the Aylesbury elections anti-machine processions paraded the town. In front was a lace pillow, mounted on a high pole; then came a band of music, followed by a car in which was seated a Lace Queen[1] "plying her vocation," the procession being closed by her court, who carried banners trimmed with lace and placards worded, "Support Bobbin lace!" "Down with the Machine Stuff!" and similar mottoes. The popular candidate, who could hardly be seen for lace, was cheered to the echo, and the other man was pelted (served him right!) "like a Shrove-tide cock."

Among the Bucks patterns imitated recently by machinery was *Fremantle*. One of the mills turned out thousands of yards which were sent to Russia, where curiously enough it was used for lining coffins.

Certainly the Bucks industry suffered terribly for years, but in time people began to recognise that machine lace has its limits, and that though much of it is effective at a distance, it is not to be spoken of in the same breath with lace made by

[1] Mrs. Whitley, who was thus honoured in 1820, died in 1884.

the hand. It is also far less durable. Cultured taste has come to admit that there is no comparison between the perfect thing made on a pillow and the make-shift imitation, however ingeniously produced.

Early in the century a licence was necessary in order " to deal in Thread Lace of British manufacture," and a copy of the Licence granted to John Morgan of Olney in 1807 is preserved in the Cowper Museum at Olney. The stamp was five shillings.

As if the blows from machinery were insufficient, resolutions were read in the House of Commons on November 17th, 1814 (that is, soon after the retirement of Napoleon to Elba), that the duties "payable on the Importation of Thread and Silk Lace into Great Britain do cease and determine."[1] The new proposals were (1) that the low *ad valorem* duty of 20 per cent. should be placed on Foreign Laces ; (2) that a stamp duty of three guineas be charged upon every Licence to be taken out by Dealers in Foreign Lace.

The lace manufacturers were now thoroughly roused. They met on December 21st, 1814, at the Swan Inn, Newport Pagnell, and resolved unanimously " That any duty imposed by the legislature on Foreign Thread Lace, except by the system of law now existing," would " entirely

---

[1] This would nullify the Act passed in the forty-sixth year of George III., by which heavy duties were placed on foreign laces.

ruin the Manufactury of this country." A committee[1] was formed, subscriptions were raised to defray expenses; deputations were appointed to wait on the Members of Parliament for Bucks, Beds and Northants, the Chancellor of the Exchequer, and others; and a petition to Parliament (dated February 15th, 1815) was drawn up, in which it was prayed that the House " would not suffer to pass into a law a Bill which must endanger the security of this interesting and Staple Manufacture which has given employment for a period of one hundred and fifty years to above 150,000 persons."

Very little good, however, came of the efforts, for after the battle of Waterloo (June 18th, 1815) large consignments of foreign lace were admitted into this country.

The unhappy Bucks workers, in their endeavour to compete with machinery, then made the fatal mistake of using inferior and cheaper thread which was obtained from Holland, as were all other threads at the time. Consequently the Valenciennes laces were soon pronounced to be more durable than the home-made fabrics, with the result that even those manufacturers who continued to use the best threads found themselves severely mauled.

---

[1] The folio volume, bound in brown calf, containing the minutes of this Committee has been preserved. On the cover are the words, " Lace Manufactory Committee Proceedings." It is in the possession of Mr. F. W. Bartlett, Port Vale, Hertford.

It may be asked whether lace made by machine will ever equal that made by hand.

62. M. Seguin on Lace. The answer is, It is an absolute impossibility. M. Seguin lucidly explains the reason. " In machine work," he says, " the operating force is absolutely uniform, and consequently a perfectly regular and perfectly flat tissue is produced. Hand work, however, is bound to be irregular." He then points out the advantage of this irregularity. " It presents," he observes, " an infinite succession of waves and little imperceptible unevennesses which catch the light and cast shadows." He illustrates his remarks by comparing the inside of a limpet shell with the inside of a sea-ear (*haliotis*). The one is a flat, dead white, while the other by its irregularities breaks the light into the prismatic colours we call mother o' pearl. Machine-made lace is the vapid, colourless, character-lacking limpet shell; hand-made lace the iridescent, light-scattering and character-presenting sea-ear. In short, machine lace is wanting in nacre.

One result of the competition brought about by machinery was to lead the Bucks **63. The Olney Crowns.** workers to devote special attention to the production of Baby Lace—that is to say, a narrow lace for ornamenting infants' caps.

The county of Buckingham and the most famous of English babies were (as we mentioned on page 30 when referring to St. Rumbald) in quite early times very closely connected ; but owing to the baby cap, the terms Buckingham and Baby were destined to become even more intimately associated.

The inventor of the Buckinghamshire "rounds" (see Plate 26), "horsehoes," and other shaped "crowns" of babies' caps was John Millward of Olney, who expended great skill upon them. On an earlier page we called him the Byron of the Lace World. The "crown" was his first great idea. He awoke and found himself famous. Those made by him from 1820 to 1828—and many of them are dated—are particularly beautiful and delicate in design.[1]

A baby's cap which must have fluttered the hearts of many ladies is in the possession of Mrs. W. W. Carlile. It is the work of Sarah Hall of Wooton,[2] and was made in 1820. The crown is hexagonal, the body is made up of point insertions and Jacob's ladder plaits, and the rim consists of point, the plaits in which form the words, " Long live the Babe."[3]

Great numbers of the Millward caps were exported to America until 1860, when the outbreak of the Civil War closed the Western market.

Another lace-designer of the period was Wil-

---

[1] The crown was surrounded by lawn, and that in its turn by edgings. The strings were of lawn.
[2] Northants.
[3] Compare the notes on Name Lace in Chapter 16, page 222.

liam Soul, a bosom friend of Millward. Soul, who affected a little straw hat and a very long coat, was in the habit as he walked of swinging his arms backwards and forwards with a regular motion; consequently, he[1] and Millward,[2] who, as already stated, had a club foot and generally wore a blue cut-away, made a curious couple as they passed through the street together, and they were usually alluded to by the profane as " Pendulum Bill " and " Dabfoot." We have reproduced a photograph (Plate 48) showing Millward, Soul, and three of their friends.

During the Regency (1810—1820) there was made in Northamptonshire a striking 64. Regency lace, with fillings of a bold character, Point. which was called Regency Point. (See Plate 25.) One peculiarity was that the plaits or leadworks, instead of being in the net ground as in the case of other Bucks Point laces, were dotted about the ornamental fillings, giving them a bizarre and very pleasing appearance. A similar pattern was being used at Padbury (Bucks) in 1891. (See Chapter 16.)

At this period the Northants workers were mostly employed in making *" Quillings ; "* and about 1830 *Insertions* found their way into popular

---

[1] Soul, who was also an astronomer and something of an author, died at Olney March 3rd, 1865. He left a biography in manuscript of Samuel Teedon, who figures so conspicuously in Cowper's letters.

[2] Millward, whose name is preserved in " Millard's Entry," a passage in the town that ran past his house, died about 1860, and was buried in the graveyard of the Independent meeting.

favour. The Bucks Point lace used by Queen
Victoria at her accession was designed by Millward, and made at Olney—the pattern being the
rose, the shamrock and the thistle ; and a similar
but narrower lace adorned the Christening Robe
of the Princess Royal. The Queen's interest in
Bucks Lace was further stimulated in 1845 during
a visit to Stowe House, when she inspected the
specimens submitted to her by the Duchess of
Buckingham.[1]

[1] In the Victoria and Albert Museum are preserved some very elaborate
and beautiful specimens of Bucks Point Lace made in the earlier half of
the 19th century.   See Plates 18, 19, 20.

CHAPTER XVI

THE MALTESE AND TORCHON PERIODS

The lace from the Midlands shown in the Exhibition of 1851 was all of the Bucks Point variety, the Gold Medal being won by an exhibit made at Olney from a parchment by Mr. John Millward, who had designed it for Messrs. Copestake and Co. (See Plate 27.)

65. Laceland in 1851.

When Queen Victoria visited the Exhibition Miss Elizabeth Clayson (afterwards Mrs. George Smith) of Olney had the honour of making this lace in her presence. The pillow was covered for the occasion with blue velvet edged with rose colour, and provided with rose-coloured bobbin bags. The Queen asked various questions about the work, one being, "Are the different coloured bobbins a guide to which thread you turn over ? " the answer being, of course, in the negative ; but, as we have already observed, the *shapes* of some of the bobbins *are* a guide—the trollies or gimps (which are larger than the others) being usually surrounded by loose rings, and the tallies (for making the tiny plaits) by tin bands.

There was also shown a Flounce made for the Queen from a copy[1] of the parchment described on page 71, the work of three sisters who lived at Stoke Goldington (Charlotte, Mary and Anne Warren).[2] It was of 14 slip thread, and it took 10 papers of pins, 26 score bobbins and 10 score trollies (gimps), that is, 750 bobbins in all.

A veil exhibited was the joint work of the mother, grandmother and great-grandmother of of a Stevington lace-maker; and the late Mr. George Hurst of Bedford contributed a piece of lace, the peculiarity of which consisted in the introduction of spun glass into the pattern.[3]

About this time there came into vogue a curiosity in the way of Bucks Point

66. Name, Monogram and Aglet Lace.

which was called *Name Lace*. Instead of a pattern some Christian name— George, John, Mary or Jane—was repeated among the net. As might be supposed, the fashion soon went out, for however fond a person might be of a sweetheart or husband named John, one wearied of seeing John, John, John[4] perpetually repeated. Six inches of him might please, but half a dozen yards led to the wish that " he was at Hanover ! "

---

[1] Both the original parchment and the copy are at Olney, the former being in the possession of Mr. G. Smith, the latter of Mrs. Joseph Peters.

[2] Charlotte, afterwards Mrs. Adams of Stoke Goldington; Mary, afterwards Mrs. Webb of Hartwell; Ann, afterwards Mrs. Garner of Hackleton.

[3] *Illustrated London News*, July 19th. 1851.

[4] A lace with this name was made at Olney about 1850 by the mother of Miss Hannah Kitchener.

At Calverton and Whaddon near Stony Stratford long bookmarkers, about an inch and a half wide, were made with mottoes such as, "Remember me," the spaces among the letters being filled with Bucks Point.[1] There was a turnpin edging in red silk.

A Bozeat lady tells me that about 1896 she saw on a pillow at Piddington (near Yardley Chase) a point lace in which an oak tree (probably Cowper's Oak) was repeated as the pattern. She remembered that it was about five inches wide, and that 16s. a yard was received for it, adding, " There was the stem of the tree as though you might take hold of it like that (suiting the action to the words) ; it had acorns, and it was the wonder of the village."

In the same period Bucks Point was occasionally made with two headsides, which were sometimes alike and sometimes different, though both as a rule were serpentine. This lace was used chiefly for insertions.

Monogram Lace, in the form of medallions— the sacred monogram I. H. S. from an antique pattern being most in demand—has been made for Mr. George Smith at Olney during the last thirty years, and sent to the Continent for ecclesiastical purposes. Outside the monogram are usually the dog tooth edgings, trails and plaits. The ornaments in the corner have raised plaits. *Bird*

[1] Mrs. Bull of Calverton has one.

Medallions—usually the Dove as emblem of the Holy Spirit—were made for the same purpose.

Aglet Lace, which had on the footside a row of aglets or eyelet-holes for the reception of a cord or a narrow ribbon, also had its little day. This lace is still occasionally made, both as an edging and as an insertion (in which case the eyelets are of course down the middle), and used for underclothing.

In 1851 the number of lace-makers in the principal lace-making counties was: Bucks, 7112; Northants, 5800; Beds, 3779; Oxford, 1197; Hunts, 442.[1]

About 1851 there was introduced from Malta
67. Maltese. 1851. the variety of lace called Maltese (see page 13), which made its special home in West Bedfordshire, whence it is sometimes called Bedfordshire Lace. It differs from the Maltese now made at Malta in several particulars. (1) The Maltese cross is absent.[2] The reason is not far to seek, for West Bedfordshire was a strong Evangelical centre, and consequently the use of the cross in the lace was discouraged. (2) The Wheat-ear (which the Maltese had borrowed from the Genoese) exchanged its pointed ends[3] for square ends, and its name for the Barley-

---

[1] These figures seem to apply to adults only. The census figures show that in 1861 there were in Beds making lace 6728 persons ; in 1881, 4792; in 1901, 1148.

[2] Now and again one sees it in very recent patterns made to order.

[3] In Bucks they are never made with pointed ends except to order. It is easier to make the square ends.

Plate 40

WINSLOW LACE INDUSTRY.   See p. 12.

1. OLD CRETE.   Width 2 inches.
2. Tray or toilet.   "The Feather"
3. Light-make Piombini.

Plate 41

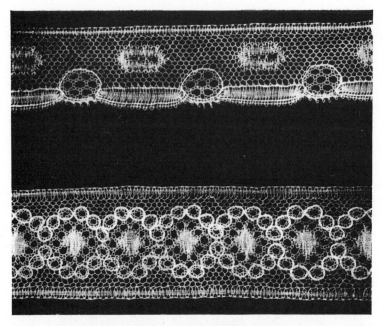

1.   POINT.   Made at Northampton.
2.   THE RING.   (Insertion.)   Made at Denton.

1.   HEXAGON INSERTION.   2.   THE ROSE PATTERN.

corn.   (3) The purl edge appeared.   (4) It contains fewer plaits.   The Maltese made in Bedfordshire and the Maltese made at Malta both differ from the original Maltese (or Genoese) in that the edges generally consist of gentle undulations, instead of vandykes and deep scallops.   (See Plates 28 to 32.)

Owing to its cheapness Maltese gradually drove Bucks Point from the market, and at the present day, where two or three persons make Bucks Point, fifty or a hundred make Maltese.   When first introduced into England Maltese was less open than it subsequently became, and birds, butterflies, etc., formed of cloth-work, were introduced into the pattern (see Plate 31), giving it some resemblance to Honiton.   Coiffures, black silk veils, parasol covers and lappets, all in Maltese, were for many years in great demand.

The principal Maltese laces are the following:

1. Legs and Turnpin Lace.   This is the lace with what is called the Maltese ground, which consists of legs forming diamond shaped openings.   The legs are ornamented with turnpins (purls or *picots*).   2. The Spider.   3. The Spider's Sister (Calverton names).   4. The Lady's Fancy (a Bozeat name).   5. The Tree of Plaits.   6. The Flower Pot.   7. The Beehive.   8. The Old Wheel.   9. The Plait.   10. The Rose and Leaf.   11. The Watch.   12. Little Dick, or the Turnpin Edge (a Bozeat name).   13. Little Dick's Mother (a Bozeat name), a narrow edging of plaits, which is also made as an insertion.   The Yardley Hastings name is Jacob's Ladder. 14. Little Dick and his Mother (a Bozeat name).

Thousands of yards of *Jacob's Ladder* have been

made at Yardley Hastings. Maltese sometimes has bold honeycomb fillings, and it has borrowed other features from Bucks Point. A mixture of Maltese and Bucks Point is made in many villages, and frequently *Raised Plaits*, sometimes called *Florentine Knots*, are introduced.

As Bucks Point had its enthusiasts so had Maltese, and one of them, who lived at Maidford near Towcester, went so far as to cause his garden gate to represent a Maltese insertion. Among the wonders of Maltese work was a shawl (2½ yds. square), made at Turweston, Northants, and exhibited some years ago in London. The parchment is still in the possession of a Turweston lace-maker.

For the Maltese Laces 3 and 4 slip gassed thread is generally used, or 6 or 8 slip for the finer patterns. In Bedfordshire the silk substitute D.M.C. No. 20 (the initials being those of Dollfus, Mieg & Co., an Alsace firm) has found favour with many workers, though for wearing qualities it cannot be compared with the specially manufactured gassed thread. Still it is the best of the sylkos, being more mellow than the others.

The Bucks Cottage Workers' Agency never use cotton in any of their productions, as laces made with it have no durability. When any new thread is offered to them, Mr. H. H. Armstrong always puts its claims to the test of soap and water. If a lace can win past and through this homely Scylla and Charybdis—the rock and whirlpool of the washtub—it has little else to fear.

Bucks Cluny (an offshoot of Maltese) which next came into fashion obtained its name on account of its having been 68. Cluny copied from certain old Italian laces and preserved in the Cluny Museum of Auvergne. Antiquities in Paris. It is made of linen thread either white or ecru, and its principal characteristic is the Divided Trail. In Maltese Laces the trail is always filled. In some of the Cluny laces made at Paulerspury wire ground of a very large mesh has been introduced; and in others, made at High Wycombe, point ground of gigantic mesh has been similarly used. Cluny, the material of which is linen, being a heavy and substantial lace, is used for curtain and table-cloth edgings—indeed as furniture lace generally, and almost anything liable to much friction. Favourite patterns are the Wheel and the Greek Pattern. (See Plate 33.) Auvergne Lace, another offshoot of Maltese, was also for a time popular.

Blonde Lace made of both white and black silk was introduced from Caen into Bedfordshire and Buckinghamshire about 1860 by Mr. E. Godfroy. The *cordonnet*, which is of thicker silk, was called in these counties the trolly.[1] (See Plate 25.)

---

[1] Thus the trolly takes the place of gimp in Blonde laces. Gimp is linen thread.

Between 1860 and 1864, and perhaps earlier,
69. The Floral Designs of 1860—1864. Mr. Sargent of Sandy, and other manufacturers, introduced from Paris an immense number of Floral Designs of a striking character. In some of them Point Ground occurred, and in others the various parts of the pattern were connected by legs. Further progress in lace designing was brought about by the Exhibition of 1862, when leaves in imitation of Nature were mingled with the Oriental arabesque of the old Maltese lace. The lace exhibits in this Exhibition, which were almost entirely Maltese, included a black silk shawl and a black silk flounce, designed by Mr. E. Godfroy, and made by the two Misses French of Buckingham. In 1864, according to *Olney and the Lace-makers*,[1] which appeared that year, the specialities of North Bucks were, in addition to black and white laces made by the yard, collars and cuffs, coiffures, lappets and parasol covers.

About 1870 there began to be made throughout
70. Yak and Gold Thread, 1840—1890. Buckinghamshire and Bedfordshire, especially at Newport Pagnell, High Wycombe and Stagsden, a coarse, strong bobbin lace, the material of which seems at first to have been obtained from the Yak animal. Most of it, however, was made of Yorkshire wool. The designs of Yak, as it was

[1] By Miss Elizabeth Wilson.

Plate 42

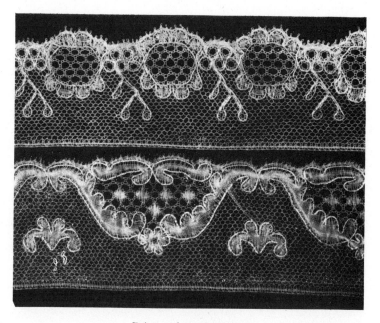

1. Point made at Northampton.
2. THE BEEHIVE, filled with Mayflower Ground. Point Ground on the footside. Made at Paulerspury.

THE WEDDING BELL PATTERN. (BUCKS POINT.)

The Bell itself and other parts of pattern are filled with Mayflower Ground. On each side of it and elsewhere are spaces filled with Wire Ground (Kat Stitch).

(Lent by Mrs. Markham, Dallington.)

Plate 43

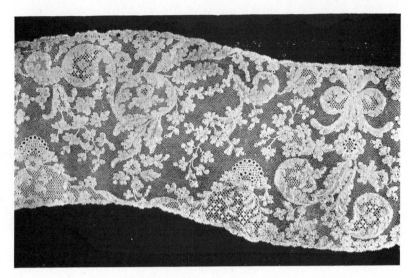

BUCKS POINT. Made near Olney.

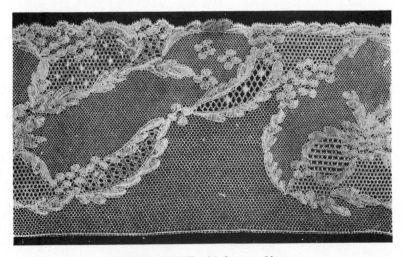

BUCKS POINT. Made near Olney.

called, were geometrical, being copied from Reticella and silk Maltese Guipure.

One of the results of its introduction was the gradual extinction of the Black Silk Lace industry, the centre of which at that time was Haddenham near Aylesbury. High Wycombe obtained a name for its wheel-like Yak design, the Town Trot, which was made in enormous quantities.[1]

A brown lace with blue plaits made in widths of two, three and four inches, which was used for dresses, valances, and for decorating furniture, occupied many pillows at Newton Blossomville and other villages in North Bucks. At Carlton (Beds) a very heavy worsted lace of every imaginable colour was made in widths from half an inch to a foot, but the black variety of Yak was most in demand. (See Plate 48.) The fashion, however, for all kinds of Yak soon declined, and eventually became almost extinct, except in respect to the cream variety which is still sold for children's clothes.[2]

A little later *Norman Lace*, made of worsted of various colours, was produced in the Newport Pagnell district, the principal market for it being the United States.[3]

Gold Thread Lace was made at Newport Pagnell, Cranfield, Bolnhurst and other towns and

---

[1] In North Bucks Mr. E. Godfroy alone used three hundred pounds weight of wool per month.

[2] Gibbs's *History of Aylesbury*, p. 622 ; Bull's *History of Newport Pagnell*, p. 196.

[3] Bull's *History of Newport Pagnell*, p. 196.

villages about 1880, but the workers disliked
making it because it " used to twipper" (curl up)
on the pillow, and they were not sorry when the
demand ceased. In 1895 the workers of Lacey
Green made some Gold Lace for the Duchess of
York.

Torchon Lace had for many years been made
on the Continent, but the English
71. Torchon.
people did not take kindly to it until
the end of the 19th century. " Torchon," a French
word, means a dishcloth or any other fabric of
coarse material, this name and that of Beggars'
Lace having been given to it in derision by the
makers of the finer fabrics. Certainly, Torchon
has a coarse appearance, but when well made it
has, to use the words of an admirer, " a beauty
and dignity all its own." Then, too, it can be devoted to uses that would be quite unsuitable to the
delicate Bucks Point and the more open Maltese.
Moreover, it has in its favour one very important
virtue, namely, its cheapness. The principal
stitches[1] in this lace are :

1. Half-stitch (in some districts also called No-stitch).
2. Whole-stitch (Cloth-stitch).
3. Torchon, with 1, 2 or 3 twists between the pins.
4. Twisted Half-stitch, with 1, 2 or 3 twists between the pins.
5. Rose, with half-stitch within each set of four pins.
6.   ,,   whole-stitch   ,,   ,,   ,, .
7.   ,,   twisted half-stitch   ,,   ,,

[1] Additional information respecting the stitches can be found in *Dentelles
aux fuseaux*, published by the D. M. C. people ; and in *English Pillow
Laces* by Miss M. Maidment.

No. 5 is by some writers called Double Rose.
All the Rose stitches are at Olney called "Fours."
Among the devices introduced are the Spider,[1]
which often occurs in a ground of Torchon Stitch
and Plaits, which, as in Maltese, are sometimes
worked into the ground and sometimes laid upon
a closer foundation, when they are known as
Leaves, *Tufts* or *Shells*. In most Torchons the Fan
and the Diamond designs are seen, and the edges
are vandyked or scalloped. The pattern is often
in parts outlined with stouter cord or coarse
coloured thread, and sometimes the raised leaves
and other parts of the pattern are also in colours.
A collection of specimens of these partially
coloured laces,—and they are very pretty,[2]—the
colours used being red, green, blue and amber, may
be seen in the Museum at Northampton. They
formed part of a pattern book that belonged to
the Northampton lace-buyer, Mr. Joseph Foddy.[3]
At Weston Underwood some of the workers add
a purl-edge to the torchon, in order that it may not
be mistaken for machine lace. The purl-edge, it
seems, cannot be made by machinery.

Some of the old European Torchons, including
"Old Naples," are made by the workers of the
Winslow (Bucks) Lace Industry. The variety of
Torchon made by Jewish workers in Syria exhibits

---

[1] Sometimes called the wheel, though it is very unwheel-like.
[2] Some were the work of Emily Clark, Ashton, near Roade.
[3] There are in the Museum 1400 specimens altogether from Mr. Foddy's
Pattern Book. One is of lace made with human hair.

as a peculiarity " the knotting stitch." Torchon is usually made of Irish linen, Nos. 28, 35, 60, 80, 100 and 120 finding most favour. The Bedfordshire workers are partial to D. M. C. No. 20. For illustration of an early Torchon see Plate 37.

Lace Pelerines and *Berthes*[1] (ornamental capes

72. Berthes, Medallions, Fichus. worn over the shoulders with evening dress) came into vogue about 1870, ousting the berthes in muslin appliqué[2]

which during the previous twenty years had dominated the market. *Fichus* made of Point or Maltese—the one called the Marie Antoinette taking the lead—were introduced about 1885 ; and *Medallions* or *Motifs*, which were used for the making up of blouses and fichus (being either let in or appliquéd), made their appearance a little later. These medallions, which are often Point Ground, French Ground, or Honeycomb, are made almost any shape, but rounds, squares and oblongs find most favour.

Owing to the influence of the various Factory

73. The Closing of the Lace Schools, 1871—1880. Acts and the legislation for Elementary Education, the many lace-making schools in the three counties were obliged to terminate their existence.

In 1871, for example, there were three at Kislingbury near Northampton. In 1879 all

---

[1] In Bucks called Berthas.

[2] They were usually appliqued on Brussels net. See *Illustrated Exhibitor*, 1852, p. 112.

were closed, and the same tale could be told of other villages.

Light on the condition of the Lace industry in the Midlands in 1891 is afforded by Mr. Alan S. Cole's " Report " of that date " on Northampton-shire, Bucks and Bedfordshire Lace-making." Mr. Cole found that in most of the villages which he visited the laces principally made were Bucks Point, Maltese and Torchon; that in many instances the designs were poor, and that in con-sequence " the average earning of the pillow lace-maker " was " very low." The lace was for the most part made by elderly women.   At *Spratton*, *Paulerspury* and *Wicken* he found several " pillows at work upon Auvergne and Cluny styles," for which many lace-buyers just then showed a preference.

At *Padbury* (Bucks) he found fine thread Bucks Point being made, and the illustration which he gives of it shows it to have been the same as that which at Brackley (Northants) was called Regency Point (see Plate 25), with the exception that it had plaits (small crosses) in the net ground.   At *Lacey Green* the workers were making in addition to narrow edgings of Bucks Point various coloured coarse thread laces suitable for curtains.   At *Ridgmont* (Beds) patterns were in use that were brought over by the French refugees in 1798. Some had the point ground with the Mechlin style of pattern, and others were Point and Maltese combined.

Among the English authors who have written charmingly on lace is John Ruskin. " If you think of it," he says, "you will find the whole value of lace as a possession depends on the fact of its having a beauty which has been the reward of industry and attention. . . . The real good of a piece of lace is that it should show first, that the designer of it had a pretty fancy; next, that the maker of it had fine fingers; lastly, that the wearer of it has worthiness or dignity enough to obtain what is difficult to obtain, and common sense enough not to wear it on all occasions."

CHAPTER XVII

LACE-MAKING TO-DAY

From the remarks made in the immediately preceding chapters it will have been judged, and correctly, that the Lace industry in the Midlands had fallen 74. The Lace Associations. into the sear, the yellow leaf. There were still good workers who obtained fair remuneration for their pains, but almost everywhere there was discouragement and a falling-off, and poor pay became the rule. The people, however, clung pathetically to their pillows, but then came the unkindest cut of all. The quality, it seems, were unable at this time to obtain maid-servants, and the word was sent round that the difficulty could best be met by ceasing to purchase lace.

The darkest hour, however, is always that before the dawn, and so the Midland workers found it. The pioneers in the attempt to revive the industry in Bucks were Mrs. Forrest of Grymsdyke, Princes Risborough, and the Countess of Buckinghamshire, whose labours extended from about 1880 to 1896.

Others who laboured indefatigably in Buckinghamshire were Mrs. W. W. Carlile (wife of

Mr. W. W. Carlile, M.P. for North Bucks), Miss Burrowes (author of *Buckingham Lace*, by T. E. D. S.), Lucy Marian (second daughter of the late Lord Addington), who was the means of leading the workers of Mid-Bucks to produce the heavy old Italian and Greek Guipures and other laces; the Hon. Rose Hubbard, Mrs. (now Lady) Inglefield, whose efforts on behalf of the Belgian lace-workers are so well known; Mr. J. Raftery, the successor of Mr. E. Godfroy; and Mr. George Smith, the successor of Mr. John Millward.

In Bedfordshire Lady Ampthill, Lady Mackenzie, Mrs. Prothero, Mrs. Fitzpatrick, Miss Haines, Mr. C. Lester, Mr. T. Lester, Mr. Thomas Coombs and others have done excellent work.

In Northamptonshire the prominent names are Mrs. J. B. Harrison (wife of the Rev. J. B. Harrison), Mrs. Chettle, Miss Sams, Mrs. Roberts, who collected patterns from all over Europe, Miss M. E. Roberts, Miss C. C. Channer, Mrs. Bostock, Miss Alice Dryden (now Mrs. Marcon), Mr. Leopold Stanton, Lady Sarah Spencer, Miss Bouverie and Mrs. Markham (wife of Major C. A. Markham).

In Huntingdonshire the most indefatigable workers have been Mrs. Fydell Rowley, Mrs. Janet Garrood and Mrs. J. E. Whitehead. Oxfordshire can boast of Mrs. Nind, Miss Sivewright, Miss C. M. Pope and Mrs. A. J. Comber.

The difficulties which had to be faced by these

Plate 44

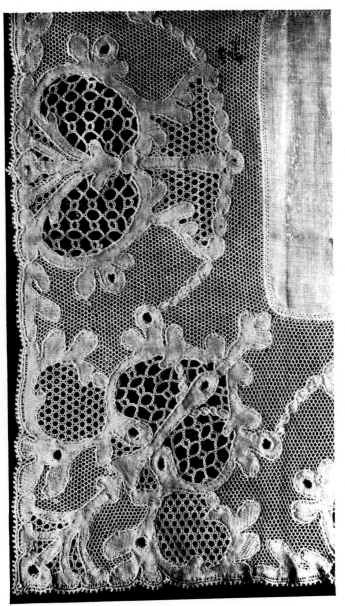

BUCKS POINT HANDKERCHIEF, WITH VARIOUS FILLINGS.

Plate 45

SAMPLER. By Miss M. Maidment. See p. 244.

Showing nearly all the stitches in Honiton Lace.

pioneers will be understood from the remarks made by Mrs. W. W. Carlile, in the *Empire Review* (Jan., 1903) : " Such lace-makers," she says, " as still plied their trade, had for the most part given up the fine Half-stitch [Bucks Point] as it is locally called, for coarse Maltese and Torchon edgings ; and those who still clung to the Bucks Point worked it in cotton with clumsy thick pins and cardboard for parchment. In the same way the old graceful flowing patterns had been abandoned for stiff and clumsy patterns devised by the workers themselves,—monotonous repetitions of one conventional flower or leaf utterly devoid of artistic merit, that showed more plainly than all else to what a low ebb the fortunes of lace-making had fallen."

I myself have seen lace-makers using cardboard patterns so worn that in places you could put your thumb through. These holes they used to " flubber "[1] over. So, whether the pattern was correct or incorrect, the work was bad.

Many of the fine old parchments had been burnt as rubbish, or melted down for glue. Inquiry, however, led to the production of a large number which, by a miracle as it were, had been preserved by some of the older workers.

Mrs. Harrison principally directed her efforts towards preserving and renewing the best old

---

[1] A variant of " fludder," to muddle over, used at North Marston and other villages.

designs and to ensure the use of proper materials, and she arranged for the sale of the lace direct from the worker to the purchaser. To her is also due the credit of having persuaded the manufacturers of thread and pins to produce, once more, linen thread fine enough for Pillow Point, and pins to correspond. Under her direction a very beautiful fan was made by Miss Gibbins of Paulerspury for Queen Alexandra, the ornaments being Her Majesty's favourite flower, the lily of the valley, her initials—A. R., and an Imperial Crown.

Mrs. Harrison was continuously helped and encouraged by her sister, Miss Sams of Paulerspury, Mrs. Moffatt of Goodrich Court, Ross on Wye, and Mrs. Wentworth Vernon of Stoke Bruern. The very beautiful lace on the frontal and pulpit-fall used at Paulerspury Church was also made under her direction.

Thanks to the efforts of the various ladies we have mentioned Associations were formed in Bucks, Beds, Northants (the Midland Lace Association) and Hunts, businesses built up, exhibitions held, and gold medals and other awards gained, and thousands of workers have been given employment. In their efforts to establish lace-making classes in the Elementary Schools of the various counties the Associations have received the support of the County Councils.

For photographs of two of these classes held at Cranfield and Olney see Plates 35 and 36.

The year 1906 was marked by the establishment at Stoke Goldington by Mr. H. H.
Armstrong of what is known as *The* **75. The Bucks Cottage Workers' Agency.**
Bucks Cottage Workers' Agency. Mr.
Armstrong's object was to set up a
sound business organization, to visit personally the
cottagers in the neighbouring towns and villages,
to distribute parchments and other materials, and
to arrange for local buyers in the various districts. Every specimen sent in was closely exam-
ined, defects were pointed out, and suggestions
for improvement made. By following this course
he was able to bring the lace to a 'higher standard
of workmanship. Lace-makers who had long
previously given up their lace work, again brought
out their pillows, and being assured of immediate
sales and remuneration, put their energies once
more into the delicate and artistic occupation of
their youth. Persistent advertising followed,
ladies' magazines and other publications perused
by ladies being chiefly used; and gradually through
careful and individual attention to every inquiry,
a connection sprang up which included many good
county families. Ladies recommended the lace
to friends, and a sound foundation was in this
manner laid.

In 1909, owing to the growth of the business,
the Agency removed to Olney, being impelled
thereto not only on account of postal and railway
advantages, but also because of the town's associ-

ation with the poet Cowper, whose name is so
intimately associated with the lace industry. A
large building was purchased, and experience soon
proved the wisdom of the choice. The industry
being carried on under more favourable conditions
went forward by leaps and bounds, orders arriving
by every mail, not only from homes in the British
Isles, but from all parts of the civilized world. In
1911 the Agency was awarded a gold medal at the
Festival of Empire and Imperial Exhibition held
in that year at the Crystal Palace.

We have already spoken in praise of the
designer, the bobbin-maker, the ladies
76. Skilled Lace-makers. who have taken upon themselves to
revive the Lace Industry, and others
to whom lovers of lace are indebted. But after
all, the highest praise is due to the workers—
those who, with an indefatigability that is even
wonderful, produce the lace. In every town and
village some names are held in special reverence—
those of the producers of marvellous pieces of lace
intended for royalty or some other distinguished
patron. All who knew these workers speak of them
with pride. Praise, too, must be bestowed on those
who are teaching the younger generation to make
lace. Every teacher, whether in the home or the
public school, who is instructing the children in
this delightful art is a benefactress of her country.
We may also mention that the mother of the
late Rev. C. H. Spurgeon was a skilled lace-
maker.

It is sincerely hoped that one of the results of the publication of this work will be to benefit the lace-makers by increasing their earnings. Dr. Lulham of Stonehouse, Gloucestershire, has written eloquently and feelingly on this subject, and it is trusted that his efforts, and the efforts of others, will, to utilize his expression, make " more satisfactory the economic position of the workers." Lace-making has never been a well paid industry. The worker fared best in the Yak period, when she could make ten shillings a week. At the present time few lace-makers, it is to be feared, can earn more than five shillings a week.

There are good collections of inscribed bobbins, of specimens of lace and other objects relative to the industry, in the Cowper and Newton Museum, Olney, the Bucks County Museum at Aylesbury, and the Museum at Northampton.

The Pillow Lace industry has almost disappeared from East Anglia, but Honiton Lace is made in parts of Norfolk, where it is encouraged by the Diss Lace Association (founded by Mrs. Thomas Slack) the object of which is " to supply work, in their own homes, to married women and girls unable to go into service either through delicate health or deformity." The lace is made in " small sprigs " which are afterwards joined together or mounted on net, with the result of many beautiful

77. East Anglia and Sussex.

flounces, scarves, fichus, veils, fans and other articles.[1]

At Great Waltham, Essex, is a Pillow Lace School which owes its origin to the efforts of Miss Tufnell of Langleys ; but the best known lace centre in Essex is that of Coggeshall, the town of the Tambour Lace industry which originated with a French refugee named Draggo, who settled there in 1812. The stitches of this lace are made with a kind of small crochet hook on machine net stretched on an oblong frame, and very beautiful designs have been shown at various exhibitions. For long the industry languished, but recently owing to the introduction of improved patterns a new era of prosperity has set in.[2]

Winchelsea, Sussex, was once a lace centre, and in 1894 an attempt was made to revive the industry.

Good work has been done in Wilts by the President (the Countess of Radnor) 78. Wilts. and the patronesses of " Ye Olde Downton Lace Industry." The lace is similar to Bucks Point (indeed the same prickings are used), but the net *(bar-work*, as they call it) is worked from the head to the foot without a pin in each mesh. It is only at the head and the foot that it is pinned. Another characteristic of Downton Lace is its straight edge.

---

[1] An illustrated account of the Diss industry appeared in *Hearth and Home*, February 6th, 1908.

[2] Coggeshall Lace is practically the same as the Tambour variety of Limerick, q.v.

A similar lace, made at Malmsbury, was for long used chiefly for babies' and old ladies' caps. " My grandmother," writes Miss G. M. Peat, of Fenstanton Manor, "used to put over six yards in the box pleats round the front alone." The revival of the Malmsbury industry is owing to the efforts of the Countess of Suffolk, in whose classes are made " The Turkey's Tail," " The Spectacles," " The Button," and other laces.

On page 35 we spoke of the two earlier stages of Devonshire Lace, namely, 1. *The Artistic Pattern and Net*, in which the 79. **Devon.** sprigs or patterns were united by net, and 2. *The Artistic Pattern and Guipure Stage*, in which they were united by purl-pin-bars. The work in both of these stages was beautiful. To them succeeded :

3. *The Ugly Guipure and Ugly Appliqué Stage.* The invention of Heathcote's machine-made net in 1809 caused great depression in the Devonshire Lace industry ; and in order to compete with the machine work the lace-makers produced what may be called a truly hideous fabric, which consisted merely of a medley of badly drawn and made sprigs joined by purl-pin-bars. The sprigs indeed were put in anywhere, and all rules of design were disregarded. In some districts the sprigs were sewn on to machine net and called Honiton Appliqué, which rivalled the Guipures in ugliness.

4. *The Present Stage.* Recently a return has

been made to the first two stages. The sprigs are sewn on blue paper and connected with a coarse net made with a needle instead of with purl-pin-bars; but Guipure and Appliqué work is also done in some of the villages. It must be borne in mind that all Honiton Lace is worked face to the pillow. In order to protect it, and also to prevent the pins in the finished work from catching in the threads from which the bobbins hang, *sliders* of horn are used.

The honour of being the first to introduce a more artistic taste in respect to this lace belongs to Queen Adelaide, whose good work was continued by Queen Victoria, who gave the order for her wedding lace to the workers of Beer and neighbourhood. The same villages are now, we understand, occupied with an order for our present Queen, the laces being of the best quality and design.

In the sampler[1] by Miss Maidment which forms one of our illustrations (see Plate 45), nearly all the stitches in Honiton lace are shown, and their names are indicated in the accompanying "key." (Plate 46.) The following is the list of the stitches:—

BRAID STITCHES.

1. Whole stitch "clothing."
2. Half-stitch.

---

[1] Miss Maidment has kindly allowed us to take the photograph of this sampler from a *Book of Instructions for the Working of English Pillow Laces* which she is preparing for publication.

Plate 46

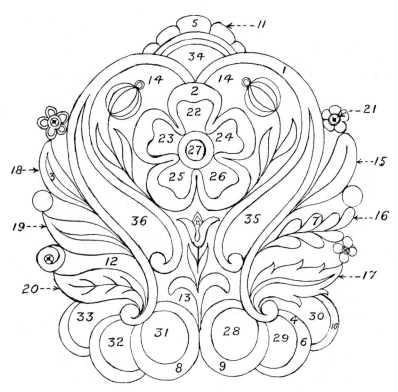

KEY TO HONITON SAMPLER. See p. 244.

Outline Guide to stitches.

Plate 47

MISS WARREN, A STOKE GOLDINGTON WORKER.

3. Mittens (vein of leaf No. 18).
4. Plain hole.
5. Four pin bud.
6. Six pin hole.
7. Ten stick raised (leaf 16).
8. Another six pin hole.
9. Zig-zag holes.
10. Line formed of twisted leaders.
11. Half and whole stitches outlined with, and divided by, gimp thread; purl pins on outer edge.

GROUNDING STITCHES.

12. Purl pin bars.
13. Point d' Angleterre net.
14. Trolly net.

LEAF TREATMENTS.

15. Half and whole stitches with centre vein of sewings.
16. Leaf worked in sections (called taps) in raised work.
17. Serrated leaf of whole stitch with vein of ten stick and cutworks.
18. Whole stitch leaf with vein of mittens.
19. Whole and half-stitch leaf with vein of cutworks and winkie pins.
20. Half-stitch leaf with raised veins.

FILLINGS.

21. Cutworks or Leadworks (centre of small flowers).
22. Diamond.   23. No pin.
24. Brick.   25. Pin.
26. Cushion.   27. Cart-wheel.
28. Blossom.   29. Point d' Esprit.
30. Double ground.   31. Toad in the hole.
32. Swing.   33. Purl.

34. Double ground and cutworks.
35. Bars and cutworks.
36. Bars and cutworks with holes.

Roughly speaking, the Honiton country consists of that strip of Devonshire coast stretching from Seaton to Exmouth, and including the town of Honiton and the villages of Beer, Branscombe, Sidbury and East Budleigh.

Among those who have applied themselves of recent years to the extension of the Devonshire industry are :—Mrs. Collier,[1] Miss Audrey Trevelyan, Mrs. Allen, Mrs. Freeman Roper, the Misses Tebbs, Mrs. Fowler and Mrs. Bernard.

In various parts of England that are not in the great lace-making centres, lace-making is taught in schools; as for example in the School for Special Instruction, Normanton Road, Derby, where the pupils make Russian Lace and Cluny, and in the Plymouth Municipal Art School.

A *Filet Lace*[2] (Guipure d' Art) Industry has been started at Odiham, Hants, by Lady Palmer, with the assistance of Miss Alice M. Healey.

Useful work has been done by the " National Association for the Organisation of the Hand-made Lace Industry in England," which was founded by Miss Isemonger, Mr. Alan Cole, C.B., and Mr. Charles Lee, J.P., of the well known firm

[1] An article on the Beer industry appeared in *The Lady of Fashion*, March 15th, 1906.
[2] Also called *lacis* or darned netting.

of Charles Lee & Son, 100 Wigmore Street. Arrangements were made in 1911 for an "All-British Shopping Week," and Mr. Lee placed a large salon at the disposal of the various Associations. The Exhibition was held from March 23rd to March 30th, and all the leading Lace Associations of England were represented.

The principal Irish "laces" are Carrickmacross, Limerick, Irish Point and Irish Crochet. It will be best to take them in the order of their inception.

80. Carrick-macross. 1820.

Of Carrickmacross, which is not, strictly speaking, lace, but an embroidery made in the hand, there are two kinds :—

(1) *Appliqué*, in which the design is made in Indian ink on stiff smooth paper. Over the design is placed machine-made net, and over the net fine muslin. The three are firmly tacked together. The pattern is then traced with close sewing stitches taken through both net and muslin and also over a thicker outlining cord, after which the work is released from the design, the muslin is cut away outside the outline, and fancy stitches are worked on the net ground. Great care is needed in order to avoid cutting the net.

(2) *Guipure*, which is made with muslin upon which a design has been traced. It has no net foundation, and the muslin is of closer texture than that used in appliqué. The design having been " corded," the centres are cut away and filled with

open stitches and wheels, and other parts that are
cut away are united with buttonhole bars.

The two varieties of Carrickmacross are some-
times happily combined in one piece of work.[1]
Carrickmacross is made chiefly in the south of the
County of Monaghan.

Limerick Lace was first made at Nottingham in
the early 19th century, the designs of
81. **Limerick.** Lille and other Continental towns
1829.
being copied, and the industry was
transferred to Ireland in 1829. It is of two
varieties:

(1) *Run*, in which the pattern is embroidered
with a running or darning stitch on machine-made
net stretched on a frame—the result being a very
light looking and dainty fabric.

(2) *Tambour*, for which the machine-made net is
also first stretched on a frame. The pattern is
embroidered with a chain stitch done with a short
crochet hook, and the effect, though very pretty,
is much heavier than that of run work. Sometimes the two varieties of Limerick are mixed—
the outline being Tambour and the other parts
Run.

Thus neither Carrickmacross nor Limerick is
lace in the strict sense of the term. Each is an

---

[1] In Carrickmacross there are no turnings taken to the applied muslin,
consequently it is not a durable lace. It may drop to pieces after once or
twice washing, and it has so decided a reverse side that its use is limited.
The Guipure variety is even less durable than the Appliqué, consequently
there are very few so-called " old " pieces in existence other than specimens under glass.—*Miss Maidment.*

embroidery, that is to say, an enrichment of an existing material. The stitches used for the fillings[1] in Carrickmacross and Limerick are the same.

Limerick lace is now made chiefly in the neighbourhood of the city of Limerick.

Irish Point, which is founded upon Italian models, was first introduced into Ireland by the Sisters of the Presentation Convent, Youghal, County Cork, as a means of alleviating the distress caused by the Great Famine of 1846—50. Produced entirely by the needle, it is at once the most difficult to make and by far the most beautiful of all the Irish laces. The richness of its designs and the remarkable variety of its stitches, " by which contrast and, as it were, a play of light and shade are obtained," have extorted admiration from all quarters. Irish Point is now made throughout the whole of that part of Ireland which extends from Wexford to Kerry, but that produced at Youghal is considered the best.

82. Irish Point [Youghal.] 1846.

In the district in the south of Donegal and north of Fermanagh, of which Innishmacsaint is the centre, is made a Rose Point lace which resembles the Venetian lace of that name, and a similar fabric is made at Cappoquin, County Waterford.

[1] Fancy stitches on the net.

Irish Crochet also owes its origin to the Great
Famine. It seems to have been first
made at the Adelaide Crochet School
at Cork, founded by the philanthropic
Mrs. Susanna Meredith[1] (1823—1901),
and the work was subsequently carried
on in convents and by private enterprise. The
city of Cork became the great centre of the
industry. It is now made throughout the county
of Cork and in parts of the adjoining counties.

What Mrs. Meredith did for the South of
Ireland, Mrs. W. C. Roberts attempted to do for
the Centre. At her home at Thornton, County
Kildare, she adapted a number of the beautiful
designs of old Venetian Needle-point and other
laces to the simplicities of crochet. She did not
meet with the success anticipated, but one of her
workers drifted to Clones, in Monaghan, where she
came into touch with Mrs. Hand, wife of the
Rector, and the seed that produced only a thin
crop at Thornton led to a plentiful harvest at
Clones. Having gathered together the young
girls of the neighbourhood, Mrs. Hand gave them
their first lessons in the art, and owing to her
insistence on good work Clones crochet came to
be unsurpassed for excellence. The principal
crochets made at Clones are Spanish, Jesuit,
Greek and Venetian.

[1] See Mrs. Meredith's work, *The Lace-makers,* and *Susanna Meredith*
by M. A. Lloyd, 1903.

Few prettier pictures could be imagined than that of the dark, merry-eyed colleens busy at their crochet, their only implements being the fine little needle projecting from the home-made cane or boxwood haft and the reel of Irish made cotton. Such pictures may be seen, for the industry has spread to almost every part of Ireland, in odorous old gardens, in front of cottage doors, by the crumbling ruins of old abbeys and wicked looking 16th century castles, in the neighbourhood of those mysterious raths,[1] and under the shadow of those equally mysterious round towers which have baffled all attempts of antiquary and historian to arrive at their origin, and in the valleys of that wild and weird region of legend and song which embraces the mountain gorges, the woods and the Lakes of Killarney. This Irish work, whether in the way of "bishops," "motifs," theatre bags or what you will, goes all over the world. Thousands of these articles have been purchased to meet actual needs, but many thousands also have been acquired, especially by Americans, merely out of love for the Island of the shamrock and all that to them the shamrock means.

At Ardee in Louth the industry of Pearl Tatting gives employment to a number of persons, and at Birr (Parsonstown), Kings County, a lace of the same character as Honiton occupies a few workers.

An important Exhibition of Irish Lace was

[1] Ancient "Mound Houses."

held at the Mansion House, London, in 1883, and in connection with it was issued *A History of the Industry, with Illustrations and a Map showing the Districts where the Lace is produced.*

Perhaps the most successful Exhibition of recent years was that held under the auspices of the *Daily Mail* at the Royal Horticultural Hall, Vincent Square, Westminster, March 9th—14th, 1908, when a charming catalogue was issued under the editorship of Mr. J. T. Herbert Baily, editor of the *Connoisseur*, to which Mr. Alan S. Cole, C.B., supplied an article on " Hand-made Laces of To-day."

Messrs. Robinson & Cleaver in their booklet, *Irish Hand-made Lace*, have the following note on the care of Lace : " Needle-point and bobbin lace should be kept in a warm, dry atmosphere, as much damage is caused by cold and damp. When not in use, lace should be taken out of the drawer, shaken, and frequently exposed to air, and the receptacle should be kept dust proof if possible."

From the same pamphlet we take the following useful remarks on " How to distinguish between Hand-made and Machine-made Lace." The threads in the latter " have a twisted and compressed look which is never seen in hand or pillow lace. If there are raised ornaments in machine-made lace the padding is worked over and over straight. In hand-made the stitches always slope.

Plate 48

AN OLD OLNEY LACE-MANUFACTURER

AND HIS FRIENDS.

Standing (left to right): John Millward, Lace Manufacturer; William Soul,
Lace Designer; Rev. James Simmons, Baptist Minister. Sitting:
Wm. Killingworth, Watch Maker; Thos. Aspray, Doctor (London).
Date about 1850. See pp. 113 & 218.

YAK LACE. The colour is chocolate. See p. 228.

Plate 49

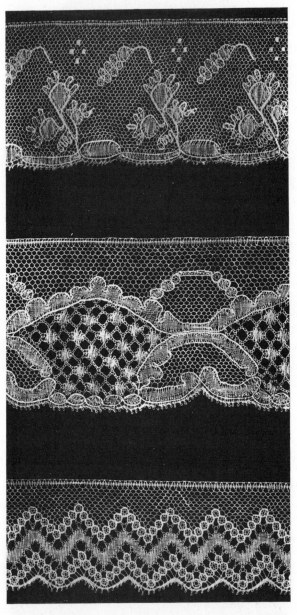

1. THE WHEAT-EAR AND CORNFLOWER. Point made at Winslow.
2. THE CROWN.   Point made at Northampton.
3. THE ZIG-ZAG.   Point made at Northampton.

If a thread in machine-made lace is unravelled it comes out easily; in needle-point on the contrary, frequent knots impede the unravelling of the thread; and in bobbin lace the unravelling is a tedious process." It is well also to examine lace with a magnifying glass, and the gimp in particular should be scrutinized. Needle-point gimp will be found to be made of loop threads; in the case of pillow lace the gimp is plaited.

Our task is done, and these words are being written just after the conclusion of the terrible War of 1914—1918. This war will probably bring about one of the **84. Conclusion.** great historical changes in lace-making—perhaps the greatest since the Revocation of the Edict of Nantes. The refugees from Belgium brought great quantities of lace with them. Their stitches and methods are likely to become mixed with ours, and our designing will probably be largely influenced. Strangely enough, the immediate result of this terrible event, which it was supposed would kill the lace industry outright, was in reality to give it an impetus. Certainly in our own great cities, and also in the great cities of America, lace has been more prominent than ever in the windows of the leading business houses. So unusual was the demand for it that indignant articles appeared in the Press denouncing so much extravagance at a time when many nations were engaged in a life and death struggle. We heard of " corsets

formed of priceless old rose point; of chemises
'encrusted' (the American term) with the choicest
laces of Buckinghamshire, of camisoles entirely
made of the rarest Alençon." Crêpe de chine and
other cobwebby materials, well-nigh lost in seas of
lace so delicate that it rose or fell with a breath,
seemed to be sought after as they never were.
There was an orgy of diaphanous garments, the
finest lace, silks, ribbons, anything, everything that
beauty unbalanced has in all ages coveted. The
lamentation was wanting in novelty. The prophets,
from Isaiah with his classic third chapter down to
George Fox, Henry Smith and many a later, have
denounced all this vanity; and yet it is possible to
protest too much. A few persons may occasionally, by putting costly fabrics to purposes for
which they were never intended, show themselves
lamentably deficient in taste, but the commonsense
of the vast majority of English and American
women will scarcely be affected by such prepos-
terous conduct. Ruskin's golden dictum, "Moderation is the girdle of beauty," is still the creed of the
ladies of both England and America; and we may
safely assume that they will use lace with the discretion that is never wanting in a cultured mind.
That in expressing their admiration for the
choicer specimens of it they will be moderate in
their language is more than can be expected or
wished. We conclude, as we commenced, by
asserting that "Lace-making is an art," and the

votaries of art never yet loved in moderation. In all matters artistic, indeed, whatever may be said of other pursuits, the Road of Excess leads, as William Blake says, to the Palace of Wisdom.

THE END.

APPENDICES

APPENDIX I.

INSCRIPTIONS ON BOBBINS.

Subsequent to the printing of this book the following notes have reached us :—

Miss Margaret Dickson of Reading writes : " I have one bobbin which was sent as a round robin present from the lads of a village to a flirt. The inscription is : ' If you don't love me leave me alone.' I also have a trolly bobbin with the pathetic inscription written in straight lines : ' You are the sweetest girl this village does afford and you don't love me—Aaron Lord.' "

Miss C. M. Tyson of Summertown, Oxford, sends the following inscriptions :

> It's all very fine but no lodge here for you my lad.
> Repent and believe the gospel.
> Betsy Brown—Henry Allen, 1842.

APPENDIX II.

GLOSSARY.

Applíque. Lace having sprigs or leaves sewn on net.

Bars. Same as legs, q.v.

Bedfordshire Trailers. The Trolly Bobbins. A Huntingdonshire name.

Bud. Bucks name for almost any ornament in the pattern.

Brides. Same as legs, q.v.

Berthe. Neckwear. Many *berthes* are made from the Rose and Leaf design. Some people call them *Berthas*.

Close-work. Same as *whole stitch*, q.v.

Clothwork. Same as *whole stitch*, q.v.

Cordonnet, or *Raised Work.* The thick thread or cord with which the pattern is sometimes outlined, as in Brussels and Honiton Laces. It is used to give boldness and relief. It must not be confused with *gimp*, which is " an essential part of a point ground pattern ' worked all across ' the parchment."[1] Gimp is a cordonnet, but all cordonnets are not gimp.

Cluny. An offshoot of Maltese. (See Plate 33.)

Dykeside. See *Head-side.*

Filet Lace, also known as Filet Brodé, Filet Guipure, Guipure d' Art, is a revival of the Lacis or Darned Netting of the Middle Ages. Its patterns are found in Vinciola's book, published in 1588.

French Ground. Same as *Kat Stitch*, q.v.

---

[1] Miss Channer's definition.

Foot-side. The inner edge of a piece of lace, as opposed to the Head-side. The Foot-side is generally straight, as it is used to sew the lace on to the material it is to decorate.

Gingles. The loose pewter rings which surround the Trolly bobbin (Bucks). It is a mistake to give this name to the *spangles*, q.v.

Guipure. (1) Old meaning of the term: A lace of which the pattern consisted of a strip of thin parchment or a " gross black thread covered or whipped about with silk." Also called *Parchment Lace.* When tape took the place of the covered thread the lace was called *Tape Guipure.* The patterns were united by net or legs.

(2) Modern meaning of the term: A lace without any net ground, the pattern being held together by legs as English-made Maltese.

Hair-pin Stitch. A Bucks name. Same as *Kat Stitch.*

Head-side. The outer edge of a piece of lace. It is generally scalloped or vandyked (when it is called the *Dykeside*). Another name is *Turnside.*

Half-Stitch. The loose work that occurs more frequently in Maltese and Torchon. (See Plate 4.)

Kat Stitch. Also called *Wire Ground, French Ground, Six-Pointed Star Ground,* and in Bucks *Hair-pin Stitch.* It takes eight bobbins to a pin instead of four like other stitches. (See Plate 3.)

Legs. The connections between the various parts of a lace design. Also called *straps, bars,* and *brides* (literally, bridges).

Leadworks (*dots, plaits, points d' esprit*). The dots with which the Lille Ground is sometimes sprinkled. The French term is *mouche* (a fly). (See Plate 25.)

Purls, or *Pearls.* Tiny loops on the head-side of lace. Also called *picots.*

Point de Paris. A narrow bobbin lace (made in Normandy and near Paris) which was much worn in the 17th century. It was also called *Point des champs,* because it was made in the country, and *Point double.*

Pelerine. (French, pélerin, a pilgrim.) Originally the cape (which had the addition of a hood) worn by pilgrims to the Holy Land. Pelerines worn by English ladies were often oramented with lace.

Pelisse. (Latin, *pellis,* a skin.) An overdress for outdoor wear. The nobles of the court of Edward the Confessor wore pelisses. In the 19th century children's pelisses were often laced.

Plain-work. Same as *whole stitch*, q.v.

Pricker. The short instrument used for making in the parchment the holes that are to receive the pins.

Points d' esprit. See *Leadworks*.

Pillow Lace. Lace made on the pillow by twisting and plaiting threads. The French term is *dentelle au fuseau*.

Picots. A French name for *purls* or *turnpins*, q.v.

Point Ground. Also called *Point de Lille, Lille Ground, Point Simple, Fond Clair, Fond Simple* (as opposed to Point de Paris, which is *Point Double* or *Fond Double*). The word Fond (Fr.) means ground.

Point Lace. Literally, lace made with the point of a needle. *Point d' Angleterre* and *Bucks Point* are misnomers, as they are made with bobbins. Fixed, however, as they are by time, these names cannot be altered. To distinguish Point from Bobbin Lace use a magnifying glass. If the solid part of the pattern—that is, the *clothwork*—is made up of looped threads the lace is needle-point ; if it is plaited it is bobbin lace.

Plastron. (French, a breast-plate.) A trimming for the front of a dress of a different material 'from the dress itself.

Quills. Bobbins with long necks on which the gimp is first wound.

Reseau. Net work.

Straps. Same as *legs*, q.v.

Spangles. Bunches of coloured beads hung to bobbins by means of brass wire in order to increase their weight.

Toile. Same as *whole stitch*.

Tatting. A reproduction of the Ragusa Gimp Laces and Knotted Laces of the 16th century, made with threads and a shuttle. It is sometimes, on account of its lace-like appearance, called Tatted Lace, but, of course, it is not lace in the true sense of the word.

Turnside. Same as *Head-side*, q.v.

Tape Guipure. See *Guipure*.

Turnpins. Tiny loops on the legs of Maltese and other laces.

Torchon. (French, a dish-cloth.) Lace of loose texture and geometrical design.

Tallies. Bucks name for *plaits*.

Trolly. Bucks name for bobbin to which the gimp is transferred from the *quill*.

Trolly Lace. (1) Bucks : Lace in which the pattern is outlined with gimp.

(2) Devon : A Lace made of coarse thread, and worked straight on—round and round the pillow. (See page 212.)

Whole Stitch. The *close-work*, *cloth-work*, or *plain-work*. The meshes are square. The French name is *toilé*. (See Plate 4.)

Wire Ground. Same as *Kat Stitch*, q.v.

APPENDIX III.

SONG: THE BOBBIN.

From Mr. Thomas Wright's Story, *The Lace-maker.*
(In the Press).

What shall I do with the money I earn ?
Up in the air it shall certainly turn[1]
Soon as I hear the first cuckoo's "cuck-oo ";
Robin will hear it the same moment too.

Come, pleasant thoughts, and sit round in a ring ;
Love is a cage in which happy birds sing ;
So I will buy a new bobbin, I may
See one to suit me on Cherry Fair day.[2]

What shall I do with the bobbin I buy ?
Give it to Robin for Robin is shy.
Then that I love him he plainly will see,
And he may buy a new bobbin for me.

What shall the motto be ? " Dear one, be true " ?
" Love me or leave me " ?   No, neither will do !
This is the motto I think I will take :
" Look at me sometimes for somebody's sake."

Then in his arms he will clasp me and I
For him will live—though for him I could die.
What a sweet world is this !   Now I have found
What it is—love it is—makes it go round.[3]

[1] In Lace-land it is the custom to turn one's money over when the cuckoo is first heard.

[2] June 29th.

[3] For the music to this song apply to Mr. H. H. Armstrong, Olney, Bucks.   Price, 2s.

APPENDIX IV.

BIBLIOGRAPHY.

Armstrong, H. H. The Bucks Cottage Workers' Agency. Articles by H. H. Armstrong and Jessie J. Williams.

Brassey, Lady. Catalogue of her Exhibition of Lace, Fans, &c., at Hastings. No date.

Burrowes, Miss M. E. B. *Buckingham Lace*, by T. E. D. S. 21 pages. No date.

Carlile, Mrs. Lace and the North Bucks Lace Association. *The Empire Review*, Jan., 1903.

Channer, Miss C. C., and Roberts, Miss M. E. *Lace-making in the Midlands*. 1900. Chapters 4 and 5 are by Miss Roberts ; the rest of the book is by Miss Channer.

Cole, Alan S. *Report on Northamptonshire, Bucks and Bedfordshire Lace-making*. 1891.

"*Devonia :*" *The Honiton Lace Book*. Bazaar Office. No date.

Daily Mail Exhibition . . . of Lace (Mar. 9th—14th, 1908) Catalogue. Edited by J. T. Herbert Baily.

Dryden, Alice. Pillow Lace in the Midlands. *Pall Mall Magazine*, Mar., 1896.

D. M. C. Bibliothèque, D. M. C. *Les Dentelles aux Fuseaux*, 1re Série. Th De Dillmont, Editeur, Mulhouse (Alsace).

Dictionary of Needlework, The. Issued in 17 parts, first by A. W. Gowan. 30 New Bridge Street, Ludgate Circus; and afterwards by L. Upcott Gill, 170 Strand, W.C. No date.

Isemonger, Mildred. English Lace. *The Lady's Realm*, Dec., 1904.

Illustrated Exhibitor and Magazine of Art. 1832. Vol. 1, p. 47. Article on Needle Lace, with plate of antique Needle Lace stitches.

Jourdain, M. *Old Lace.* 121 pages. 1908.

Jackson, Mrs. F. Nevill. *A History of Hand-made Lace.* 1900.

Liberty & Co. *Buckinghamshire Lace.* No date.

Lowes, Mrs. *Chats on Old Lace,* &c. 1908.

Moule, Rev. H. R. (Vicar of Bozeat). The Making of Lace. *The Church Monthly*, July, 1903.

Moody, A. Penderel. *Devon Pillow Lace.* 1907.

Moody, A. Penderel. *Lace-Making and Collecting.* 1909.

Mincoff (Elizabeth) and Marriage (Margaret). *Pillow Lace.* 1907.

Marshall & Snelgrove. *A Short History of Honiton Lace.*

Maidment, Miss M. *A Book of Instructions for the working of English Pillow Laces.* (In the Press.)

North Bucks Lace Association. *Examples of Lace.* No date.

Owen-Mackenzie, Lady (Tempsford Hall). *Revival of Point Ground Lace-Making in Beds.* Mar., 1910.

Palliser, Mrs. Bury. *History of Lace.* 1st Ed., 1869; latest Ed., 1910.

Pollen, Mrs. John Hungerford. *Seven Centuries of Lace.* 1908.

Robinson & Cleaver. *Irish Hand-made Lace.* No date.

Ratcliff, Oliver, and H. Brown. *Olney: Past and Present.* 1893.

Sharp, Miss Mary. *Point and Pillow Lace,* by A. M. S. 1899.

Sime, A. M. *Torchon Lace Book.* Part I., 1904; Part II., 1909.

Stewart, Hon. Mrs. Fitzroy. Lace and Bobbins. *Woman at Home.*

Tebbs, The Misses L. and R. *The Art of Bobbin Lace.* 1911.

Tebbs, The Misses L. and R. *Supplement.* 1911.

Times, The. Real Lace and its Story. Dec. 1, 3, 6, 8, 10, 1904.

Victoria and Albert Museum. *Catalogue of Samplers.* Edited by Mr. P. G. Trendell.

Victoria County History.   Bucks.
     ,,   ,,   Beds.
     ,,   ,,   Northants.
     ,,   ,,   Herts.

Viccars, R.   *A Succinct History of Buckingham Lace.*   Issued by Peter Robinson.

Watson, W. G. Willis.   *Mate's Illustrated Honiton : its History, Past and Present.*

Welldon's :

   No. 115, Vol. 10 :   *Practical Point Lace.*
        124   ,,   11 :   ,,   *Torchon Lace.*
        129   ,,   11 :   ,,   *Point Lace.*
        153   ,,   13 :   ,,   *Honiton Lace.*
        200   ,.   17 :   ,,   *Carrickmacross Lace.*
        213   ,,   18 :   ,,   *Limerick Lace.*
        229   ,,   20 :   ,,   *Pillow Laces.*

INDEX